THE BOOK OF CHEESE

THE BOOK OF CHEESE

CHARLES THOM,
WALTER WARNER FISK

ISBN: 978-93-89614-12-1

Published: 1918

LECTOR HOUSE LLP
E-MAIL: lectorpublishing@gmail.com

Fig. 1.— A cheese laboratory in the New York State College of Agriculture at Cornell University.

THE BOOK OF CHEESE

BY

CHARLES THOM

INVESTIGATOR IN CHEESE, FORMERLY AT CONNECTICUT
AGRICULTURAL COLLEGE

AND

WALTER W. FISK

ASSISTANT PROFESSOR OF DAIRY INDUSTRY (CHEESE-MAKING),
NEW YORK STATE COLLEGE OF AGRICULTURE
AT CORNELL UNIVERSITY

1918

PREFACE

Certain products we associate with the manufactures of the household, so familiar and of such long standing that we do not think of them as requiring investigation or any special support of science. The older ones of us look back on cheese as an ancient home product; yet the old-fashioned hard strong kind has given place to many named varieties, some of them bearing little resemblance to the product of the kitchen and the buttery. We have analyzed the processes; discovered microorganisms that hinder or help; perfected devices and machines; devised tests of many kinds; studied the chemistry; developed markets for standardized commodities. Here is one of the old established farm industries that within a generation has passed from the housewife and the home-made hand press to highly perfected factory processes employing skilled service and handling milk by the many tons from whole communities of cows. This is an example of the great changes in agricultural practice. Cheese-making is now a piece of applied science; many students in the colleges are studying the subject; no one would think of undertaking it in the old way: for these reasons this book is written.

This book is intended as a guide in the interpretation of the processes of making and handling a series of important varieties of cheese. The kinds here considered are those made commercially in America, or so widely met in the trade that some knowledge of them is necessary. The relation of cheese to milk and to its production and composition has been presented in so far as required for this purpose. The principles and practices underlying all cheese-making have been brought together into a chapter on curd-making. A chapter on classification then brings together into synoptical form our knowledge of groups of varieties. These groups are then discussed separately. The problems of factory building, factory organization, buying and testing milk, and the proper marketing of cheese, are briefly discussed.

Such a discussion should be useful to the student, to the beginner in cheese-making, as a reference book on many varieties in the hands of makers who specialize in single varieties, and to the housekeeper or teacher of domestic science. The material has been brought together from the experience of the writers, supplemented by free use of the literature in several languages. Standard references to this literature are added in the text.

No introduction to the subject of cheese should fail to mention the work of J. H. Monrad, who has recently passed away. Mr. Monrad never collected his material into a single publication, but his contributions to chees-emaking information, scattered widely in trade literature over a period of thirty years, form an encyclopedia of the subject.

Bulletins of the Agricultural Experiment Stations and United States Department of Agriculture have been quoted extensively, with citation of the sources of the material. Personal assistance from Professor W. A. Stocking and other members of the Dairy Department of Cornell University, and C. F. Doane of the United States Department of Agriculture, is gladly acknowledged.

Students cannot learn out of books to make cheese. They may, however, be aided in understanding the problems from such study. To make cheese successfully they must have intimate personal touch with some person who knows cheese. Sympathetic relations with such a teacher day by day in the cheese-room are essential to success in making cheese which, at its best, is one of the most attractive of food-products.

THE AUTHORS.

CONTENTS

CHAPTER I

GENERAL STATEMENT ON CHEESE

CHAPTER II

THE MILK IN ITS RELATION TO CHEESE

CHAPTER III

COAGULATING MATERIALS

CHAPTER IV
LACTIC STARTERS

CHAPTER V
CURD-MAKING

CHAPTER VI
CLASSIFICATION

CHAPTER VII
CHEESES WITH SOUR-MILK FLAVOR

CHAPTER XIII

COMPOSITION AND YIELD OF CHEDDAR CHEESE

CHAPTER XIV

CHEDDAR CHEESE RIPENING

CHAPTER XV

THE SWISS AND ITALIAN GROUPS

CHAPTER XVI

MISCELLANEOUS VARIETIES AND BY-PRODUCTS

THE BOOK OF CHEESE

CHAPTER I

GENERAL STATEMENT ON CHEESE

Nature of cheese; Cheese-making as an art; Cheese-making as a science; Problems in cheese-making; History.

Cheese is a solid or semi-solid protein food product manufactured from milk. Its solidity depends on the curdling or coagulation of part or all of the protein and the expulsion of the watery part or whey. The coagulum or curd so formed incloses part of the milk-serum (technically whey) or watery portion of the milk, part of the salts, part or all of the fat, and an aliquot part of the milk-sugar. The loss in manufacture includes a small fraction of the protein and fat, the larger proportion of the water, salts and milk-sugar.

1. Nature of cheese.—Milk of itself is an exceedingly perishable product. Cheese preserves the most important nutrient parts of the milk in condition for consumption over a much longer period. The duration of this period and the ripening and other changes taking place depend very closely on the composition of the freshly made cheese. There is an intimate relation between the water, fat, protein and salt-content of the newly made cheese and the ripening processes which produce the particular flavors of the product when it is ready for the consumer. This relation is essentially biological. A cheese containing 60 to 75 per cent of water, as in "cottage cheese" (the sour-milk cheese so widely made in the homes), must be eaten or lost in a very few days. Spoilage is very rapid. In contrast to this, the Italian Parmesan, with 30 to 32 per cent of water, requires two to three years for proper ripening.

The cheeses made from soured skim-milk probably represent the most ancient forms of cheese-making. Their origin is lost in antiquity. The makers of Roquefort cheese cite passages from Pliny which they think refer to an early form of that product. It is certain that cheese in some form has been familiar to man throughout historic times. The technical literature of cheese-making is, however, essentially recent. The older literature may be cited to follow the historical changes in details of practice.

2. Cheese-making as an art has been developed to high stages of perfection in widely separate localities. The best known varieties of cheese bear the geographical names of the places of their origin. The practices of making and handling such cheeses have been developed in intimate relation to climate, local conditions and the habits of the people. So close has been this adjustment in some cases, that the removal of expert makers of such cheeses to new regions has resulted in total failure to transplant the industry.

3. Cheese-making as a science has been a comparatively recent development. It has been partly a natural outgrowth of the desire of emigrant peoples to carry with them the arts of their ancestral home, partly the desire to manufacture at home the good things met in foreign travel. Its development has been largely coincident with the development of the agricultural school and the science of dairy biology. Even now we have but a limited knowledge of a few of the 500 or more varieties of cheese named in the literature. It is desirable to bring together the knowledge of underlying principles as far as they are known.

No technical description of a cheese-handling process can replace experience. Descriptions of appearances and textures of curd in terms definite enough to be understood by beginners have been found to be impossible. It is possible, however, to lay down principles and essentials of practice which are common to the industry and form the foundation for intelligent work. Cheese-making will be a science only as we depart from the mere repetition of a routine or rule-of-thumb practice and understand the underlying principles.

4. Problems in cheese-making.—Any understanding of these problems calls for a working knowledge of the very complex series of factors involved. These include the chemical composition of the milk, the nature of rennet and character of its action under the conditions met in cheese-making, the nature of the micro-organisms in milk, and the methods of controlling them, their relation to acidity and to the ripening of the cheese. To these scientific demands must be added acquaintance with the technique of the whole milk industry, from its production and handling on the farm through the multiplicity of details of factory installation and organization, to those intangible factors concerned with the texture, body, odor and taste of the varied products made from it. Some of these factors can be adequately described; others have thus far been handed on from worker to worker but have baffled every effort at standardization or definition.

5. History.—The recorded history of the common varieties of cheese is only fragmentary. Practices at one time merely local in origin followed the lines of emigration. Records of processes of manufacture were not kept. The continuance of a particular practice depended on the skill and memory of the emigrant, who called his cheese after the place of origin. Other names of the same kind were applied by the makers for selling purposes. The widely known names were thus almost all originally geographical. Some of them, such as Gorgonzola, are used for cheeses not now made at the places whose names they bear. Naturally, this method of development has produced national groups of cheeses which have many common characteristics but differ in detail. The English cheeses form a typical group of this kind.

Emigration to America carried English practices across the Atlantic. The story of cheese-making in America has been so closely linked with the development of the American Cheddar process that the historical aspects of the industry in this country are considered under that head in Chapter VIII.

CHAPTER II

THE MILK IN ITS RELATION TO CHEESE

Factors affecting the quality; Chemical composition; Factors causing variation in composition; Milk constituents; Water; Fat; Casein; Milk-sugar; Albumin; Ash; Enzymes; The flavor of feeds eaten by the cow; Absorption of odors; Effect of condition of the cow; Bacteria in the milk; Groups of bacteria in milk; Acid fermentation of milk; Bacterium lactis-acidi group; Colon-aërogenes group; Acid peptonizing group; Bacillus bulgaricus group; Acid cocci or weak acid-producers; Peptonizing organisms; Inert types; Alkali-producing bacteria; Butyric fermenting types; Molds and yeasts; Bacterial contamination of milk; Germicidal effect of milk; Sources and control of bacteria in milk; The cow; Stable air; The milker; Utensils; The factory; The control of bacteria; Fermentation test; The sediment test.

The opaque whitish liquid, secreted by the mammary glands of female mammals for the nourishment of their young, is known as milk. The milk of the cow is the kind commonly used for cheese-making in America.

6. Factors affecting the quality.—The process of cheese-making begins with drawing the milk from the udder. The care and treatment the milk receives, while being drawn, and its subsequent handling, have a decided influence on its qualities. The process of cheese-making is varied according to the qualities of the milk. There are five factors that influence the quality of the milk for cheese-making: (1) its chemical composition; (2) the flavor of feed eaten by the cow; (3) the absorption of flavors and odors from the atmosphere; (4) the health of the cow; (5) the bacteria present. The first factor is dependent on the breed and individuality of the cow. The other four factors are almost entirely within the control of man. Of these factors, number five is of the most importance, and is the one most frequently neglected.

7. Chemical composition.—The high, low and average composition of milk is approximately as follows:

TABLE I

COMPOSITION OF MILK

	WATER PER CENT	FAT PER CENT	CASEIN PER CENT	SUGAR PER CENT	ALBUMIN PER CENT	ASH PER CENT
High	88.90	5.50	3.00	5.00	.72	.73
Low	85.05	3.00	2.10	4.60	.70	.70
Average	87.47	3.80	2.50	4.80	.71	.71

8. Factors causing variation in composition.—The composition of cow's milk varies according to several factors. The composition of the milk of different breeds differs to such a degree that whole series of factories are found with lower or higher figures than these averages on account of dominant presence of particular kinds of cattle.

The following table shows the usual effect of breed on fat and total solids of milk:

TABLE II

THE USUAL EFFECT OF BREED OF COWS ON FAT AND TOTAL SOLIDS OF MILK

BREED OF COWS	AVERAGES	
	FAT PER CENT	TOTAL SOLIDS PER CENT
JERSEY	5.62	14.74
GUERNSEY	5.34	14.70
SHORTHORN	4.17	13.41
AYRSHIRE	3.61	12.72
HOLSTEIN-FRIESIAN	3.30	11.89

The figures[1] in Tables I and II are compiled and averaged from a large number of analyses made at different agricultural experiment stations.

[1] Ont. Exp. Sta. Rept. 1890, pages 237-241.
Maine Exp. Sta. Rept. 1890, part II, pages 52-57.
Conn. (Storrs) Exp. Sta. Rept. 1886, pages 119-130.
Vt. Exp. Sta. Rept. 1890, pages 97-100.
Vt. Exp. Sta. Rept. 1891, pages 61-74.
N. Y. Exp. Sta. Rept. 1892, pages 299-392.
N. Y. Exp. Sta. Rept. 1893, pages 39-162.
Wis. Exp. Sta. Rept. 1890, pages 115-119.
Conn. (Storrs) Exp. Sta. Rept. 1907, pages 152-156.
N. Y. Exp. Sta. Rept. 1891, pages 139-142.
N. Y. Exp. Sta. Rept. 1894, pages 31-86, 118-121.
N. J. Exp. Sta. Rept. 1895, pages 136-137.

This variation not only affects the fat, but all constituents of the milk. While there is a difference in the composition of the milk from cows of different breeds, there is almost as wide variation in the composition of the milk from single cows[2] of the same breed. With the same cow the stage of lactation causes a wide variation in the composition of the milk.[3] As the period of lactation advances, the milk increases in percentage of fat and other solids.

9. Milk constituents.—From the standpoint of the cheese-maker, the significant constituents of milk are water, fat, casein, milk-sugar, albumin, ash and enzymes. These will be discussed separately.

10. Water.—The retention of the solids and the elimination of the water are among the chief considerations in cheese-making. Water forms 84 to 89 per cent of milk. Cheese-making calls for the reduction of this percentage to that typical of the particular variety of cheese desired with the least possible loss of milk solids. This final percentage varies from 30 to 70 per cent with the variety of cheese. The water has two uses in the cheese: (1) It imparts smoothness and mellowness to the body of the cheese; (2) it furnishes suitable conditions for the action of the ripening agents. To some extent the water may supplement or even replace fat in its effect on the texture of the cheese. If the cheese is properly made, the water present is in such combination as to give no suggestion of a wet or "leaky" product.

11. Fat.—Fat is present in the milk in the form of suspended small transparent globules (as an emulsion). These globules vary in size with the breed and individuality of the cow and in color from a very light yellow to a deep yellow shade as sought in butter. Milk with small fat globules is preferred for cheese-making, because these are not so easily lost in the process. Milk-fat is made up of several different compounds called glycerids,[4] which are formed by the union of an organic acid with glycerine as a base.

Fat is important in cheese-making for two reasons: (1) Its influence on the yield of cheese; (2) its effect on the quality of the cheese. Many of the details of cheese-making processes have been developed to prevent the loss of fat in manufacture. The yield of cheese is almost directly in proportion to the amount of fat in the milk; nevertheless, because the solids not fat do not increase exactly in pro-

---

Eckles, C. H., and R. H. Shaw. The influence of breed and individuality on the composition and properties of milk, Bur. An. Ind. Bul. 156, 1913.

Eckles, C. H., and R. H. Shaw, Variations in the composition and properties of milk from the individual cow, U. S. Dept. Agr. Bur. An. Ind. Bul. 157, 1913.

[2] Morrow, G. A., and A. G. Manns, Analyses of milk from different cows, Ill. Exp. Sta. Bul. 9, 1890.

[3] Eckles, C. H., and R. H. Shaw, The influence of the stage of lactation on the composition and properties of milk, U. S. Dept. Agr. Bur. An. Ind. Bul. 155, 1913. N. Y. Exp. Sta. Rept. 1892, pages 138-140.

[4] N. Y. Exp. Sta. Rept. 1891, pages 143-162, 316-318.

Wis. Exp. Sta. Rept. 1890, pages 238-247.

Van Slyke, L. L., Conditions affecting the proportions of fat and protein in cow's milk, Jour. Am. Chem. Soc., 30 (1908), no. 7, pages 1166-1186.

portion to the fat, the cheese yield is not exactly in proportion to the fat. The fat, however, is a good index of the cheese-producing power of the milk.

12. Casein.—Cheese-making is possible because of the peculiar properties of casein. This is the fundamental substance of cheese-making because it has the capacity to coagulate or curdle under the action of acid and rennet enzymes. Casein is an extremely complex organic compound.[5] Authorities disagree regarding its exact composition, but it contains varying amounts of carbon, oxygen, nitrogen, hydrogen, phosphorus and sulfur, and it usually is combined with some form of lime or calcium phosphate. It belongs to the general class of nitrogen-containing compounds called proteins. It is present in milk in the form of extremely minute gelatinous particles in suspension. Casein is insoluble in water and dilute acids. The acids, when added, cause a heavy, white, more or less flocculent precipitate. Rennet (Chapter III) causes the casein to coagulate (curdle), forming a jelly-like mass called curd, which is the basis of manufacture in most types of cheese. In the formation of this coagulum (curd), the fat is imprisoned and held. The casein compounds in the curd hold the moisture and give firmness and solidity of body to the cheese. Casein contains the protein materials in which important ripening changes take place. These changes render the casein more soluble, and are thought to be the source of certain characteristic cheese flavors.

13. Milk-sugar.—Milk-sugar (lactose) is present in solution in the watery part of the milk. It forms on the average about 5 per cent of cow's milk. Since it is in solution, cheese retains the aliquot part of the total represented by the water-content of the cheese, plus any part of the sugar which has entered into combination with the milk solids during the souring process. The larger part of the lactose passes off with the whey. Lactose[6] is attacked by the lactic-acid bacteria and by them is changed to lactic acid. Cheeses in which this souring process goes on quickly, soon contain a large enough percentage of acid to check the rotting of the cheese by decay organisms. Without this souring, most varieties of cheese will begin to spoil quickly. For each variety there is a proper balance between the souring, which interrupts the growth of many kinds of putrefactive bacteria, and the development of the forms which are essential to proper ripening.

14. Albumin.—This is a form of protein which is in solution in the milk. Albumin forms about 0.7 per cent of cow's milk. It is not coagulated by rennet. Most rennet cheeses, therefore, retain only that portion of the total albumin held in solution in the water retained, as in the case of milk-sugar. Albumin is coagulated by heat, forming a film or membrane upon the surface. There are certain kinds of cheese, such as Ricotte, made by the recovery of albumin by heating.

---

[5] Van Slyke, L. L., and A. W. Bosworth, Composition and properties of some casein and paracasein compounds and their relations to cheese, N. Y. Exp. Sta. Tech. Bul. 26, 1912.

Forbes, E. B., and M. H. Keith, A review of the literature of phosphorus compounds in animal metabolism, Ohio Exp. Sta. Tech. Bul. 5, pages 32-36, 42-45.

Van Slyke, L. L., and A. W. Bosworth, Condition of casein and salts in milk, N. Y. Exp. Sta. Tech. Bul. 39.

[6] Wis. Exp. Sta. Rept. 1901, pages 162-166.

15. Ash.—The ash or mineral constituents make up about 0.7 per cent of cow's milk. This total includes very small amounts of a great many substances. The exact form of some of the substances is still unknown. Of these salts, the calcium or lime and phosphorus salts are most important in cheese-making. They are partially or completely precipitated by pasteurization. After such precipitation rennet fails to act[7] or acts very slowly; hence pasteurized milk cannot be used for making rennet cheese unless the lost salts are replaced, or the condition of the casein is changed by the addition of some substance, before curdling is attempted.

16. Enzymes.—Milk also contains enzymes. These are chemical ferments secreted by the udder. They have the power to produce changes in organic compounds without themselves undergoing any change. Minute amounts of several enzymes are found in milk as follows: Diastase, galactase, lipase, catalase, peroxidase and reductase. Just what part they play in cheese-making is not definitely known.

17. The flavor of feeds eaten by the cow.—Undesirable flavors in the milk are due many times to the use of feed with very pronounced flavors. The most common of these feeds are onions, garlic, turnips, cabbage, decayed ensilage, various weeds and the like. These undesirable flavors reach the milk because the substances are volatile and are able to pass through the tissues of the animal. While feed containing these flavors is being digested, these volatile substances are not only present in the milk, but in all the tissues of the animal. By the time the process of digestion is completed, the volatile flavors have largely passed away. Therefore, if the times of milking and feeding are properly regulated, a dairy-man may feed considerable quantities of strong-flavored products, such as turnip, cabbage and others, without any appreciable effect on the flavor of the milk. To accomplish this successfully, the cows should be fed immediately before or immediately after milking, preferably after milking. This allows time for the digestive process to take place and for the volatile substances to disappear. If, however, milking is performed three or four hours after feeding, these volatile substances are present in the milk and flavor it.[8]

In the case of those plants which grow wild in the pasture, and to which the cows have continued access, it is more difficult to prevent bad flavor in the milk. The cows may be allowed to graze for a short time only, and that immediately after milking, without affecting the flavor of the milk. This will make it necessary to supplement the pasture with dry feed, or to have another pasture where these undesirable plants do not grow.

Undesirable flavors are usually noticeable in the milk when the cows are turned out to pasture for the first time in the spring; and when they are pastured on rank fall feed, such as second growth clover.

18. Absorption of odors.—Milk, especially when warm, possesses a remark-

<hr>

[7] Sammis, J. L., and A. T. Bruhn, The manufacture of cheese from pasteurized milk, Wis. Exp. Sta. Research Bul. 27, 1912.

[8] Baer, U. S., and W. L. Carlyle, Quality of cheese as affected by food, Wis. Exp. Sta. Bul. 115, 1904.

able ability to absorb and retain odors from the surrounding atmosphere.[9] For this reason, the milk should be handled only in places free from such odor. Some of the common sources of these undesirable odors are bad-smelling stables, strong-smelling feeds in the stable, dirty cows, aërating milk near hog-pens, barnyards and swill barrels. The only way to prevent these undesirable flavors and odors is not to expose the milk to them. The safest policy is to remove the source of the odor.

19. Effect of condition of the cow.—Any factor which affects the cow is reflected in the composition and physiological character of the milk. (1) Colostrum. Milk secreted just before or just after parturition is different in physical properties and chemical composition from that secreted at any other time during the lactation period. This milk is known as colostrum. It is considered unfit for human food, either as milk or in products manufactured from the milk. Most states[10] consider colostrum adulterated milk, and prohibit the sale of the product for fifteen days preceding and for five days after parturition. (2) Disease. When disease is detected in the cow, the milk should at once be discarded as human food. Some diseases are common both to the cow and to man, such as tuberculosis, foot-and-mouth disease. If such diseases are present in the cow, the milk may act as a carrier to man. Digestive disorders of any sort in the cow are frequently accompanied by undesirable flavors in the milk. These are not thought to be due to the feed, but to the abnormal condition of the cow. When the normal condition is restored, these undesirable flavors disappear.

20. Bacteria in the milk.—Bacteria are microscopic unicellular plants, without chlorophyll. Besides bacteria, there are other forms of the lower orders of plants found in milk, such as yeasts and molds. While the bacteria are normally the more important, frequently yeasts and molds produce significant changes in milk and other dairy products. Bacteria are very widely distributed throughout nature. They are so small that they may easily float in the air or on particles of dust. Many groups of bacteria are so resistant to adverse conditions of growth that they may be present in a dormant or spore stage, and, therefore, not be easily recognized; when suitable environments for growth are again produced, development begins at once. They are found in all surface water, in the earth and upon all organic matter. There are a great many different groups of bacteria; some are beneficial, and some are harmful. As they are so small, it is difficult to differentiate between the beneficial and harmful kinds, except by the results produced, or by a careful study in an especially equipped laboratory. The bacteria multiply very rapidly. This is brought about by fission; that is, the cell-walls are drawn in at one place around the cell, and when the walls unite at the center, the cell is divided. There are then two bacteria. In some cases, division takes place in twenty to thirty minutes. Like other plants, they are very sensitive to food supply, to temperature and to moisture, as conditions of growth. Inasmuch as the bacteria are plant cells, they must

[9] King, F. H., and E. H. Farrington, Milk odor as affected by silage, Wis. Exp. Sta. Bul. 59, 1897.

[10] N. Y. Agricultural Law, 1913, section 30.
    Mich. Agricultural Law, 1915, section 77.
    Wis. Agricultural Law, 1913, section 4601.

absorb their food from materials in solution. They may live on solid substances, but the food elements must be rendered soluble before they can be used. Most bacteria prefer a neutral or slightly acid medium for growth, rather than an alkaline reaction. Ordinary milk makes a very favorable medium for the growth of bacteria, because it is an adequate and easily available food supply.

In milk, certain groups of bacteria are commonly present, but many others which happen to get into it live and multiply rapidly. A favorable temperature is very necessary for such organisms to multiply. There is a range of temperature, more or less wide, at which each group of bacteria grows and multiplies with the greatest rapidity. This range varies with the different groups, but most of them find temperatures between 75° F. and 95° F. the most favorable for growth. Excessive heat kills the bacteria. Low temperatures stop growth, but kill few if any bacteria. Temperatures of 50° F. and lower retard the growth of most forms of bacteria found commonly in milk. Many forms will slowly develop, however, below 50° and some growth will occur down to the freezing point. Milk held at 50° F. or lower will remain in good condition long enough to be handled without injury to quality until received in the cheese factory. In the place of seeds, some groups of bacteria form spores. The spores are exceedingly resistant to unfavorable conditions of growth, such as heat, cold, drying, food supply and even chemical agents. This property makes it difficult to destroy such bacteria.

21. Groups of bacteria in milk.—Milk when first drawn usually shows an amphoteric reaction; that is, it will give the acid and alkaline reactions with litmus paper. Under normal conditions, milk soon begins to undergo changes, due to the bacteria. Changes produced in this way are called "fermentations"; the agents causing them, "ferments." Normally the acid fermentation takes place first, and later other fermentations or changes begin, which, after a time, so decompose the milk that it will not be suitable for cheese-making or human consumption.

The following grouping of the organisms in milk is based on their effects on the milk itself[11]:

I. Acid-producing types.

II. Peptonizing types.

III. Inert types.

IV. Alkali-producing types.

[11] Conn. (Storrs) Exp. Sta. Rept. 1899, pages 13-68.
Conn. (Storrs) Exp. Sta. Rept. 1903, pages 33-98.
Conn. (Storrs) Exp. Sta. Rept. 1904, pages 27-88.
Esten, W. M., and C. J. Mason, Sources of bacteria in milk, Conn. (Storrs) Exp. Sta. Bul. 51, 1908.
Rogers, L. A., and B. J. Davis, Methods of classifying the lactic acid bacteria, U. S. Dept. Agr. Bur. An. Ind. Bul. 154, 1912.
Bergey, D. H., The colon-aerogenes group of bacteria, Jour. Med. Research, Boston, Vol. XIX, pages 175-200, 1908.
Conn, H. W., Classification of dairy bacteria, Conn. (Storrs) Exp. Sta. Rept. 1906.
Rogers, L. A., Bacteria in milk, U. S. Dept. Agr., Farmers' Bul. 490, 1912.

V. Butyric fermenting types.

Each type of bacteria produces more or less specific changes in the milk. As a general rule, the predominance of one of these types is an aid in the interpretation of the quality of the product at the time of analysis, such as the age, the temperature at which it has been held, the conditions under which it was produced and, in some cases, the general source of the contamination. The reaction due to certain bacteria is utilized in the manufacture and handling of dairy products; other groups have deleterious effects. (See Fig. 2.)

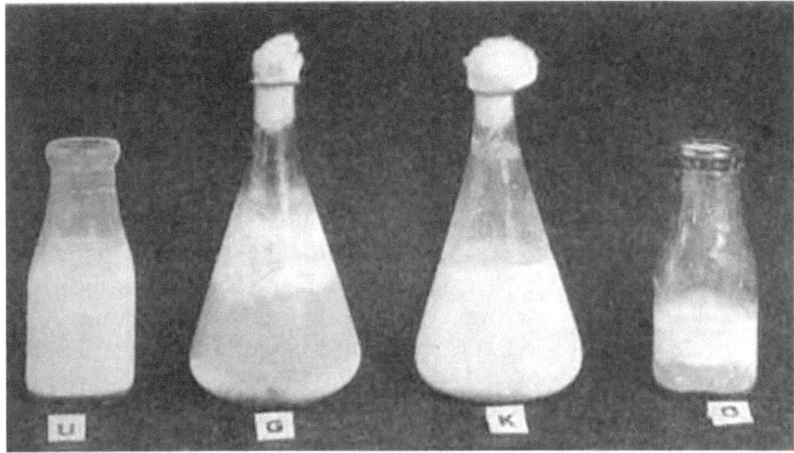

Fig. 2.—Effect of different fermentations of milk: U, Curd pitted with gas holes; G and O, gassy curds which float; K, smooth, solid desirable curd.

22. Acid fermentation of milk.—By far the most common and important fermentation taking place in milk is due to the action of the lactic acid-forming bacteria on the milk-sugar or lactose. The bacteria that bring about this fermentation may be divided into several groups on the basis of their morphology, proteolytic activity, gas production, temperature adaptation and production of substances other than lactic acid. The larger number of organisms producing lactic acid in milk also produce other organic acids in greater or less abundance. Inasmuch as lactic acid is the principal substance produced, they are called lactic acid organisms. This group contains different kinds of organisms which may be subdivided into small groups as follows:

(a) *Bacterium lactis-acidi* group

(b) *Bacterium colon-aërogenes* group.

(c) Acid peptonizing group.

(d) *Bacillus bulgaricus* group.

(e) Acid cocci or weak acid-producing group.

23. Bacterium lactis-acidi group.—There are many strains or varieties in this group which are closely related in their activities. They are universally present in milk and are commonly the greatest causal agent in its souring. They are widely distributed in nature. At a temperature of 65° F. to 95° F., these bacteria grow and multiply very rapidly; at 70° F. (approximately 20° C.) these forms usually outgrow all others. The total amount of acid produced in milk by these organisms varies from 0.6 of one per cent to 1 per cent acid calculated as pure lactic acid. These forms coagulate milk to a smooth curd of uniform consistency. In addition to the lactic acid, there are produced traces of acetic, succinic, formic and proprionic acids, traces of certain alcohols, aldehydes and esters. Substances other than lactic acid are not produced by organisms of this group to such an extent as to impart undesirable flavors to the milk. The action of this group on the milk proteins is very slight. They produce no visible sign of peptonization. The *B. lactis-acidi* group of organisms are essential to the production of the initial acidity necessary in most types of cheese. The practical culture and utilization of them for this purpose under factory conditions are discussed in Chapter IV, entitled "Lactic Starters."

24. Colon-aërogenes group.—This group takes its name from a typical species, *Bacterium coli communis*, which is a normal inhabitant of the intestines of man and animals, and from *Bacterium coli aerogenes*, which is similar in many respects to *B. coli communis*. The initial presence of these bacteria in milk is indicative of fecal contamination or unclean conditions of production. These organisms, however, grow and develop in milk very rapidly at high temperatures of handling. The total acidity produced by these forms is less than that by the *Bacterium lactis-acidi* group. Of the acid produced, less than 30 per cent is lactic acid; the other acids are formic, acetic, proprionic and succinic. The large percentage of these acids, with comparatively large amounts of certain alcohols, aldehydes and esters, invariably impart undesirable flavors and odors to the milk. Members of this group uniformly ferment the lactose with the production of the gases, carbon dioxide and hydrogen. The milk is coagulated into a lumpy curd, containing gas pockets.

25. Acid peptonizing group.—These are often associated with colon organisms. The group includes those bacteria which coagulate milk with an acid curd and subsequently partly digest it. They grow and multiply rapidly at a temperature between 65° and 98° F. They impart undesirable flavors and odors to the milk, which appear to be due to the formation of acids other than lactic acid, and to action on the milk proteins.

26. Bacillus bulgaricus group.—These organisms grow best at a temperature of 105° to 115° F. They will develop at lower temperatures, but not so rapidly. They survive heating to 135° F. without loss of vigor, as occurs in Swiss cheese-making. They produce from 1 to 4 per cent of acid in milk, which is practically all lactic acid. They do not produce gas. They impart no undesirable flavors to the milk.

27. Acid cocci or weak acid-producers.—This group of organisms is not very well defined. It consists mostly of coccus forms, commonly found in the air and in the udder. Their presence in the milk may indicate direct udder contamination. These are regarded as of little importance, unless in very large number, and they have been only partially studied. They produce little or no lactic acid, and small amounts of acetic, proprionic, butyric and caproic acids. These forms rarely create enough acid to coagulate milk.

28. Peptonizing organisms.—This group includes all bacteria which have a peptonizing effect on the milk. It includes the acid peptonizing organisms, although they are of primary importance in the acid type of bacteria, because the acid-producing power is greater than the peptonizing power. Some of the specific organisms in this class are *Bacillus subtilis*, *Bacterium prodigiosus* and *Bacterium liquefaciens*. These are commonly found in soil water and in fecal material. The presence of these organisms denotes contamination from such sources.

29. Inert types.—As the name indicates, these are organisms not known to have an appreciable effect on milk. The ordinary tests fail to connect them with important processes; hence they appear to feed upon, but not to affect the milk in any serious way. Milk ordinarily contains more or less of these organisms, but no particular significance is attached to their presence.

30. Alkali-producing bacteria.—This group of organisms has only recently been studied in relation to its action on milk. Investigators still disagree as to the usual percentage in the normal milk flora. Their presence in milk has been considered to be relatively unimportant.

31. Butyric fermenting types.—Organisms causing butyric fermentation may be present in the milk, but seldom become active, because they are commonly anaërobic and so will not develop in milk kept under ordinary conditions, and the rapid growth of the lactic acid-forming bacteria prevents their growth. These organisms act on the milk-fat, decomposing it. Butyric acid fermentations are more common in old butter and cheese. In these, the fermentation causes a rancid flavor.

32. Molds and yeasts.—The cattle feed and the air of the barn always contain considerable numbers of yeasts and mold spores. Yeasts have been found by Hastings[12] to cause an objectionable fermentation in Wisconsin cheese. No further study of this group as factors in cheese-handling has been reported. Mold spores, especially those of the blue or green molds (Penicillum sp.) and the black molds (Mucors), are always abundant in milk. These spores are carried into all cheeses made from unpasteurized milk, in numbers sufficient to cover the cheeses with mold if they are permitted to grow. Pasteurization[13] kills most of them. The border-line series commonly referred to as the streptothrix-actinomyces group are also very abundant in all forage and are carried in large numbers into all milk and its products.

33. Bacterial contamination of milk.—When drawn from the cow, milk is seldom if ever sterile. Organisms usually work their way from the tip of the teat into the udder and multiply there. The fore milk usually contains more organisms than does that drawn later. Most of the bacterial contamination of the milk is due to the handling after it is drawn from the cow.

34. Germicidal effect of milk.—Authorities agree that when a bacterial examination of the milk is made, hour by hour, beginning as soon as it is drawn from

[12] Hastings, E. G., Distribution of lactose-fermenting yeasts in dairy products, Wis. Exp. Sta. Rept. 23, pages 107-115.

[13] Thom, C., and S. H. Ayers, Effect of pasteurization upon mold spores, Jour. Agr. Research 6 (1916), no. 4, pages 153-156.

the cow, there is no increase in the number of organisms for a period of several hours at first, but an actual reduction not infrequently takes place. This is called the "germicidal"[14] property of milk. The lower the temperature of the milk, the longer and less pronounced is the germicidal action; the higher the temperature, the shorter and more pronounced is this action.

This is explained as either: (1) a period of selection within which types of bacteria entering by accident and unadapted for growth die off; or (2) an actual weak antiseptic power in the milk-serum itself; or (3) the forming of clusters by the bacteria and so reducing the count.

In working on a small scale or on an experimental basis, this property at times introduces a factor of difficulty or error which is not to be lost sight of in the selection of the milk for such purposes.

35. Sources and control of bacteria in milk.—Most of the bacterial infection of milk is due to lack of care in handling. Some of the common sources[15] of contamination are: the air in the stable; the cow's body; the milker; the utensils; the method of handling the milk after it is drawn from the cow; unclean cheese factory conditions.

Since bacteria cause various kinds of fermentation, not only in the milk but in the products manufactured from it, the question of their control is of prime importance. There are two ways in which the bacterial growth in milk used for cheese-making may be controlled: (1) prevention of infection; (2) the retardation of their development when present. The former is accomplished by strict cleanliness, the latter by adequate cooling.

36. The cow.—The body of the cow may be a source of bacterial contamination. Bacteria adhere to the hair of the animal, and to the scales of the skin, and during the process of milking these are very liable to fall into the milk. To prevent this, the cow should be curried to remove all loose material and hair. Just before

[14] Hunziker, O. F., Germicidal action of milk, N. Y. (Cornell) Exp. Sta. Bul. 197.

Stocking, W. A., Germicidal action of milk, Conn. (Storrs) Exp. Sta. Bul. 37, 1905.

U. S. Treasury Dept., Hygienic Laboratory, Bul. 41, Milk and its relation to the public health, 1908, also revised as Bul. 56, 1909.

[15] U. S. Dept. Agr., Farmers' Bul. 602, Dairy Division, Production of clean milk, 1914.

Lauder, A., and A. Cunningham, Some factors affecting the bacteriological content of milk, Edinburgh and East of Scotland Coll. of Agr. Rept. XXVIII, 1913.

Prucha, M. J., and H. M. Weeter, Germ content of milk, Ill. Exp. Sta. Bul. 199, 1917.

Harding, H. A., et al., The effect of certain dairy operations upon the germ content of milk, N. Y. Exp. Sta. Bul. 365, 1913.

Fraser, W. J., Sources of bacteria in milk, Ill. Exp. Sta. Bul. 91, 1903.

Frandsen, J. H., Care of milk and cream on the farm, Neb. Exp. Sta. Bul. 133, 1912.

Conn, H. W., The care and handling of milk, Conn. (Storrs) Exp. Sta. Bul. 26, 1903.

Stocking, W. A., Jr., Quality of milk as affected by certain dairy operations, Conn. (Storrs) Exp. Sta. Bul. 42, 1906.

milking, the udder and flank should be wiped with a damp cloth; this removes some of the material, and causes the remainder to adhere to the cow.

37. Stable air.—If the air of the stable is not clean, it will be a source of contamination. Particles of dust floating in the air carry more or less bacteria, and these fall into the milk during the process of milking. To keep the stable air free from dust at milking time, all operations which stir up dust, such as feeding, brushing the cows, cleaning the floor, should be practiced after milking or long enough before so that the dust will have settled. It is a good plan to close the doors and to sprinkle the floor just before milking.

38. The milker himself may be a source of contamination. He should be clean and wear clean clothing. The hands should not be wet with milk during milking.

Fig. 3.—Types of small-top milk pails.

39. Utensils.—The utensils are an important source of bacterial contamination. The bacteria lodge in the seams and corners unless these are well-flushed with solder. From these seams they are not easily removed. When fresh warm milk is placed into such utensils, the bacteria begin to grow and multiply. All utensils with which milk comes in contact should first be rinsed with cold water and then thoroughly washed and finally scalded with boiling water, and drained or blown absolutely dry. They should then be placed in an atmosphere free from dust until wanted for use again. If an aërator is used, this should be operated in pure air, free from odors and dust. One of the greatest sources of bacterial contamination of cheese milk is the use of the milk-cans to return whey to the farms for pig feed. Frequently, sour whey is left in the cans until ready to feed. These cans are then not properly washed and scalded. The practice of pasteurizing the whey at the cheese factory is a great help in preventing this source of infection and the spreading of disease.

The use of a small-top milk pail[16] is to be especially recommended in preventing bacterial contamination. Because of the small opening, bacteria cannot easily fall into the milk in as large numbers as when the whole top of the pail is

[16] Harding, H. A., J. K. Wilson and G. A. Smith, Tests of covered milk pails, N. Y. Exp. Sta. Bul. 326, 1910.

Stocking, W. A., Tests of covered milk pails, Conn. (Storrs) Exp. Sta. Bul. 48, 1907.

open. (See Fig. 3.)

If a milking machine[17] is used, great care must be exercised to see that all parts that come in contact with the milk are cleaned after each milking, and then put in a clean place until ready to use again.

40. The factory.—Another source of contamination is the cheese factory itself. The cheese-maker should keep his factory in the cleanest condition possible, not only because of the effect on the milk itself, but as a stimulus for the producers to follow his example. All doors and windows in the factory should be screened to keep out flies.

41. The control of bacteria.—If, in spite of preventive measures, bacteria get into the milk, their growth can be retarded by controlling the temperature. If the temperature of the milk, as soon as drawn, can be reduced below that at which the bacteria grow and multiply rapidly, it will retard their development. In general, all milk should be cooled to 50° F. or below. In cooling the milk, it should not be exposed to dust or odors. One of the best methods of cooling is to set the can containing the milk into a tub of cold running water, and then stir. If running water is not available, cold well-water[18] may be used, but the water should be changed several times. If the milk is not stirred during the cooling process, it will not cool so rapidly, because the layer of milk next the can will become cold and act as an insulator to the remainder in the center of the can.

One way to destroy many of the bacteria in milk is by pasteurization. This consists in heating the milk to such a degree that the bacteria are killed, and then quickly cooling it. After pasteurization, the milk is so changed that some kinds of cheese cannot be made successfully.

42. Fermentation test.—When a cheese-maker is having trouble with gas in his cheese, or bad flavors, he can generally locate the source of difficulty. This can be done by making a small amount of cheese from each patron's milk, called a fermentation test.[19] Pint or quart fruit jars or milk bottles make suitable containers. They should be thoroughly washed and scalded, to be sure they are clean and sterile, and then covered to prevent contamination. As the milk is delivered to the factory, a sample is taken of each patron's milk. The best way to secure the sample is to dip the sterile jar in the can of milk as delivered and fill two-thirds full of milk.

The jars are then set in water at 110° F. to bring the temperature of the milk to 98° F. The jar should be kept covered. A sink or wash-tub makes a convenient place in which to keep the jars. When the temperature of the milk is 98° F., ten drops of rennet extract or pepsin is added to each jar. A uniform temperature of 98° F. should be maintained in the jars. This will necessitate the addition of warm water occasionally to the water surrounding the jars. When the milk is coagulated,

---

[17] Wing, L. W., Milking machines; their sterilization and their efficiency in producing clean milk, N. Y. (Cornell) Exp. Sta. Circ. 18, 1913.

[18] Ruddick, J. A., and G. H. Barr, The cooling of milk for cheese making, Ottawa Dept. of Agr. Bul. 22, 1910.

[19] Wis. Exp. Sta. Rept. 1895, pages 14-150, Fermentation test for gas-producing bacteria in milk. This is commonly called the Wisconsin curd test.

the curd is broken up with a sterile knife. Precaution should be taken to sterilize the knife after using it in one jar before putting it into another. The best way to do this is to hold the knife for a minute in a pail of boiling water, after taking it out of each jar. The same precaution should be observed with the thermometer. Unless care is taken, contamination is liable to be carried from one jar to the other. After cutting, the whey is poured off. The temperature should be kept at 98° F. so that the organisms will have a suitable temperature for growth. The whey should be poured from the jars occasionally, usually about every half hour.

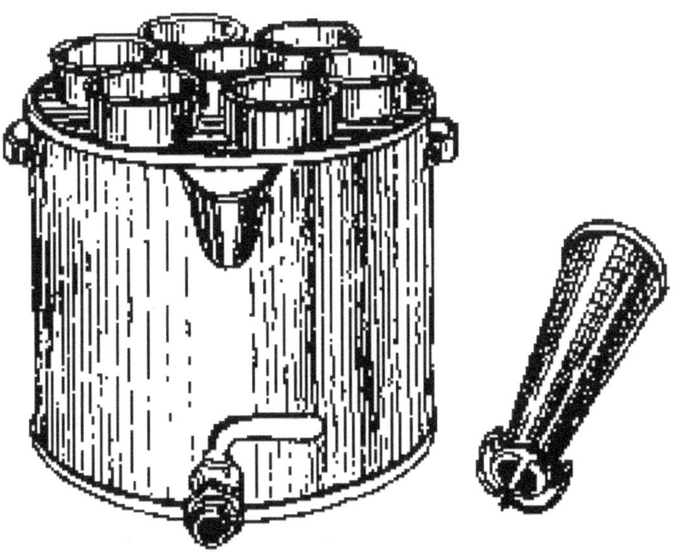

Fig. 4.—A gang sediment tester, one tester removed.

As the fermentation takes place, different odors will be noticed in different jars. In ten to twelve hours the jar should be finally examined for odors and the curd taken out and cut to examine it for gas pockets. By this means, bad flavors and gas in the cheese can be traced to their sources.

43. The sediment test.—The presence of solid material or dirt in the milk is always accompanied by bacterial contamination. By means of the sediment test, the amount of solid material can be determined. The test consists of filtering the milk through a layer of cotton; the foreign material is left on the cotton filter. Various devices for filtering the milk have been manufactured. (Figs. 4 and 5.) In order to be able to compare the filters from the different dairy-men's milk, the same amount of each patron's milk is filtered, usually about a pint. These tests are usually made once or twice a month at the factory and the filters placed on a card where the dairy-men can see them. Much improvement in the quality of the milk has been accomplished by the use of the sediment test. The purpose of this test may be and often is defeated by the use of efficient strainers. Milk produced in an unclean way may be rendered nearly free from sediment if carefully strained. It must be remembered that the strainer takes out only the undissolved substances and that bacteria and soluble materials which constitute a very large part of the filth pass through with the milk.

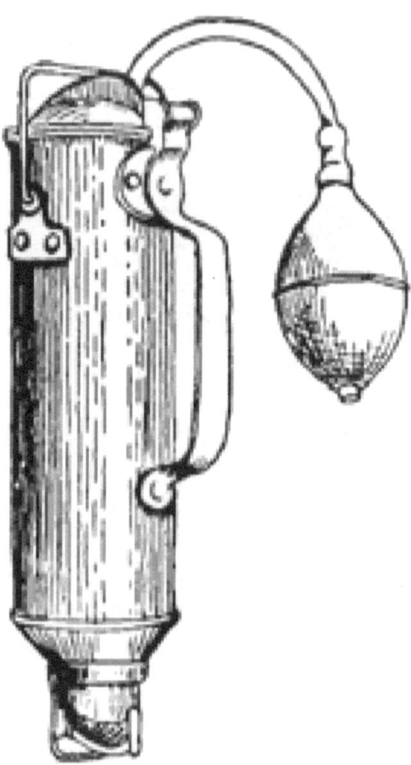

Fig. 5.—A single sediment tester.

CHAPTER III

COAGULATING MATERIALS

Ferments; Nature of rennet; Preparation of rennet extract; Pepsin; Chemistry of curdling; Use of acid; Robertson's theory; Rennet curd; Hammarsten's theory; Duclaux theory; Bang's theory; Bosworth's theory.

At the present time, two substances are used to coagulate milk for cheese-making,—rennet extract and commercial pepsin.[20] Many substances will coagulate milk, such as acids and other chemicals. Enzymes in certain plants will also coagulate it.

The curing or ripening of the cheese seems to depend on the physical and chemical properties of the curd, on the activity of certain organisms and on enzymes produced by them or in the milk. Rennet extract and pepsin are the only known substances which will produce curd of such character as will permit the desired ripening changes to take place. Until recently, rennet extract was principally used to coagulate the milk, but because of the scarcity, pepsin is now being substituted.

44. Ferments.—Many of the common changes taking place in milk are due to fermentations. The souring of milk is one of the most familiar cases of fermentation. The important change taking place is the formation of lactic acid from the milk-sugar. The change is brought about by certain living organisms, namely, the lactic acid-forming bacteria. Another familiar case of fermentation is the coagulation of milk by rennet extract or pepsin. In this case, the change is produced by a chemical substance, not a living organism. Fermentation may be defined as a chemical change of an organic compound through the action of living organisms or of chemical agents.

There are two general classes of ferments: (1) living organisms, or organized

---

[20] Stevenson, C., Pepsin in cheesemaking, Jour. Agr. (New Zeal.) 14 (1917), pages 32-34.

Todd, A., and E. C. V. Cornish, Experiments in the preparation of homemade rennet, Jour. Bd. Agr. (London) 23 (1916), no. 6, pages 549-555.

Besana, C., Lack of coagulating ferment in cheesemaking, Staz. Sper. Agr. Ital. 49 (1916), pages 10-12.

Van Dam, W., Rennet economy and substitutes, Verslag. Ver. Exploit. Proefzuivelbo-erderij. Hoorn, 1914, pages 45-46.

ferments; (2) chemical, or unorganized ferments. Organized ferments are living microorganisms, capable, as a result of their growth, of causing the changes. Unorganized ferments are chemical substances or ferments without life, capable of causing marked changes in many complex organic compounds, while the enzymes themselves undergo little or no change. These unorganized ferments are such as rennin, pepsin, trypsin, ptyalin. The rennet and pepsin must, therefore, be very thoroughly mixed into the milk to insure complete and uniform results, because they act by contact, and theoretically, if they could be recovered, might be used over and over again. Practically, the amount used is so small a percentage that recovery would be impractical even if possible.

45. Nature of rennet.—Two enzymes or ferments are found in rennet extract, rennin and pepsin. They are prepared from the secreting areas of living membranes of the stomachs of mammalian young. For rennet-making, these stomachs are most valuable if taken before the young have received any other feed than milk. Rennin at this stage appears to predominate over pepsin which is already secreted to some extent. With the inclusion of other feed, the secretion of pepsin comes to predominate. Rennin has never been separated entirely from pepsin. Both of these enzymes are secreted by digestive glands in the same area, perhaps even by the same glands. They are so closely related that many workers have regarded them as identical. In practical work the effectiveness of rennet preparations has been greatest when stomachs which have digested feed other than milk are excluded. The differences, therefore, however difficult to define, appear to be important in the commercial preparation of rennet.

It was the practice until a few years ago for each cheese-maker to prepare his own rennet extract. Each patron was supposed to supply so many rennets. Now commercial rennet extract and pepsin are on the market; however, some Swiss cheese-makers prefer to make their own rennet extract. For sheep's and goat's milk cheese, some makers hold that rennet made from kid or lamb stomachs is best for handling the milk of the respective species. The objection to the cheese-maker preparing his own rennet extract is that it varies in strength from batch to batch and is liable to spoil quickly. Taints and bad odors and flavors develop in it and so taint the cheese.

46. Preparation of rennet extract.—This extract may be manufactured commercially from digestive stomachs of calves, pigs or sheep. An animal is given a full meal just before slaughtering; this stimulates a large flow of the digestive juices, containing the desired enzymes.

The stomach is taken from the animal, cleaned, commonly inflated and dried. It may be held in the dry condition until needed for use. Such stomachs are usually spoken of as "rennets" in the trade. Such old rennets may be seen to-day hanging from the rafters of some of the older cheese factories. When wanted for use, rennets are placed in oak barrels and covered with water. Before placing them in the barrel, they are cut open so that the water may have easy access. Salt is usually added to the water at the rate of 3 to 5 per cent. They are stirred and pounded in this solution from five to seven days. At the end of this time, they are wrung through a clothes-wringer to remove the liquid. The rennets are put back into a fresh solution of salt and water, the object being to obtain all the digestive juices possible. They are usually soaked from four to six weeks. At the end of this time, most of the digestive juices will have been removed. The liquid portion is passed through a filter made of straw, charcoal and sand. When clean, an excess of salt is added to preserve it.

Such extracts cannot be sterilized by heat because the necessary temperature would destroy the enzyme. Effective disinfectants cannot be used in food products. The extract, therefore, should be kept cool to retard bacterial growth. The extract is kept in wooden barrels, stone jugs or yellow glass bottles to protect it from light, which is able to destroy its activity. Rennet extract should be clear, with a clean salty taste and a distinct rennet flavor. There should be no cloudy appearance and no muddy sediment in properly preserved rennet. Rennet extract is on the market in the form of a liquid and a powder, the former being much more common. The commercial forms of rennet have the advantage in the skill used in their preparation and standardization. The combined product from large numbers of stomachs may not be as effective a preparation as the most skillfully produced sample from the very choicest single stomach, but it gives a uniformity of result which improves the average product greatly.

47. Pepsin.—Pepsin is on the market in several commercial forms, as a liquid, scale pepsin and in a granular form known as spongy pepsin. Some commercial concerns put out a preparation which is a mixture of rennet extract and commercial pepsin.

48. Chemistry of curdling.—The chemistry of casein[21] and of curd formation under the influence of acid and rennet extract and pepsin has been the subject of many years' research. While many points remain unsettled, the general considerations together with a large mass of accepted facts may be presented and some of the unsolved problems pointed out as left for future researches.

Casein is a white amorphous powder, practically insoluble in water. It is an acid and as such readily dissolves in solutions of the hydroxides or the carbonates of alkalies and alkaline earths by forming soluble salts.

Pure casein salt solutions and fresh milk do not coagulate on boiling, but in the presence of free acid coagulation may take place below the boiling temperature. The coagulum formed in the case of milk includes fat and calcium phosphate. The slight pellicle which coats over milk when it is warmed is of the same composition.

---

[21] The paragraphs on the chemistry of casein and on rennet action have been selected from a complete discussion of the subject by E. B. Forbes and M. H. Keith in Ohio Exp. Sta. Tech. Bul. 5 entitled, "A review of the literature of phosphorus compounds in animal metabolism." The original references cited in this discussion are given at the end of the chapter in the order of their citation in the text.

See also, Van Slyke, L. L., and D. D. Van Slyke, I, The action of dilute acids upon casein when no soluble compounds are formed; II, The hydrolyses of the sodium salts of casein, N. Y. (Geneva) Exp. Sta. Tech. Bul. 3, pages 75-162, 1906.

Sammis, J. L., S. K. Suzuki and F. W. Laabs, Factors controlling the moisture content of cheese curds, U. S. Dept. Agr. Bur. An. Ind. Bul. 122, pages 1-61, 1910.

49. Use of acid.—A commonly accepted explanation of the precipitation of casein by acids is that the casein is held in solution by chemical union with a base (lime in the case of milk); that added acid removes the base, allowing the insoluble casein to precipitate; and that excess of acid unites with casein, forming a compound which is more or less readily soluble.

50. Robertson's theory.—According to Robertson's conception, in a soluble solution of a protein or its salt, the molecules of the protein unite with each other to a certain extent, in this way forming polymers. The reaction is reversible, and the point of equilibrium between the compound and its polymeric modification varies under the influence of whatever condition affects the concentration of the protein ions. Addition of water, or of acid, alkali or salt, or the application of heat has such an effect, and consequently alters the relative number of heavier molecule-complexes. Robertson's experiments give evidence that one of the effects of increase of temperature on a solution of casein is a shifting of the equilibrium in the direction of the higher complexes. He explains coagulation as being a result of these molecular aggregates becoming so large as to assume the properties of matter in mass and to become practically an unstable suspension and then a precipitate. The acid curd then is casein or some combination of casein with the precipitant acid.

51. Rennet curd.—Rennet extract and pepsin coagulation differs from coagulation by acids, and cannot be looked on as a simple removal of the base from a caseinate. The presence of soluble calcium salts (or other alkaline earth salts) seems to be essential, and the precipitate formed is not casein or a casein salt, but a salt of a slightly different nucleoalbumin called "paracasein." Many writers, following Halliburton, call this modification produced by rennin the "casein" and that from which it is derived, "caseinogen." Foster and a few others have used the term "tyrein" for the rennet clot.

A number of investigations have been made on the conditions essential or favorable to formation of the coagulum, especially with regard to the effects of the degree of acidity and of conditions affecting the amount of calcium present, either as free soluble salt or bound to the casein. Soluble salts of calcium, barium and strontium favor or hasten coagulation, while salts of ammonium, sodium and potassium retard or prevent coagulation.

The bulk of the coagulum from milk is a calcium paracaseinate, but it carries down with it calcium phosphate and fat, both of which bodies have been helped to remain in their state of suspension in milk by the presence of the casein salt. Lindet (1912) has concluded that about one-half of the phosphorus contained in the rennet curd is in the form of phosphate of lime (probably tricalcic), the other half being organically combined phosphoric acid.

52. Hammarsten's theory.—According to Hammarsten (1877, 1896), whose view has been commonly held, the distinctive effect of the ferment is not precipitation but the transformation of casein into paracasein. This is evidenced by the fact that if rennet be allowed to act on solutions free from lime salts no precipitate occurs; but there is an invisible alteration of the casein, for now, even if the ferment be destroyed by boiling the solution, addition of lime salts will cause immediate coagulation. (See also Spiro, 1906.) Hence the process of rennet coagulation is a two-phase process; the first phase is the transformation of casein by rennin, the second is the visible coagulation caused by lime salts.

Furthermore, if the purest casein and the purest rennin were used, Hammarsten always found after coagulation that the filtrate contained very small amounts of a protein. This protein he designated as the "whey protein."

In accordance with these observations, Hammarsten (1911) explains the rennin action "as a cleavage process, in which the chief mass of the casein, sometimes more than 90 per cent, is split off as paracasein, a body closely related to casein, and in the presence of sufficient amounts of lime salts the paracasein-lime precipitates out while the proteose-like substance (whey-protein) remains in solution."

By continued action of rennin on paracasein, a further transformation has been found in several cases (Petry, 1906; Van Herwerden, 1907; Van Dam, 1909), but perhaps due to a contamination of the rennin with pepsin, or to the identity of these two enzymes. The action which forms paracasein and whey-protein takes place in a short time (Hammarsten, 1896; Schmidt-Nielson, 1906). The composition and solubilities of paracasein have received considerable attention. (See Loevenhart, 1904; Kikkoji, 1909; Van Slyke and Bosworth, 1912.) It is more readily digested by pepsin-hydrochloric acid than is casein (Hosl, 1910).

53. Duclaux theory.—Duclaux (1884) and Loevenhart (1904) and others do not accept Hammarsten's theory; but to most workers it seems probable, at least, that the action of the rennin is to cause a cleavage of casein with formation of paracasein. However, the chemical and physical differences observed between casein and paracasein appear to be so slight that Loevenhart and some others think that they are only physical, perhaps differences in the size of the colloid or solution aggregates. Loevenhart conceives of a large part of the work of the rennet (or of the acid, in acid and heat coagulation) as being a freeing of the calcium to make it available for precipitation. Some think that the aggregates of paracasein are larger than those of casein, but there is more evidence of their being smaller, which idea corresponds with the findings of Bosworth, though he looks on the change as a true cleavage.

54. Bang's theory.—Another description of the precipitation is given by Bang (1911), who studied the progress of the coagulation process by means of interruptions at definite intervals. His observations confirm the idea that rennin causes the formation of paracasein, and that the calcium salt serves only for the precipitation of the paracasein; the rennin has to do also with the mobilizing of lime salts. According to Bang, before coagulation occurs, paracaseins with constantly greater affinity for calcium phosphate are produced. These take up increasing amounts of calcium phosphate, until finally the combination formed can no longer remain in solution.

55. Bosworth's theory.—By a very recent work of L. L. Van Slyke and A. W. Bosworth (Van Slyke and Bosworth, 1912, 1913; and Bosworth and Van Slyke, 1913), in which ash-free casein and paracasein were compared as to their elementary composition, and as to the salts they form with bases, and the properties of these salts, it is indicated that the two compounds are alike in percentage composition and in combining equivalent, the paracasein molecule being one-half of the casein molecule. Moreover, Bosworth (1913) has shown that, if the rennin cleavage be carried out under conditions which avoid autohydrolysis, no other protein is formed; also that, if the calcium caseinate present be one containing four equivalents of calcium, the paracaseinate does not precipitate, save in the presence of a soluble calcium salt, while, if the calcium caseinate be one of two equivalents of base, rennin does cause immediate coagulation. Bosworth concludes that the rennin action is a cleavage (probably hydrolytic) of a molecule of caseinate into two molecules of paracaseinate, the coagulation being a secondary effect due to a change in solubilities, dicalcium paracaseinate being soluble in pure water but not in water containing more than a trace of calcium salt, and the monocalcium caseinate being insoluble in water. The alkali paracaseinates, as well as caseinates, are soluble. This explanation seems to promise to harmonize the observations with regard to acidity and the effects of the presence of soluble salts. This theory represents, therefore, many years of continuous work at the New York Experiment Station centered primarily on American Cheddar cheese. Disputed points remain for further study but these workers have contributed much toward a clear description of the chemical constitution of casein as affected by rennet action and bacterial activity.

The investigations of these authors and of Hart with regard to the changes which the paracasein, the calcium and the phosphorus undergo during the ripening of cheese (Van Slyke and Hart, 1902, 1905; Van Slyke and Bosworth, 1907, 1913; Bosworth, 1907) contributed to this interpretation.

BANG, IVAR, Ueber die chemische Vorgang bei der Milchgerinnung durch Lab, Skand. Arch. Physiol. 25, pages 105-144; through Jahresb. u. d. Fortsch. d. Thierchem. 41, pages 221-222, 1911.

BOSWORTH, A. W., The action of rennin on casein, N. Y. Exp. Sta. Tech. Bul. 31, 1913.

BOSWORTH, A. W., Chemical studies of Camembert cheese, N. Y. Exp. Sta. Tech. Bul. 5, 1907.

BOSWORTH, A. W., and L. L. VAN SLYKE, Preparation and composition of basic calcium caseinate and paracaseinate, Jour. Biol. Chem. Vol. 14, pages 207-210, 1913.

DUCLAUX, ÉMILE, Action de la présure sur le lait, Compt. Rend. Acad. Sci. 98, pages 526-528, 1884.

HAMMARSTEN, OLOF, Zur Kenntnis des Caseins und der Wirkung des Labfermentes, Nova. Acta Regiae Soc. Sci. Upsaliensis in Memoriam Quattuor Saec. ab Univ., Upsaliensi Peractorum, 1877.

HAMMARSTEN, OLOF, Ueber das Verhalten des Paracaseins zu dem Labenzyme, Zeit. physiol. Chem. 22, pages 103-126, 1896.

HAMMARSTEN, OLOF, A text book of physiological chemistry, from the author's 7th German edition, 1911.

HOSL, J., Unterschiede in der tryptischen und peptischen Spaltung des Caseins, Paracaseins und des Paracaseinkalkes aus Kuh- und Ziegenmilch, Inaug. Diss. Bern., 31 pp., 1910.

KIKKOJI, T., Beitrage zur Kenntniss des Caseins und Paracaseins, Zeit. physiol. Chem. No. 61, pages 130-146, 1909.

LINDET, L., Solubilité des albuminoides du lait dans les éléments du sérum; rétrogradation de leur solubilité sous l'influence du chlorure, Bul. Soc. Chim. (ser. 4) 13, pages 929-935.

LINDET, L., Sur les éléments mineraux contenus dans la caseine du lait, Rep. Eighth Internat. Congr. of Applied Chem. 19, 199-207, 1912.

LOEVENHART, A. S., Ueber die Gerinnung der Milch, Zeit. physiol. Chem. 41, pages 177-205, 1904.

PETRY, EUGEN, Ueber die Einwirkung des Labferments auf Kasein, Beitrage z. Chem. Physiol. u. Path. 8, pages 339-364, 1906.

ROBERTSON, T. BRAILSFORD, On the influence of temperature upon the solubility of casein in alkaline solutions, Jour. Biol. Chem. 5, pages 147-154, 1908.

SCHMIDT-NIELSON, SIGVAL, Zur Kenntnis des Kaseins und der Labgerinnung, Upsala läkaref. Förh. (N. F.) No. 11, Suppl.

Hammarsten Festschrift No. XV, 1-26; through Jahresb. u. d. Fortschr. d. Thierchem. No. 36, pages 255-256, 1906.

SPIRO, K., Beeinflussung und Natur des Labungsvorganges, Beitrage z. Chem. Physiol. u. Path. 8, pages 365-369, 1906.

VAN DAM, W., Ueber die Wirkung des Labs Auf. Paracaseinkalks, Zeit. physiol. Chem. No. 61, pages 147-163, 1909.

VAN HERWERDEN, M., Beitrag zur Kenntnis der Labwirkung auf Casein, Zeit. physiol. Chem. 52, pages 184-206, 1907.

VAN SLYKE, L. L., and A. W. BOSWORTH, I. Some of the first chemical changes in Cheddar cheese. II. The acidity of the water extract of Cheddar cheese, N. Y. Exp. Sta. Tech. Bul. 4, 1907.

VAN SLYKE, L. L., and A. W. BOSWORTH, Composition and properties of some casein and paracasein compounds and their relations to cheese, N. Y. Exp. Sta. Tech. Bul. 26, 1912.

VAN SLYKE, L. L., and A. W. BOSWORTH, Method of preparing ash-free casein and paracasein, Jour. Biol. Chem. Vol. 14, pages 203-206, 1913.

VAN SLYKE, L. L., and A. W. BOSWORTH, Preparation and composition of unsaturated or acid caseinates and paracaseinates, *Ibid.* Vol. 14, pages 211-225, 1913.

Van Slyke, L. L., and A. W. Bosworth, Valency of molecules and molecular weights of casein and paracasein, *Ibid.* Vol. 14, pages 227-230, 1913.

Van Slyke, L. L., and A. W. Bosworth, Composition and properties of the brine-soluble compounds in cheese, Jour. Biol. Chem. 14, pages 231-236, 1913.

Van Slyke, L. L., and E. B. Hart, A study of some of the salts formed by casein and paracasein with acids; their relations to American Cheddar cheese, N. Y. Exp. Sta. Bul. 214, 1902.

Van Slyke, L. L., and E. B. Hart, Casein and paracasein in some of their relations to bases and acids, American Chem. Jour. 33, pages 461-996, 1905.

Van Slyke, L. L., and E. B. Hart, Some of the relations of casein and paracasein to bases and acids, and their application to Cheddar cheese, N. Y. Exp. Sta. Bul. 261, 1905.

CHAPTER IV

LACTIC STARTERS

Acidifying organisms; Starter; Natural starter; Commercial starter or pure cultures; Manufacturer's directions; Selecting milk; Pasteurization; Containers; Adding cultures; Cleanliness; "Mother" starter or startoline; Examining starter; Second day's propagation; Preparations of larger amount of starter; Amount of mother starter to use; Qualities; How to carry the mother starter; Starter score-cards; Use of starter; The amount of starter to use; Starter lot-card.

Acidity in cheese-making arises almost exclusively from the lactic acid produced from the fermentation of milk-sugar (lactose) by bacteria. Hydrochloric acid is used in the Wisconsin[22] process of making pasteurized milk cheese and sometimes for making skimmed-milk curd for baking purposes. It is regularly used in precipitating casein not for food but for manufacturing purposes.

56. Acidifying organisms.—Many species of bacteria have been shown to possess the power to produce lactic acid by fermenting lactose. In practice, however, the cheese-maker seeks to control this fermentation by the actual introduction of the desired organisms and by the production of conditions which will insure this dominance through natural selection. For this purpose the initial souring for most types of cheeses is produced by some variety of the species originally described by Esten[23] and commonly referred to as *Bacterium lactis-acidi*, but variously named as *B. acidi-lactici, Streptococcus lacticus, B. guntheri* by different authors. Organisms of this series dominate all other species in milk which is incubated at 70° F. They produce a smooth solid mass without a sign of gas holes and without the separation of whey from the curd, and develop in milk a maximum acidity of about 0.90 of one per cent when titrated as lactic acid. (For titration see Chapter V.) This species is usually present in small numbers in fresh milk. There are many varieties or strains of the species with differing rates of activity and measurable differences in acid produced but with approximately the same qualitative characters. Most commercial starters for cheese- and butter-making belong to this group of species, although special mixtures with other organisms are prepared for special purposes. In addition to this group, most varieties of cheese contain some members of the colon-aërogenes group. When the milk is in proper condition, the activity of this

[22] Sammis, J. L., and A. T. Bruhn, The manufacture of Cheddar cheese from pasteurized milk, Wis. Exp. Sta. Research Bul. 27, 1912.

[23] Esten, W. M., Bacteria in the dairy, Conn. (Storrs) Rept. 1896, pages 44-52.

group should be held in check by the early and rapid development of acid. Free development of members of this group usually shows itself in the presence of gas holes in the curd.

57. Starter.—The practice of using pure cultures in cheese-making has brought about the development of factory methods of producing day by day cultures of the organisms desired, in quantities sufficient to inoculate the total quantity of milk used in manufacture. For this purpose milk is mostly used and the product is known as "starter." For cheese-making purposes, a starter is a substance used in the manufacture of dairy products having a predominance of lactic acid-forming microorganisms in an active state. There are two general classes of starter: (1) Natural starter; (2) commercial starter.

58. Natural starter.—Milk, or other similar substance, which has become sour or in which large numbers of lactic acid-forming organisms are present, is called a natural starter when used in the manufacture of dairy products. To secure clean-flavored milk, the cheese-maker usually selects the milk of some producer who usually brings good milk and allows it to sour naturally for use the next day. There is often a variation from day to day in the milk delivered by the same producer, so that the cheese-maker is not certain of a uniform quality in his fundamental material. While the lactic acid-forming organisms are developing, other organisms may also be present in numbers sufficient to produce bad flavors. If a starter has any objectionable flavor, it should not be used. Natural starters very commonly develop objectionable flavors which at first are very difficult to recognize. When natural starters with objectionable but not easily recognizable odors are used, the effect may be seen on the cheese. Milk, sour whey and buttermilk are materials commonly used as natural starter. A common difficulty in skimmed-milk cheese is caused by the use of buttermilk as a starter.

59. Commercial starter or pure cultures.—The alternative practice consists in the introduction of pure cultures of known strains of lactic bacteria into special milk to make the starter. Since these cultures must be prepared by a bacteriologist, commercial laboratories have developed a large business in their production. Many such commercial brands are manufactured under trade-marked names. Some of these cultures represent races of lactic bacteria cultivated and cared for efficiently, hence uniformly valuable over long periods of time. Others carelessly produced are worthless, or even a peril to the user.

These organisms are usually shipped in small quantities in bottles of liquid or powder, or in capsules of uniform size. The contents may be either the culture medium upon which the organisms grew or inert substance designed merely to hold the bacteria in inactive form. In either solid or liquid form, the producer of the culture should guarantee its activity up to a plainly stated date.

It is the problem[24] of the cheese-maker or butter-maker to increase this small

[24] Bushnell, L. D., and W. R. Wright, Preparation and use of butter starter, Mich. Exp. Sta. Bul. 246, 1907.

Hastings, E. G., Preparation and use of starter, Wis. Exp. Sta. Bul. 181, 1909.

Larsen, C., and W. White, Preparation and use of starter, S. D. Exp. Sta. Bul. 123, 1910.

amount of lactic acid-forming organisms to such numbers and in such active condition that it may be used in the factory; while being built up, these organisms must be kept pure. The usual practice is to allow them to develop in some material, usually whole milk or skimmed-milk; dissolved milk powder may be used in the place of milk.

60. Manufacturer's directions.—The manufacturer usually sends directions with his starter preparation, telling how it should be used to secure the best result. These directions apply to average conditions and must be varied to suit the individual instances so that a good starter will be the result. The directions usually state the amount of milk necessary for the first inoculation. It is usually a small amount, one or two quarts. After the specific amount has been selected, this milk should be pasteurized.

61. Selecting milk.—The milk for use in starter-making should be selected with very much care. Only clean-flavored sweet milk, free from undesirable micro-organisms, should be used in the preparation of starter. The milk is ordinarily chosen from a producer whose milk is usually in good condition. The quality of the milk can be determined by the use of the fermentation test. (See Chapter II.) It is better to choose only the morning's milk for the making of starter, because the bacteria have not had so much opportunity to develop. In no case should the mixed milk be used in the preparation of starter, as this eliminates all opportunity for selection. The flavor of the starter will be the same as that of the milk from which it is made.

62. Pasteurization is the process of heating to a high temperature for a given length of time and quickly cooling. It kills most of the micro-organisms in the milk. In other words, it makes a clean seed-bed for the pure culture. The temperatures of pasteurization recommended for starter-making differ with the authority. A temperature of 180° F. for thirty minutes or longer seems to be very satisfactory, since under these conditions nearly all the micro-organisms in the milk are killed.

63. Containers.—Various kinds of containers may be used for starter-making. One-quart glass fruit jars or milk bottles make very satisfactory containers, because the condition of the starter may be seen at any time. They are also easily cleaned. They have the disadvantage, however, of being easily broken, if the temperature is suddenly changed, or if severely jarred. Tin containers may also be used. Such containers are not easily broken, but they are harder to clean and must be opened to examine the contents; hence the liability of contamination is very much greater.

This small amount of milk may be pasteurized by placing the container in water heated to the desired temperature. A very satisfactory arrangement is to cut of a barrel, and place a steam pipe in it. The barrel can then be filled partly full of water and heated by steam. The bottles of milk to be pasteurized are hung in the water in the barrel. Two or three more bottles should be prepared than it is expected will be used as some of the bottles are liable to be broken while cooling or heating. The bottles should be filled about two-thirds full. This leaves room enough to add the mother starter and later to break up the starter to examine it. It is desirable not

Guthrie, E. S., and W. W. Fisk, Propagation of starter for butter-making and cheese-making, N. Y. (Cornell) Exp. Sta. Circ. 13, 1912.

to have the milk or starter touch the cover since contaminations are more likely. It is a good plan when pasteurizing to have one bottle as a check. This may be filled with water and left open and the thermometer placed in it. A uniform temperature may be obtained by shaking the bottles.

64. Adding cultures.—After being pasteurized, the milk should be cooled to a temperature of 80° F. This is a suitable temperature for the development of the lactic acid-forming organisms. The commercial or pure culture should now be added to the milk at the rate specified in the directions. Care should be exercised in opening bottles not to put the covers in an unclean place. A sterile dipper is a good place to put them. After the culture has been added to the milk, it should be mixed thoroughly by shaking the bottle. This should be repeated every fifteen or twenty minutes for four or five times. This is done to make certain that the culture is thoroughly mixed with the milk. The milk should be placed in a room or incubator as near 80° F. as possible, in order to have a uniform temperature for the growth of the organisms. The bacteria in the pure culture are more or less dormant so that a somewhat higher temperature than the ordinary is necessary to stimulate their activity. This milk should be coagulated in eighteen to twenty-four hours, depending largely on the uniformity of the temperature during incubation.

65. Cleanliness.—To produce a good starter, great care should be exercised that all utensils coming in contact with the milk are sterile. After the milk is in the container in which the starter is made, it should be kept covered as continuously as possible. Thermometers should not be put into it to ascertain the temperature. When examining the starter, do not dip into it, but pour out, as this prevents contamination. The cover, when removed from the container, should be put in a sterile place in such way that the dirt will not stick to it and later get into the starter.

66. "Mother" starter or startoline.—The thickened sour milk obtained by inoculating the sweet pasteurized milk with pure culture of lactic acid-forming bacteria is known as "mother starter" or "startoline."

67. Examining starter.—This starter should be examined carefully as to physical properties, odor and taste. The coagulation should be smooth, free from whey and gassy pockets or bubbles. Sometimes the first few inoculations from a new culture will show signs of gas, but, usually, this will quickly disappear, and not injure the starter. It should have a clean sour cream odor and clean, mild, acid flavor. After breaking up it should be thick and creamy, entirely free from lumps. This starter may have an objectionable flavor, due to the media in which the organisms were growing when shipped. In such cases it is necessary to carry the starter one or two propagations to overcome the flavor, to enliven the micro-organisms and to secure the quantity desired.

68. Second day's propagation.—For the second day, the milk for the starter is selected as on the first day. It is pasteurized, and this time cooled to 70° F. The milk is cooled a trifle colder the second day than the first, because the organisms have become more active and hence do not require as high a temperature to grow. Instead of inoculating with powder, as was done the first day, the mother starter prepared the first day is used. This requires only a very small amount, perhaps a tablespoonful to a quart bottle. It should be thoroughly mixed with the milk. This starter may have the flavor of the media used in the laboratory culture, therefore may need to be carried one or two days more to eliminate it. After the flavor has become normal, the mother starter is ready for commercial use.

Fig. 6.—An improved starter-can.

69. Preparation of larger amount of starter.—The first thing to determine is the quantity of starter required. As much milk should be carefully chosen as the amount of starter desired. This milk should then be pasteurized. An improved starter-can (Fig. 6) may be used in the pasteurization of the milk and the making of starter, or a milk-can (Fig. 7) placed in a tub of water in which there is a steam pipe. The former requires mechanical power to operate the agitator, but the latter can be used where mechanical power is not available. In the latter the milk and starter are stirred by hand. This is the kind of apparatus more often found in cheese factories. If possible, this milk should be pasteurized to 180° F. for thirty minutes; this kills most of the bacteria and spores. The milk should be cooled to 60°-65° F., the temperature of incubation. This temperature may be varied with conditions, so that the starter will be ready for use at the desired time. The higher the temperature, the less time is required to ripen the starter.

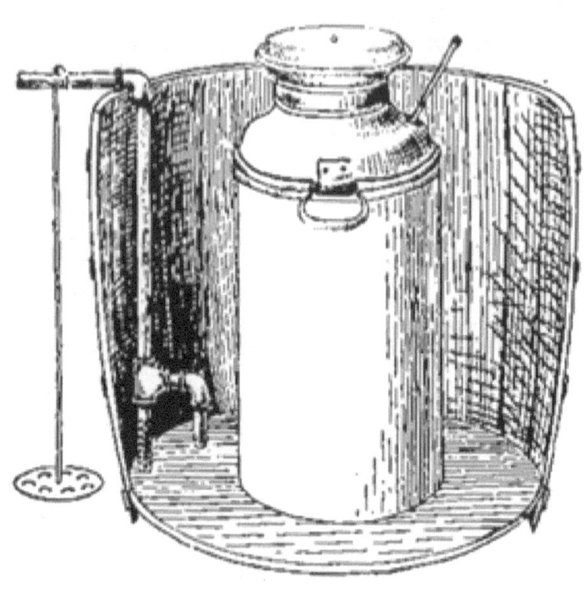

Fig. 7.—A simple device for the preparation of starter.

70. Amount of mother starter to use.—The mother starter prepared the day before is now used to inoculate the starter milk. The amount to use will depend on:

1. Temperature of milk when mother starter is added;

2. Average temperature at which the milk will be kept during the ripening period;

3. Time allowed for starter to ripen before it is to be used;

4. Vigor and acidity of the mother starter added. There is a very wide range as to the amount of mother starter required, from 0.5 of one per cent to 10 per cent being used under different conditions.

Some operators prefer to add the mother starter while the milk is at a temperature of about 90° F., before it has been cooled to the incubating temperature. This reduces the amount of mother starter necessary.

If an even incubating temperature can be maintained, it will require less mother starter than if the temperature goes down.

If the ripening period is short, it will require a larger amount of mother starter, than if the ripening period is longer. If the starter has a low acidity or weak body indicating that organisms are of low vitality, it will require more mother starter.

71. Qualities.—The starter, when ready to use, may or may not be coagulated; a good idea of the quality of the starter may be gained by the condition of the coagulation. The coagulation should be jelly- or custard-like, close and smooth, entirely free from gas pockets and should not be wheyed off.

When broken up, the starter should be of a smooth creamy texture and entirely free from lumpiness or wateriness. It should have a slightly pronounced acid aroma. The starter should be free from taints and all undesirable flavors; the flavor should be a clean, mild acid taste.

72. How to carry the mother starter.—Some mother starter must be carried from day to day to inoculate the large starter. This may be carried or made in several ways:

1. Independently: By this method a mother starter is made and carried entirely separately from the large starter. It requires more time and work, but is by far the best method. With a good mother starter, there is not so much danger of the larger starter becoming poor in quality.

2. Mother starter may be made by dipping pasteurized milk from that prepared for the large starter with sterile jars and then inoculating these jars separately. By this method, if the milk selected for the large starter is poor, the mother starter for the next day will be the same. It is very difficult by this method to carry a uniform, high quality mother starter.

There is danger that the container used for the mother starter may not be sterile, and there is also danger of contamination in transferring the milk.

3. Another practice is to hold over some of the large starter used to-day for mother starter. This is by far the easiest method. By this practice, there is no certainty of the quality of the starter, because there is little or no control of the mother starter. If the large starter is for some reason not good, there is no separate reserve of mother starter on which to rely.

73. Starter score-cards.—The use of a score-card tends to analyze the observations in such a way as to emphasize all the characteristics desired in the starter. Such an analysis seeks to minimize the personal factor and produce a standardization of the quality. The score-card finally reduces the qualities of the starter to a numerical basis for ease of comparison. Many score-cards have been proposed but the one preferred by the authors is that used by the Dairy Department of the New York State College of Agriculture, which is as follows:

CORNELL SCORE-CARD

Flavor	50	Clean, desirable acid.
Aroma	20	Clean, agreeable acid. No undesirable aroma.
Acidity	20	0.6 per cent-0.8 per cent.
Body	10	Before breaking up: jelly-like, close, absence of gas holes. No free whey. After breaking up: smooth, creamy, free from granules or flakes.

The qualities mentioned in this score-card can be quickly and easily determined by examining and tasting the starter and by making an acid test of a sample. The acid test is conducted as with milk (see Chapter II) except the starter must be rinsed out of the pipette with pure water. Some starter score-cards call for a bacterial examination and counting of the starter organisms. This takes a considerable period of time and is not entirely necessary. The physical properties and acid test are closely correlated with the presence of the desired organisms.

74. Use of starter.—If all milk could be clean and sweet and the only fermentation from it were the clean acid type, a starter would be useless. Such milk is hard to obtain; therefore, a starter is used to overcome the bad fermentation. This improves the flavor, body and texture of the cheese. The common contaminations which the starter will tend to correct are:

1. Gas-producing bacteria.
2. Yeasts.
3. Bad flavors or taints.

The length of time a starter may be carried depends on the accuracy and carefulness of the maker. This calls for scrupulous attention to the temperature, the selection of milk and keeping out contaminations. The maker must remember that a starter is not merely milk, but milk full of a multitude of tiny plants, very sensitive to food, temperature, clean surroundings and the quantity of their own acid.

75. The amount of starter to use depends on the amount of acid desired in the milk for any particular kind of cheese. The great abuse of starter is the practice of using too much. It is better and safer to add starter a little at a time and several times than to add too much at once. When starter is added to milk for cheese-making, it should be strained to remove any lumps; otherwise an uneven color is likely to result.

76. Starter lot-card.—For certain dairy operations, a permanent record is desired. This is especially true in the making of starter and certain varieties of cheese. A lot-card not only serves as a record but also points out the succeeding steps of the operation. This latter is especially useful for beginners and students. Page 53 shows a desirable lot-card to be used when making starter. Each operation has been referred to the page in the text where it is discussed. This makes this particular lot-card an index to the whole process of starter-making as here treated.

NEW YORK STATE COLLEGE OF AGRICULTURE AT CORNELL UNIVERSITY

STARTER LOT–CARD   Department of Dairy Industry.

Day and Date...

MILK:
Kind....................% fat.................... % solids not fat.......................
Flavor..
Amount of milk.................................... Hours old...................

PASTEURIZATION:
Method..
Milk when received: Temperature....................°
    Acidity....................%
Heating: Turning on heat....................APM.
    Desired temp. reached....................APM.
    Turning off heat....................APM.
    Length of time at desired temp....................
    Beginning to cool....................
    Cooled....................APM; to....................°
Acidity: After pasteurization....................
    When inoculated....................

INOCULATION:
    Time....................   Temperature....................
    Amount....................lbs.   ....%

INCUBATION:
    Temperature....................   Time....................

MOTHER STARTER USED:
    Source....................   % used....................
    Times propagated....................   Acidity....................
    Amount used....................   Appearance....................
                Flavor....................
    Comments....................

STARTER:
    Time of examining....................
    Temperature....................

SCORE–CARD:

Flavor....................50	Clean, desirable acid.	
Aroma....................20	Clean, agreeable acid. No undesirable aroma.	
Acidity....................20	0.6%–0.75%.	
Body....................10	Before breaking up: jelly-like, close, absence of gas holes. No free whey.	
———	———After breaking up: smooth, creamy, free from granules or flakes.	
Total........ 100		

The above is a tentative score-card.

COMMENTS: ....
....
....
....

Work and observation by..

CHAPTER V

CURD-MAKING

The composition of the milk; Cheese color; The acidity factor; Acidity of milk when received; The acid test; Rennet tests; Marschall rennet test; Comparison of acid and rennet test; Control of acid; Acidity and rennet action; Acidity and expulsion of the whey; Acidity in relation to cheese flavor; Acidity in relation to body and texture of cheese; Acidity in relation to cheese color; Control of moisture; Relation of moisture to manufacture and quality; Relation of moisture to acidity; Setting temperature; Strength of coagulating materials; Amount of coagulating materials to use; Method of adding rennet; The curdling period; Cutting or breaking the curd; Curd knives; Heating or "cooking,; Draining; Application to cheese.

Aside from the purely sour-milk cheeses, the coagulum or curd resulting from rennet action is the basis of cheese-making. The finished cheese, whatever its final condition, is primarily dependent on a particular chemical composition and fairly definite physical characters in the freshly made curd mass. These characters are determined by a series of factors under control of the cheese-maker. Assuming the milk to be normal in character, success depends on the use of a proper combination of these factors. The possible variations in each factor together with their number makes an almost infinite series of such combinations possible. The essential steps in the process are, therefore, presented as underlying all cheese-making. The special adaptations of each factor are considered in the discussion of the varieties group by group.

These factors follow:

A. The coagulation group:

 1. Fat-content of the milk.
 2. The acidity of the milk.
 3. The temperature of renneting.
 4. The effective quantity of rennet.
 5. Curdling period or the time allowed for rennet action.

B. The handling group:

 6. Cutting or breaking the curd.
 7. Heating (cooking) or not heating.
 8. Draining (including pressing, grinding and putting into hoops

or forms).

77. The composition of the milk.—The fat percentage in the milk in the cheese-vat should be known to the cheese-maker and be strictly under his control. The fat tester and the separator make this clearly possible. He can go further. Milk from particular herds whose quality is a matter of record from the routine test of each patron's milk may be selected and brought together for the manufacturer of cheese of special quality. Control of casein or lactose, on the contrary, is not nearly so practicable. The purchase of milk on the fat test has become so well established in most dairy territories, as to insure the presence and constant use of the tester. A fat test of the mixed product in the cheese-vat in connection with established tables thus insures an accurate knowledge of the materials which go into each day's cheese. For some varieties of cheese, whole milk should always be used. For other varieties, the addition or removal of fat is regularly recognized as part of the making process. The presence of added fat or the removal of fat affects the texture of the product and the details of the process of making.

78. Cheese color.—An alkaline solution of annatto is usually used as a cheese color. This colors both casein and fat in contrast to butter color which is an oil solution of the dye and mixes only with the fat. Cheese color is added to the milk in making some varieties of cheese, and not for others. When lactic starter is used, the color should be added after the starter and just before the addition of the rennet. The amount is determined by the color desired in the cheese. The usual amount varies from one to four ounces to each thousand pounds of milk. Before adding, the color should be diluted in either milk or water, preferably water. It should then be mixed thoroughly with the milk.

79. The acidity factor.—Milk as drawn shows a measurable acidity when titrated to phenolphthalein with normal sodium hydroxide. This figure varies with the composition of milk. Casein itself gives a weakly acid reaction with this indicator. Calculated as lactic acid, this initial acidity varies within fairly wide limits, records being found from 0.12 to 0.21 of one per cent or even more widely apart. Commonly, however, such titration shows 0.14 to 0.17 per cent. Some forms of cheese (Limburger, Swiss, Brie) are made from absolutely fresh milk. Acidity from bacterial activity is important as a factor in the making of most types of cheese and probably in the ripening of all types.

Increasing the acidity of the milk hastens rennet action and within limits produces increased firmness of the curd. If carried too high, acidity causes a grainy or sandy curd. Normally fresh milk is sufficiently acid in reaction when tested to phenolphthalein to permit rennet to act, but the rate of action increases rapidly with the development of acid. Increase of acidity may be accomplished: (a) by the addition of acid as has been done by Sammis[25] and Bruhn in pasteurized milk for Cheddar cheese; or (b) by the development of acid through the activity of lactic organisms, which is the usual way. For renneting, the acidity necessary for particular cheeses runs from that of absolutely fresh milk still warm (as in French Brie, Limburger, Swiss, Gorgonzola) through series calling for increase of acidity,

[25] Sammis, J. L., and A. T. Bruhn, The manufacture of cheese of the Cheddar type from pasteurized milk, U. S. Dept. Agr. Bur. An. Ind. Bul. 165, pages 1-95, 1913.

hundredth by hundredth per cent calculated as lactic acid. This ranges from 0.17 to 0.20 per cent as is variously used in American factory Cheddar to about 0.25 to 0.28 per cent as obtained by adding acid in Sammis' method. This method is discussed under the heading "Cheddar Cheese from Pasteurized Milk" (p. 229) since it requires special apparatus and has not thus far been used with other types of cheese. For the development of acidity by the action of bacteria, lactic starter is almost universally used. This may be added in very small quantities and the acidity secured by closely watching its development or by adding starter in amount sufficient to obtain the required acidity at once. In either case, the cheese-maker needs to know the rate of action of the culture to insure the proper control of the process. The amount of acid already present when the rennet is added affects not only the texture of the curd as first found, but within limits indicates also the rate at which further acidity may be expected to develop.

A series of experiments in making Roquefort were tabulated to show the rate of acidification from various initial points. In the graphs (Fig. 8) the curves for acid development are parallel after the determination reaches 0.30 per cent. These experiments were made at a temperature 80° to 84° F. Milk at the lowest acidities tried developed titratable acid very slowly. A period of several hours was required to produce sufficient acid to affect the curd texture. When the acid reached 0.25 per cent by titration, the further rise was rapid and all the lines became almost straight and parallel after the titration reached 0.30 per cent. If this rapid souring occurred after the completion of the cheese-making process, the texture of the experimental cheese was not measurably affected. In those cases, however, in which 0.30 per cent was reached before the cheese reached its final form in the hoop, the texture of the ripened cheese was entirely different from that desired for this variety under experiment. These curves apply directly to but one cheese process in which a particular combination of acidity, rennet and time is used to obtain a very delicately balanced result. In other varieties it is equally important to obtain exactly the adjustment of these factors which will bring the desired result.

80. Acidity of milk when received.—If proper care has been taken, milk should be delivered to the factory fresh, clean and without the development of acid. If the milk has not been handled properly, the early stages of souring or some other unfavorable fermentation will have developed. Such milk may develop too much acid, or gas, or any one of several objectionable flavors during the making and ripening of the cheese. Some cheese-makers become very expert in detecting the first traces of objectionable qualities, but most makers are dependent on standardized tests to determine whether milk shall be accepted or rejected, and when accepted to determine the rate at which it may be expected to respond during the cheese-making process.

Various tests have been devised to determine the amount of acid present in milk. There are two tests commonly used in cheese-factories. One is known as the "acid test" and the other the "rennet test."

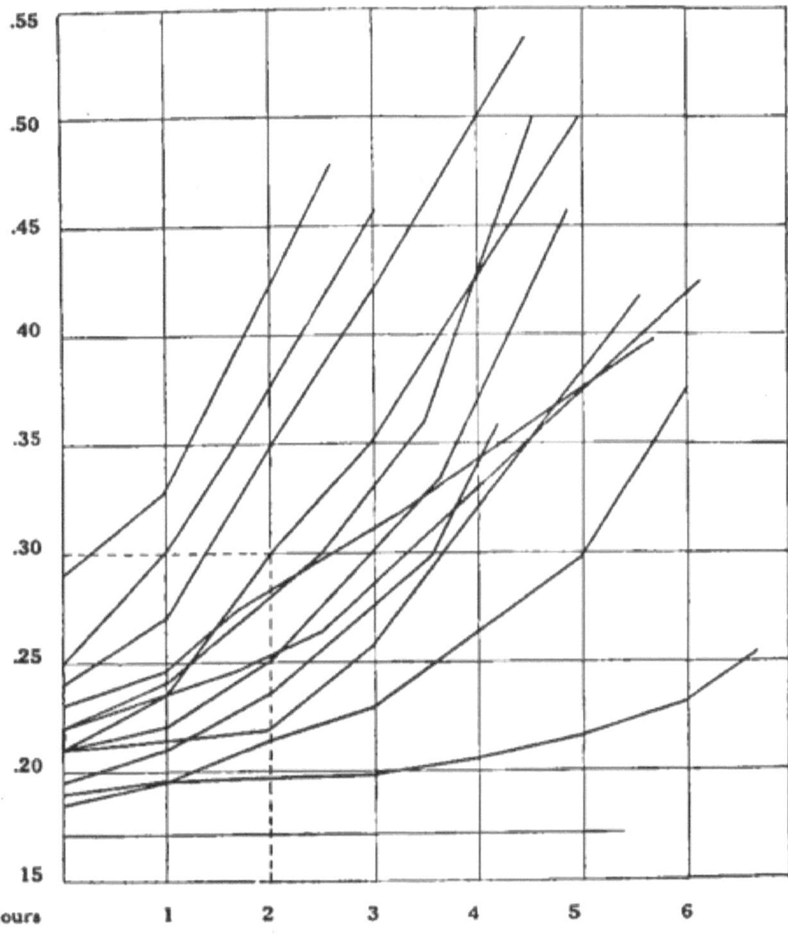

Fig. 8.—The acidification of Roquefort cheese.

81. The acid test[26] is made by titrating a known amount of milk (Fig. 9) against an alkali solution of known strength, using phenolphthalein as an indicator. The object of the indicator is to tell the condition of the milk, whether it is acid, alkaline or neutral. The indicator does not change in an acid solution but turns pink when the solution is or becomes alkaline. To make the test, a known quantity of the material to be tested is placed in a white cup, and to this several drops of indicator are added. As an indicator, a 1 per cent solution of phenolphthalein in

[26] Publow, C. A., An apparatus for measuring acidity in cheesemaking and butter-making, Cornell Exp. Sta. Circ. 7, pages 17-20, 1909.

Hastings, E. G., and A. C. Evans, A comparison of the acid test and the rennet test for determining the condition of milk for the Cheddar type of cheese, U. S. Dept. Agr. Bur. An. Ind. Circ. 210, pages 1-6, 1913.

95 per cent alcohol is commonly used. As an alkali solution, sodium hydroxide (NaOH) is used in the standardized strength usually either tenth (N/10) normal or twentieth (N/20) normal. This solution should be obtained in some one of the standardized forms commercially prepared. The alkali is added, drop by drop, from a graduated burette until a faint pink color appears. This shows that the acid in the milk has been neutralized by the alkali. The amount of alkali that has been used can be determined from the burette. Knowing the amount of milk and alkali solution used, it is easy to calculate the amount of acid in the substance tested. The results are usually expressed either as percentages of lactic acid or preferably as cubic centimeters of normal alkali required to neutralize 100 or 1000 c.c. of milk. This kind of test is on the market under different names, such as Mann's, Publow's, Farrington's and Marschall's.

Fig. 9.—An acid tester.

82. Rennet tests.—Several rennet tests have been devised, but the one most widely used is the Marschall (Fig. 10). This consists of a 1 c.c. pipette to measure the rennet extract, a small bottle in which to dilute the extract, a special cup to hold the milk and a spatula to mix the milk with the rennet extract. This cup has on the inside from top to bottom a scale graduated from 0 at the top to 10 at the bottom. There is a hole in the bottom to allow the milk to run out.

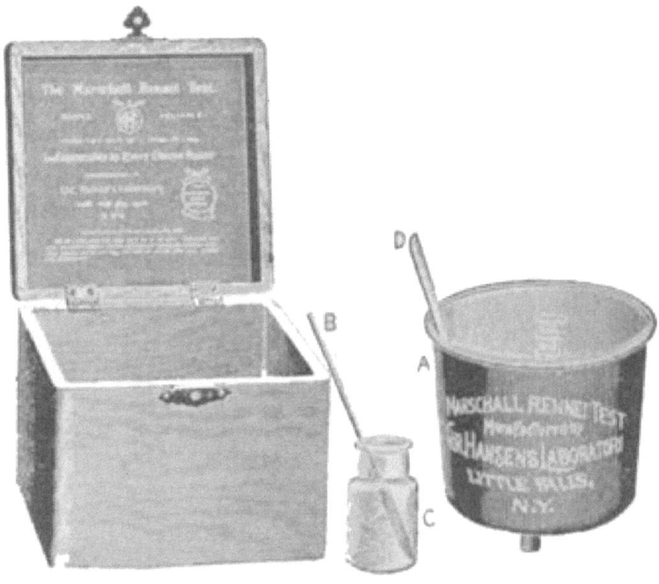

Fig. 10.—Marschall rennet test.

83. Marschall rennet test.—To make a Marschall rennet test, 1 c.c. of rennet extract is measured, with the 1 c.c. pipette, and placed in the bottle. Care should be exercised to rinse out the pipette. The bottle is then filled to the mark with cold water. After the milk has been heated to the setting temperature, 84°-86° F., the cup is filled with milk and set on the edge of the vat so that the milk running out through the hole in the bottom of the cup will flow into the vat. Just as the surface of the milk reaches the 0 mark on the cup, the diluted rennet extract is added and thoroughly mixed with the milk, using the small spatula to stir it. The rennet and milk should be mixed until it has run down at least one-half space on the scale in the cup. As the rennet begins to coagulate the milk, it runs slower from the hole in the bottom of the cup, until it finally stops. When it stops, the point on the scale indicated by the surface of the coagulated milk is noted. The test is recorded by the number of spaces the surface of the milk lowers from the time the rennet is added until it is coagulated. This test depends on three factors: the strength of the rennet extract, the temperature of the milk, the acidity of the milk. The more acid, the quicker the milk will coagulate. To measure any one of these factors, the other two must be constant. The variable factor is the acidity of the milk. This test will not indicate the percentage of acid in the milk, but is simply a comparative test to be used from day to day; for example, if the rennet test to-day shows three spaces, and the operator makes that milk into cheese and the process seems to be normal, it shows that for good results in this factory, milk should be ripened to show three spaces every day. If the next day the milk showed four spaces, it should be allowed to ripen more until it shows three spaces. If it shows only two spaces, this indicates that the milk has too much acid development or is over-ripe. A cheese-maker will have to determine at what point to set his milk, because the test will vary from one factory to another.

84. Comparison of acid and rennet test.—Each of these tests has its advantages and disadvantages. The advantage of the acid test is that it can be made as well of warm as cold milk. This is of great importance in determining whether the milk delivered by any patron is too ripe to be received. The acidity of other materials, such as whey and starter, can be determined as well as that of milk. The disadvantages are that it is difficult to get the alkali solution of the proper strength and the solution is liable to deteriorate on standing. It requires a careful exact operator to make the test.

The advantages of the rennet test are that it is easy to make, and it requires no materials that are hard to replace. The disadvantage is that the milk must be warmed to the same temperature before a comparative test can be made. The size of the outlet in cups varies. It does not indicate the percentage of acid present in the milk. It is simply a comparative test. To obtain the best result, both tests should be used in conjunction.

85. Control of acid.—The control of acidity in curd and cheese is dependent on the control of the moisture or water-content. The control of both factors is very important in relation to the quality[27] of the cheese. Often acidity is spoken of when moisture is really intended, and vice versa. The close relation between the moisture and acidity is due to the presence of the milk-sugar in solution in the milk-serum which becomes the whey of cheese-making. Water or moisture in cheese consists of the remnant of this whey which is not expelled in the making process. During manufacture and the ripening process, the milk-sugar is changed to lactic acid. A cheese may be sweet when first made and after a time become sour because it contains too much moisture in the form of whey. Excess of whey carries excess of milk-sugar from which fermentation produces intense acidity.

Various tests have been devised to determine the amount of acid developed at the different stages of manufacture. These tests are described on page 61. By the use of such tests, the development of acid during the manufacturing process can be very accurately determined. There is no quick, accurate test to determine the amount of moisture in the curd. The cheese-maker has to rely on his own judgment, guided largely by the appearance, feeling and condition of the curd.

After the rennet extract has been added, all control of the acid development is lost. The cheese-maker can determine rather accurately how fast the acid will develop during the ripening of the milk. This shows the importance of the proper ripening. The amount of acid developed during the different stages of the manufacturing process can be approximately followed with the various acid tests. The manufacturing process should then be varied to obtain the proper relation between the moisture and the acid present. The only time that the acidity may be controlled is when the milk is being ripened. If too much acid is developed before the rennet is added, there is apt to be too much acid at each stage of the manu-

---

[27] Doane, C. F., The influence of lactic acid on the quality of cheese of the Cheddar type, U. S. Dept. Agr. Bur. An. Ind. Bul. 123, pages 1-20, 1910.

facturing process. This is liable to hurry the cheese-making process and to cause a loss, both in quality and quantity of cheese, and may cause a high acid or sour cheese. If sufficient acid is not developed at the time the rennet is added or if the milk is not sufficiently ripened, the acid is liable not to develop fast enough so that there will not be sufficient at each step in the cheese-making process. Such a cheese is called "sweet." There are several conditions which will cause an over-development of acid. Such a cheese is called "acidy" or "sour." These factors are within the control of the cheese-maker, hence should be avoided. A sour cheese shows lack of skill and care on the part of the cheese-maker.

Conditions causing an acidy or sour cheese:

Receiving sour or high acid milk at the cheese-factory.
Use of too much starter.
Ripening the milk too much before the rennet is added.
Removing the whey before the curd is properly firmed, hence leaving it with too much moisture.
Development of too much acid in the whey before the whey is removed.
Improper relationship between the moisture and acidity at the time of removing the whey.

Conditions causing deficient acid:

Adding the rennet before sufficient acid has developed.
Not using sufficient starter.
Not developing sufficient acid in the whey.

86. Acidity and rennet action.—The rennet extract acts only in an acid medium. The greater the acid development, within certain limits, the faster the action of the rennet. If enough acid has developed to cause a coagulation of the casein, the rennet will not coagulate the milk. This is one reason why Cheddar cheese cannot be made from sour milk.

87. Acidity and expulsion of the whey.—The contraction of the curd and expulsion of the whey are so closely related that they may be treated under the same heading. The more acid, the faster the whey separates from the curd, other conditions being uniform. The relation of acidity and firmness of the curd to temperature of the curd is another important factor in the successful manufacture of cheese. The higher the acidity, the faster the temperature of the curd can be raised without any harmful effects. If the temperature is raised too fast in relation to the acidity, the film surrounding each piece of curd will become toughened so that the moisture will not be able to escape. When this condition exists, the curd will feel firm but when the pieces are broken open the inside is found to be very soft. This results in a large loss later or may cause a sour cheese. It usually causes an uneven texture and color in the cheese.

88. Acidity in relation to cheese flavor.—Just what part the acid plays in the development of cheese flavor is not known. If a certain amount of acid is not present, the characteristic cheese flavor does not develop. If too much acid is developed, it gives the cheese a sour flavor which is unpleasant. If sufficient acid is not developed, the other undesirable factors seem to be more active, causing very disagreeable flavor and may cause the cheese to putrefy. A cheese with a low acid usually develops a very mild flavor, and if carried to extremes, as in the case of some washed curd cheese, the true cheese flavor never develops.

89. Acidity in relation to body and texture of cheese.—If a cheese is to have a close, smooth, mellow, silky body and texture, a certain amount of acid development is necessary. If too much acid is developed, the body and texture will be dry, harsh, sandy, mealy, corky. If the acid is not sufficient the cheese may be soft or weak bodied, and is usually characterized by "Swiss curd holes," which are spaces of various sizes usually more or less round and very shiny on the inside.

90. Acidity in relation to cheese color.—An over-development of acidity affects the color of a cheese. If this development of acidity is uniform throughout the cheese, it causes the color to become pale or bleached. If this development is uneven, due to the uneven distribution of moisture, the color will be bleached in spots, causing a mottled effect.

91. Control of moisture.[28]—The cheese-maker must use skill and judgment in regulating the amount of moisture in relation to the firmness of the curd and the acid. Since there are no quick accurate tests to determine the amount of moisture, this is left entirely to the judgment of the operator. Certain methods of handling the curd reduce the moisture-content, while others increase it. The cheese-maker must decide how to handle the curd. If the curd becomes too dry, methods should be employed to increase the moisture, and vice versa.

Causes of excessive moisture:

> Cutting the curd coarse.
> Cutting the curd after it has become too hard.
> Setting the milk at a high temperature.
> Use of excessive amount of rennet extract.
> Low acid in the curd at the time of removing the whey.
> Not stirring the curd with the hands as the last of the whey is removed.
> High piling of the curd during the cheddaring process.
> Piling the curd too quickly after removing the whey.
> Use of a small amount of salt.
> Holding the curd at too low a temperature after the whey is removed.
> Soaking the curd in water previous to salting.
> Allowing the curd to remain in the whey too long so that it reabsorbs the whey.
> Heating the curd too rapidly.

Causes of insufficient moisture:

> Cutting the curd too fine or breaking up the pieces with the rake into too small pieces.

[28] Fisk, W. W., A study of some factors influencing the yield and moisture content of Cheddar cheese, Cornell Exp. Sta. Bul. 334, 1913.

Cutting the curd too soft.

Stirring the curd too much by hand as the last of the whey is being removed.

Developing high acid in the curd at the time of removing the whey.

Insufficient piling of the curd during the cheddaring process.

Using a large amount of salt.

High temperature and low humidity in the curing room.

92. Relation of moisture to manufacture and quality.—(1) *Flavor:* If the cheese contains too much moisture, it is likely to develop a sour or acidy flavor. A cheese with a normally high moisture-content usually ripens or develops a cheese flavor much faster than one with a lower moisture-content, other conditions being uniform. A cheese with a high moisture-content is much more liable, during the curing process, to develop undesirable flavors than is one with a lower moisture-content. (2) *Body and texture:* A cheese containing too much moisture is very soft and is difficult to hold in shape. Such a product breaks down very rapidly and is usually pasty and sticky in texture. If too little moisture is present, the cheese is very dry and hard, and cures or ripens very slowly because of the lack of moisture together with milk-sugar from which acid may be formed. Dry cheeses are usually harsh, tough and rubbery in texture. Such cheeses also have poor rinds. (3) *Color:* If the ideal conditions exist, the moisture will be evenly distributed throughout the cheese. The spots containing more moisture will be lighter in color. If a cheese contains so much moisture that it becomes "acidy," the effect is the same as when too much acid is developed, that is, the color becomes pale from the action of the acid. (4) *Finish:* A cheese containing too much moisture is usually soft. A good rind does not form. Such a cheese loses its shape very easily, especially in a warm curing room. (5) *Quality:* A cheese with a high moisture-content is usually marketable for only a very short period. Such a product usually develops flavor very quickly in comparison to a dry cheese. It must be sold very soon because if held too long, the flavor becomes so strong as to be undesirable, and objectionable flavors are liable to develop. In some cases, such cheeses rot.

93. Relation of moisture to acidity.—From the preceding discussion, it is evident that the relation between the moisture and acidity is very close, in fact so intimate that in some cases it is difficult to distinguish one from the other when the quality of the cheese is considered. The proper relation of the moisture and the acidity determines the quality of the resulting cheese. If too much acid is developed during the manufacturing process, the product will be sour. If too much moisture is retained in the form of whey, the cheese will be sour. The less acid in the curd, the more moisture in the form of whey may be retained in the curd without causing a sour cheese. The proper relationship between the moisture and the acidity must be maintained or a sour cheese will result.

The relation of the moisture to the acidity also has an influence on the curing. If the cheese has a low development of acidity and a low moisture-content, it will cure very slowly. The increasing of either the acidity or moisture usually increases the rate of cheese ripening, other factors being the same.

The relation of the acidity and the moisture is so important that it cannot be neglected without injuring both the quality and quantity of cheese. This knowledge can be obtained only by experience.

94. Setting temperature.—The temperature of renneting makes very much difference in the texture of the product. The enzyme rennin is sensitive to very slight changes in temperature. Below 70° F., its rate of action is very slow. Beginning with approximately 20 per cent of its maximum effectiveness at 70° F. (the curdling point for Neufchâtel), it has risen to 65 per cent at 84° F., to 70 per cent at 86° F., as used in Cheddar, to about 80 to 85 per cent at 90-94° F., as used in Limburger. At 105° F. it reaches its maximum effective working rate to fall from that efficiency to about 50 per cent at 120° F. Curdling at low temperature lengthens the time required for the same amount of rennet to curdle a given quantity of the same milk. The texture of curd produced at temperatures between 70° F. and 84° F. is soft, jelly-like, friable rather than rubbery. At 86° F. it begins to show toughening or rubbery characters which become very marked at 90° F. to 94° F. as used in Limburger. With the increased vigor of action as it passes its maximum rate of action at 105° F., the texture tends to become loose, floccose to granular. Aside from the Neufchâtel group, the working range of temperatures for the renneting period runs from about 84° F. to about 94° F., a range of barely 10° F., or the use of 65 per cent to 80 or possibly 85 per cent of the maximum efficiency of the rennet. Within this range of temperature, the curd has the physical characters demanded for making most varieties of cheese.

95. Strength of coagulating materials.—Rennet and pepsin preparations vary in strength and in keeping quality. With a particular stock, changes go on to such a degree that the last samples from a barrel of rennet are much weaker than the earlier ones. Each sample, barrel, keg or bottle should be tested before used. In continuous work the results of each day's work furnish the guide for the next day's use of a particular lot of rennet.

96. Amount of coagulating materials to use.—For most varieties of cheese, sufficient rennet extract or pepsin is added to the milk to give a firm curd in twenty-five to forty minutes. Of the ordinary commercial rennet extract, this requires from two and one-half to four ounces to one thousand pounds of milk. This gives a maximum of one part rennet for each four to six thousand parts of milk. The great strength of the rennet extract is thus clearly shown.

97. Method of adding rennet.—Before rennet is added to the milk, it is diluted in about forty times its volume of cold water, which chills the enzyme and retards its action until it can be thoroughly mixed with the milk. If the material is added without such dilution, the concentrated extract produces instant coagulation in the drops with which it comes in contact, forming solid masses from which the enzyme escapes only slowly to diffuse throughout the mass. Uniform coagulation thus becomes impossible. After the rennet extract has been diluted with cold water, it should be distributed the entire length of the vat in an even stream from a pail. It should then be mixed with the milk by stirring from top to bottom for about three to four minutes. For this purpose, either a long-handled dipper or a wooden rake may be used. A dipperful should be drawn from the gate and stirred into the vat, otherwise the milk in the gate will fail to coagulate properly because the rennet diffuses too slowly to reach and affect all the milk at that point. The milk should be stirred on the top, preferably with the bottom of a dipper, until signs of coagulation begin to appear. This stirring keeps the cream from rising. There are various ways or signs to indicate when the coagulation has gone to the stage at which the mix is about to become thick: (1) The milk becomes lazy or thicker as the finger is passed through it; (2) bubbles caused by moving the finger remain on the milk longer, usually until one can count ten when ready to thicken.

If the milk is stirred too long or after it begins to thicken, the result is a granular sort of curd, and there will be an abnormally large loss of fat in the manufacturing process. The addition of the rennet and subsequent stirring require the exercise of great care and constant attention to details. The cheese-maker can do nothing else for those few minutes. When through stirring, it is a good plan in cold weather to cover the vat with a cloth as this will keep the surface of the curd warm. In summer the same cover will keep out the flies.

Causes of a delayed coagulation:

(1) Weak rennet extract or too small an amount.
(2) Low temperatures due to inaccurate thermometers.
(3) Pasteurized milk.
(4) Presence of abnormal bacterial ferments.
(5) Presence of preservatives.
(6) Heavily watered milk.
(7) Use of badly rusted[29] cans.
(8) Milk containing small amounts of casein or calcium salts.

Causes of uneven coagulation:

(1) Uneven temperature of the mix in the vat, due to lack of agitation.
(2) Uneven distribution of the rennet extract.
(3) Adding rennet to vat too soon after heating, while the sides and bottom are still hot, causes curd to stick to sides and bottom of the vat making cutting difficult.

98. The curdling period. — The time allowed for rennet action also affects the texture of the curd. The enzymes of rennet (rennin and pepsin) do not cease acting with the thickening of the milk. In many cheeses, the handling process begins as soon as the curd has become solid enough to split cleanly before a finger thrust into it. If let stand further, the same curd mass will continue to harden with the progressive separation of whey; this shows first as drops ("sweating") on its surface, which then increase in number and size until they run together and form a sheet of whey. The limit of such action is difficult to measure. The solidifying process ceases in a period of hours. The further action of the enzymes is digestive in character and goes on slowly. It requires a period of weeks or even months to accomplish measurable results at the working temperatures in use in the trade.

[29] Olson, G. A., Rusty cans and their effect upon milk for cheese-making, Wis. Exp. Sta. Bul. 162, pages 1-12, 1908.

Other ripening agents with more rapid action intervene to shape the final result. It follows that the rennet factor in the ripening changes found at the end of the period is almost negligible for most varieties of cheese, although it appears to be measurable in some varieties.

99. Cutting or breaking[30] the curd.—As soon as curd is formed, separation of whey begins upon the surface and perhaps around the sides of the vessel. This is accompanied by shrinkage and hardening of the mass. If the curd remains unbroken, the separation is extremely slow. In cheese-making practice, such curd masses may be dipped at once into hoops as in Camembert, dumped in mass into cloths for drainage as in Neufchâtel or, as in the larger number of cheeses, cut or broken in some characteristic manner. After the curd mass is firm, the rate at which subsequent changes take place depends largely on the size of the particles into which the curd is cut. The smaller the particles, the quicker the water is expelled. Consequently the development of the acidity and other changes take place more slowly. For this reason the curd should be cut into pieces of uniform size. If the work is not properly performed, the pieces of curd of various sizes will be at different stages of development. The fine particles will be firm and elastic while the larger particles are still soft and full of whey and may be developing too much acid. The knives should be inserted into the curd obliquely so that they will cut their way into the curd and not break it. The horizontal knife is used lengthwise of the vat and cuts the curd into layers of uniform thickness. The perpendicular knife then is used lengthwise and crosswise of the vat. It first cuts the curd into strips and then into cubes. The knives may have wire blades or steel blades, some operators preferring one and some the other. Whichever is used, the blades should be close enough together to give the fineness of curd desired.

After the knife passes through, the cut faces quickly become covered with a smooth coating, continuous over all exposed areas. This surface has the appearance of a smooth elastic coating or film. This can be seen by carefully breaking a piece in the hand. It is this film which holds the fat within the pieces of curd. If the film is broken, some of the fat globules are lost because the rennet extract acts only on the casein and that in turn holds the fat. All the fat globules which come in contact with the knives as they pass through the curd will be left between the pieces of curd and will pass off in the whey. If care is exercised in cutting, the loss of fat will be confined to what may be called a mechanical loss. This is similar to the loss of the sawdust when sawing a board. This loss in American Cheddar is about 0.3 per cent and cannot be avoided. If it is greater than this, it is due to negligence on the part of the cheese-maker or the poor condition of the milk. The cutting of the curd into small pieces may be considered a necessary evil. If the moisture could be expelled from the whole mass without disturbing it, this fat loss could be prevented. The cutting, breaking or turning should be done with the greatest care, that the loss may be as small as possible.

[30] The term "broken" is included here because the use of some curd-breaking tool has always formed a step in certain commercially successful processes. In every case in which careful experimental work has been done the curd knife has been successfully substituted for the breaking tool and has reduced the losses of fat and casein and in addition aided in obtaining more uniform cheese.

100. Curd knives.—For cutting curd, special knives have been devised (Fig. 11). They consist of series of parallel blades fixed in a frame to make cuts equidistant. The blades run vertically in one, horizontally in another. They are spaced according to the demands of the variety of cheese to be made. Wires stretched in a frame take the place of blades in some makes of curd knife.

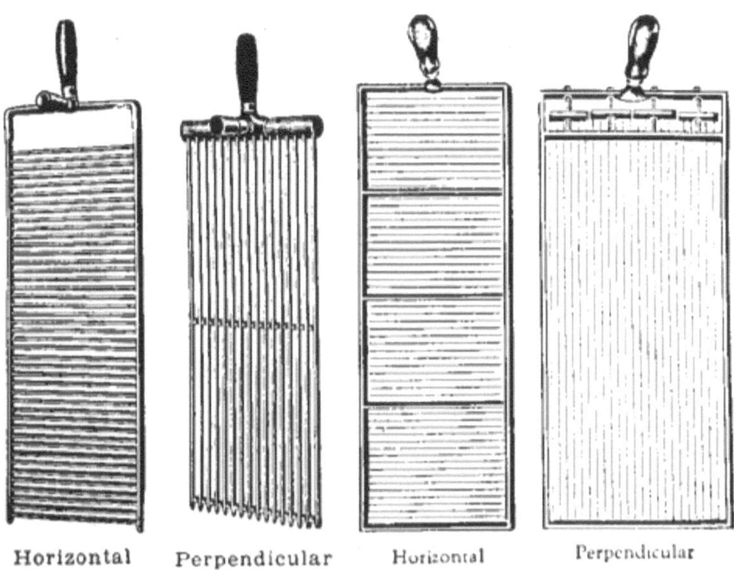

Fig. 11.—Blade and wire curd knives.

101. Heating or "cooking."—Curdling by rennet has already been shown to be markedly hastened by moderate heating. After the coagulum or curd is formed, the making process may be completed without the application of further heat, as in Neufchâtel, Camembert and related forms (Fig. 12) and in some practices with Limburger. In other forms and especially in the hard cheeses in which cutting of curd is a prominent part of the process, the curd after being cut is reheated or "cooked." The cooking process hastens the removal of the whey, thus shortening the time required to reduce the water-content of the mass to the percentage most favorable for the type of cheese desired. The process also produces marked changes in the physical character of the curd mass. With the rise in temperature the casein becomes elastic first, then approaches a melting condition and assumes a tough, almost rubbery consistency. The final texture is the result of the combination of the amount of rennet added, the temperature, the acidity reached during the process, and the final water-content of the mass.

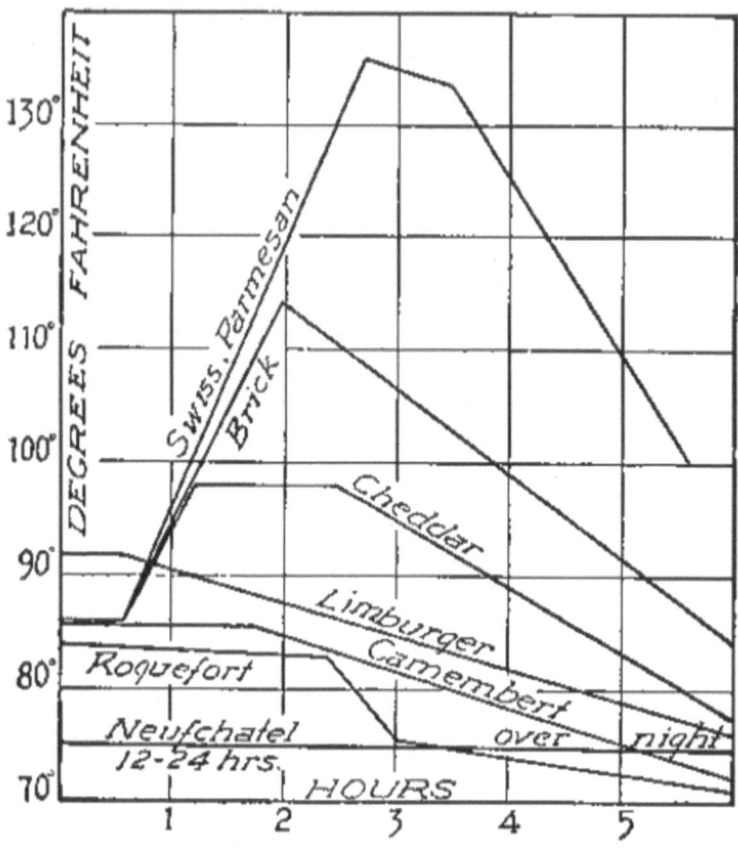

Fig. 12.—The heat relation. See pages 77 and 87.

102. Draining (including grinding, putting into hoops or forms and pressing).—The reduction of the water in the curd begins almost as soon as the curd becomes firm. It is aided by cutting or breaking, by the retention of the heat applied before renneting and by the secondary heating or cooking used in making certain groups of cheeses. In many varieties special apparatus is provided in the form of draining boards, draining racks or bags to hasten the removal of the whey as fast as it separates. The draining process continues until the cheese has reached its final form and weight. The intervening process of matting in the Cheddar group involves a combination of a souring process with the removal of whey, during which the cubes of curd become fused into semi-solid masses. If such masses are formed, they must be ground up before the cheese can be given its final form in the hoop. The draining process, therefore, may take any one of many forms varying from the direct transfer of freshly formed curd into hoops in which the entire draining process is completed, to an elaborate series of operations which end in pressing curd drained to approximately its final condition before it is placed in the hoop.

103. Application to cheese.—From the discussion of these factors, it is evident that the cheeses produced will differ widely with the differences in manipulation. If one considers essential constituent substances separately, the water-content of the finished product is found to vary from 30 per cent in Parmesan to 75 per cent in cottage cheese. The fat-content runs from a trace in some varieties to 60 per cent in some cream cheeses. The texture of the casein, which gives character to the product, varies from the tough or glue-like consistency of freshly made Swiss to the buttery condition of a cream or Neufchâtel cheese. Inside such limits the tastes of different peoples have led to the manufacture of many kinds of cheese. Each of these varieties represents some particular combination of curd-making factors and ripening conditions which produces a cheese suited to the taste of the maker and consumer of that country or community.

CHAPTER VI
CLASSIFICATION

Basis of classification; Processed cheeses; Whey cheeses; Soft and hard
cheeses; Relation of moisture to classes; Relation of heat to classes.

The literature of cheese-making contains reference to more than 500 names
for varieties of cheese. Many of these can be thrown readily into great groups or
families in which there are variations in unessential detail without modifying the
characteristic texture and flavor of the product. Many varietal names are attached
to the product of single factories or factory groups. Such varieties frequently differ
only slightly in size or shape, or in stage of drainage or of ripening, from widely
known varieties or other similar local forms. The descriptions recorded for such
varieties commonly emphasize minor differences in manipulation without showing differences in essential factors. Vessels of particular size are prescribed to be
made of wood, earthenware, or of a special metal. These details specify the exact
size and shape of hoops, the use of particular styles of cutting or breaking in-
struments and of certain stirring tools, the material and construction of mats and
draining racks.

The descriptions themselves are very commonly inadequate. The variable factors in cheese-making are fat-content of the milk, acidity, temperature of setting,
amount of rennet, time allowed for curdling and the method of draining the curd.
The differences in practice lie, with few exceptions, in the amount or intensity of
particular factors, not differences in kind or quality of treatment. Such contrasts
are quantitative, not qualitative. A great number of combinations is possible by
small variations of these factors.

Varieties selected as types of groups give marked contrasts in character, but
comparison of large numbers of forms shows that almost every gradation from
group to group can actually be found. Within groups frequently the same physical
results in texture and flavor can be obtained by combinations or adjustments of
factors for the purpose of offsetting or counteracting the effects of one change in
practice by the manipulation of other factors. In ripening, an equally large range
of practices makes possible the development of very different qualities in mature
cheeses from the same lot.

Only a few of the large number of described varieties have obtained even national importance; fewer still are known outside the country of origin. In spite of
the success of special products when properly advertised, the largest place in the
market is clearly accorded to the standard forms which are widely known.

104. Basis of classification.—A series of these widely known forms has been chosen as typical of groups in a system of classification adapted from the French of Pouriau. No completely satisfactory scheme of classifying all of these varieties has been devised. The grouping proposed here is based on the principles of curd-making already discussed together with consideration of the ripening processes to be discussed with each group. The factors that actually influence the quality of the final product are separated as completely as possible from non-essential operative details.

The common use of the terms "soft" and "hard" cheese is based on the single arbitrary fact of texture. The term "semi-hard" cheese may be conveniently applied to a miscellaneous group of unrelated families which are intermediate in texture between such soft forms as Neufchâtel or Camembert and really hard cheeses like Cheddar or Parmesan. Although these terms are not made the main basis of the proposed grouping, their application to sections is indicated. Classification based on the essential facts of manufacture is, however, really helpful.

ANALYTICAL TABULATION OF GROUPS

Subsection B. Semi-hard cheeses, firm, well-drained. (38 to 45% water)

    a. Curd not cooked, ripened by molds.

      * Made from friable curd—Roquefort   94-95

      ** Made from firm or tough curd—Gorgonzola, Stilton   99
and such French forms as Gex, Septmoncel

    b. Curd cooked and ripened by bacteria,—brick, Munster,   103-104
Port du Salut (Oka)

Subsection C. Hard cheeses, cooked and pressed (30 to 40% water)

    a. Ripened without gas holes.   103-104

    1. Dutch—Edam, Gouda.   108-109

    2. Danish.   108-109

    3. The Cheddar group.

      * English—Cheddar and numerous related forms   115
known principally in Great Britain

      ** American—the factory Cheddar of related forms   10-109
United States and Canada

    b. Ripened with the development of gas holes.   103-104

    * Holes large—Swiss-Emmenthal Gruyère, American   108-109
Swiss.

    ** Holes small—Parmesan and related varieties.   108-109

Such a classification brings together series of products in which there is essential similarity in the final output, however great the differences in manipulation. It does not consider all varieties and specialties. Some of these groups are important enough to demand special mention.

105. Processed cheeses.—Cheese of any group may be run through mixing and molding machines and repackaged in very different form from that characteristic of the variety. In such treatment, the texture and appearance may be so changed as to give the effect of a new product. Substances (such as pimiento) are added to change the flavor. Or the product may be canned and sterilized with equally great change of flavor and texture. One thus finds Club made from Cheddar; Pimiento from Cream, Neufchâtel or Cheddar; similarly olive, nut and other combinations are made. The possible variations are numerous.

106. Whey cheeses.—Several products bearing cheese names are made from whey. These take the forms of the recovery of the albumin and casein separately or in a single product, and the recovery of the milk-sugar either alone or with the albumin. Whey cheeses have been especially developed by the Scandinavian people, although some of them have their origin in the south of Europe. Certain of these varieties are produced on a limited scale in America.

There are a number of forms fairly widely known that are difficult to place in this scheme of groups. Among these are Caciocavallo, Sap Sago.

107. Soft and hard cheeses.—Another commonly used classification makes two groups: (1) soft cheeses; (2) hard cheeses. In such a classification the semi-hard group presented here is included with the soft cheeses. Some cheeses of this group are soft in texture. This is correlated with high water-content, high fat-content or both together.

108. Relation of moisture to classes.—In this classification the water-content reflected in the texture of the cheese assumes first place. To carry the analysis somewhat further by showing the correlation between water-content and certain factors, a tabulation of well-known varieties of typical groups is presented (Table III). In this table the series of typical dairy products are first arranged according to water-content of the final product. Approximate limits of percentages of milk-fat are also given, because milk-fat frequently affects texture to a degree almost equal to water. Column 4 gives the period within which the more quickly perishable cheeses are usable, and the length of the ripening for the more solid forms. The correlation between water-content, texture and the time of keeping is clearly shown for most varieties.

TABLE III

CORRELATION WATER- AND FAT-CONTENT WITH RIPENING				
VARIETY OF	PER CENT WATER	PER CENT FAT	PERIOD REQUIRED	RIPENING AGENT
Cheese: Soft,				
Cottage	70	trace	a few days	Bacteria
Skim Neufchâtel	70	trace	a few days	Bacteria
Neufchâtel	50-60	12-28	a few days	Bacteria
Camembert	50	22-30	3-5 weeks	Molds
Cream cheese	40-50	35-45	a few days	Primarily bacteria
Semi-hard:				
Limburger	40-45	24-30	3-6 months	Bacteria
Roquefort	38-40	31-34	3-6 months	Mold
Brick	37-42	31-35	3-6 months	Bacteria
Hard:				
Cheddar	30-39	32-36	6-12 months	Bacteria
Swiss	31-34	28-31	9-18 months	Bacteria and yeasts
Parmesan	30-33		2-3 years	Bacteria

The soft cheeses are quickly perishable products. Bacteria and molds find favorable conditions for growth in products with 45 to 75 per cent of water. If such growth is permitted, enzymic activities follow quickly with resultant changes in appearance, texture, odor and taste. Refrigeration is necessary to transport such cheeses to the consumer, if properly ripened. Trade in these forms may continue throughout the year in cool climates and in places where adequate refrigeration is available. Practically, however, outside the large cities this trade in America is at present limited to the cold months; inside the large cities much reduced quantities of these cheeses continue to be handled through the year.

In the stricter sense, the soft group of cheeses falls naturally into two series: (1) the varieties eaten fresh; and (2) the ripened soft cheeses. Those eaten fresh have a making process which commonly involves the development of a lactic acid flavor by souring, but no ripening is contemplated after the product leaves the maker's hands. In the ripened series, after the making process is completed, the essential flavors and textures are developed by the activity of micro-organisms during ripening periods varying in length but fairly well-defined for each variety.

In contrast to the soft cheeses, the hard kinds are low in water-content, ripen more slowly and may be kept through much longer periods. They retain their form through a wider range of climatic conditions. They develop flavor slowly and correspondingly deteriorate much more slowly. Such cheeses are in marketable condition over longer periods. In their manufacture the cooking of the curd takes a prominent place.

109. Relation of heat to classes.—The close relation between the heat applied and the product sought forms the basis of a striking series of graphs (Fig. 12, page 78). These show the changes hour by hour in the heat relation during the making process of a series of widely known forms, each of which is chosen as typical. In some of these forms, heat is applied but once to bring the milk to the renneting temperature typical for the variety. Subsequent manipulations are accompanied by a steady fall in temperature. In other forms, the curd when solid is specially heated or "cooked" to bring about the changes characteristic of the variety. These contrasts are clearly brought out by the graphs which represent practices well recognized for the varieties. The detailed process for these groups is considered in succeeding chapters.

CHAPTER VII

CHEESES WITH SOUR-MILK FLAVOR

Skim series; Cottage cheese; Household practice; Factory practice;
Buttermilk cheese; Neufchâtel group; Domestic or American Neufchâtel cheeses; The factory; Cans; Draining racks; Cloths; Molding machinery; Milk for Neufchâtel; Starter; Renneting or setting;
Draining; Cooling Neufchâtel; Pressing; Working and salting
Neufchâtel; Storage; Molding; Skimmed-milk Neufchâtel; Baker's
cheese; Domestic Neufchâtel; Partially skim Neufchâtel; Cream
cheese; Neufchâtel specialties; Gervais; European forms occasionally imported.

The cheeses with flavor of sour milk are probably more widely used than
any other group. Historically and to a very large degree at present, they are farm
cheeses.[31] No estimate of volume of such production in the household has ever
been made. The utilization of surplus milk in this way is of ancient origin.

With the introduction of the factory system of handling milk, the manufacture
of such cheese in the household was largely dropped. The rise in price of all food
substances and increasing appreciation of the food value of milk products have
made the recovery of all surplus milk in some form very necessary. The manufacture of cottage, Neufchâtel and cream cheese is one of the best forms of such
recovery which may be adapted to utilize any grade from skimmed-milk to cream.
Large quantities of skimmed-milk have frequently been lost from the total of human food by the manufacture of casein for industrial uses, and by use as stock
feed.

110. Skim series.—The kinds of cheeses eaten fresh have in common a very
soft texture and the flavor of sour milk, principally lactic acid. The group falls
naturally into two sections: (1) the cheeses made from milk curdled by souring;
(2) those for which the milk is curdled by souring and rennet. In the latter group
both agencies are necessary to the resulting product. The time required to curdle
by souring alone is longer than when rennet is used; this period is usually longer

[31] Frandsen, J. H., and T. Thorsen, Farm cheese-making, Univ. Neb. Ext. Serv. Bul.
47, pages 1-16, 1917.

Michels, J., Improved methods for making cottage and Neufchâtel cheese, N. C. Exp.
Sta. Bul. 210, pages 29-38.

Fisk, W. W., Methods of making some of the soft cheeses, Cornell Exp. Sta. Circ. 30,
pages 41-62, 1915.

than necessary for the cream to rise by gravity; hence the cream is either skimmed off or removed with the separator beforehand. The curd, therefore, is essentially a skimmed-milk curd. Casein curdled in this way tends to become granular or "rough," to feel "sandy" when rubbed between the fingers. Heating is commonly necessary to lower the water-content of the mass even to 75 per cent. Such curd tends to become hard or rubbery when heat is applied. In this group, the best known form is variously called "cottage" cheese, "clabber" cheese, schmierkäse.

111. Cottage cheese is made from skimmed-milk, soured by lactic bacteria until a curd is formed. This is done preferably at about 20° C. (70° F.), because at this temperature the purely lactic type of organism has been found to outgrow competing forms which may be present. Starter containing the desired culture, if properly used, saves much time in the curdling period. Such curdling requires at least twelve to twenty-four hours, frequently much longer unless abundant starter is introduced.

112. Household practice.—The details of cottage cheese making in the home differ widely in separate sections and even in different families in the same part of the country. The essentials of the practice, common to all, include: (1) curdling the whole milk by natural souring; (2) removing the sour cream which is usually used for butter-making; (3) scalding the curdled skimmed-milk either by slowly heating it in the original vessel surrounded by hot water or by actually pouring an approximately equal volume of boiling water into the curdled mass; (4) bagging and draining the mass until it reaches the desired texture; (5) the kneading of the mass with the addition of salt and cream. The resulting product varies greatly in quality. Unfavorable fermentations frequently affect the flavor.[32] The "scalding" varies from a temperature of 90° F. almost to boiling with a resultant texture varying from almost the smooth buttery consistency of Neufchâtel to hard coarse granular lumps. The best practice, using clean well-cared-for milk and draining at low temperature, produces a very attractive cheese. Such cheese is heated to 90° to 100° F. on the maker's judgment, drained carefully, kneaded well by hand or by machine with the addition of cream to give it an attractive texture and flavor.

113. Factory practice.—When cottage cheese is made in the factory,[33] separated milk is taken; it should be pasteurized and then soured by a lactic starter. The souring can be accelerated by the use of a starter, which may be added at the rate of 0.5 to 5 per cent of the skimmed-milk used, depending on the amount of starter that can be made. Generally, the more starter added, the more rapid will be the coagulation and the better will be the flavor of the cheese. As soon as the milk has thickened, the curd is ready to be broken up and separated from the whey. This separation is hastened by the application of heat. Usually the temperature of the curd is raised slightly before it is broken up; since this makes the curd firmer, there will be a smaller loss of curd particles in the whey. The curd may be cut with coarse Cheddar cheese knives or broken with a rake. The temperature of the

[32] Tolstrup, R. M., Cheese that farmers should make, Iowa Agr. 15 (1914), 2, pages 89-90.

[33] Van Slyke, L. L., and Hart, E. B., Chemical changes in the souring of milk and their relations to cottage cheese, N. Y. (Geneva) Exp. Sta. Bul. 245, pages 1-36, 1904.

curd should be raised very slowly, at least thirty minutes being taken to reach the desired final temperature. No set rule can be given as to the exact temperature to which the curd should be heated. The temperature should be raised until a point is reached at which the curd, when pressed between the thumb and the fingers, will stick together and not go back to the milky state. This temperature is usually from 94° to 100° F., but the cheese-maker must use his own judgment in this respect. If the curd is heated too much, it will be hard and dry; on the other hand, if it is not heated sufficiently, the whey will not separate from the curd and the latter will be very soft and mushy.

When the curd has been heated sufficiently and has become firmed in the whey, it should be removed from the whey. This may be done either by letting down one end of the vat and piling the curd in the upper end, or by dipping out the curd into a cloth bag and allowing the whey to drain, which it does very rapidly. No treatment can prevent the "roughness" of an acid curd (this is a fine gritty feeling when rubbed between the fingers), but the coarse hard grainy texture and lumps characteristic of the highly heated curd do not develop. Experimental workers have agreed that to have the proper texture, such curd should contain when finished about 70 to 75 per cent of water. It should have a mild but clean acid flavor. Such a cheese will carry about 1 to 2 per cent of salt, without an objectionably salty taste. This cheese is commonly sold by measure, sometimes in molds or cartons. The manufacture of all forms of cottage cheese has been largely superseded by the making of skimmed-milk Neufchâtel or Baker's cheese.

The yield from one hundred pounds of skimmed-milk runs up to fourteen to nineteen pounds of cheese, when made very wet or from pasteurized milk. The yield varies with the moisture-content of the cheese, being greater for cheese with a high content. Too much moisture or whey should not be left in the curd, however, as this will render it too soft to be handled.

Cottage cheese made by either the home or factory practice is a quickly perishable article. Although the acid restrains bacteria at first, the high percentage of water favors the growth of molds which tolerate acidity, especially *Oidium (Oospora) lactis* and the Mucors or black molds. These molds destroy acidity rapidly and thus permit the bacteria of decay to develop and to produce objectionable taste and odors. Spoilage in these products is accelerated by the kneading process which distributes air throughout the mass and with it all forms of microbial contamination.

114. Buttermilk cheese.—A cheese closely resembling cottage may be made from buttermilk. If the buttermilk came from cream which was churned before it became sour, the process is the same as that already described for the making of cottage cheese from skimmed-milk. If the buttermilk came from sour cream the process of manufacture is much more difficult. The casein of sour cream has already been coagulated with acid and broken during churning into very minute rather hard particles. These fine particles are difficult to recover. They are so fine that they pass through the draining cloth or at other times clog it and prevent drainage. They do not stick together at ordinary temperatures. They cannot be collected by the use of acid because they have already been coagulated with acid.

After casein has been coagulated with acid, rennet extract will not recoagulate the particles. The buttermilk may be mixed with sweet skimmed-milk; then as the latter coagulates, it locks in the casein of the buttermilk so that it can be collected. If buttermilk from soured cream is used alone, the casein may be collected[34] by neutralizing and heating to 130 to 150° F., and holding until the casein gathers together. The whey can then be drawn off. Often there is further difficulty in getting the casein to collect, since the pieces remain so small that they go through the strainer.

Cheese made entirely from buttermilk is sandy in texture and often not palatable. If the buttermilk with good flavor is mixed with skimmed-milk, it makes a good cheese closely resembling cottage.

115. Neufchâtel group.[35]—The Neufchâtel process originated in northern France where a number of varieties are included under this as a group name. Among these are Bondon, Malakoff, Petit Suisse, Petit Carré. The name designates a general process of curd-making which is applied to skimmed-milk, whole milk or cream. Some of the resultant cheeses are ripened; some are eaten fresh. The Neufchâtel cheeses of France gained such wide recognition for quality that the process of making has become widely known. In America the manipulations of the French process were early dropped. The essentials were made the basis of a successful factory practice which has been widely adopted. The American factory practice is discussed here and the French process briefly considered under the heading Ripened Neufchâtel. (See Chapter VIII.)

116. Domestic or American Neufchâtel cheeses are soft, have clean sour milk (lactic acid) flavor and are quickly perishable. In all but the coldest weather, they require refrigeration to reduce deterioration and loss. They range in fat-content from traces only to 50 per cent and more; in water from 40 to 75 per cent, according to the milk used. In texture Neufchâtel is smooth, free from gas, free from lumps or roughness when rubbed between the fingers. This flavor and texture is obtained by a combination of slow rennet curdling with developing acidity. No further ripening is permitted.

117. The factory.—Neufchâtel factories require the standard dairy equipment for receiving, weighing, testing, separating, heating, pasteurizing and cooling the milk. Since many factories produce several products, the same general dairy equipment may serve for all. In addition to such equipment, Neufchâtel requires a curdling apparatus which can be held at 70-75° F. This may be a room properly controlled, or a tank where temperature control is obtained by water and steam. For draining, a room kept at 60° F. gives nearly the ideal temperature, which must be supplemented by relative humidity high enough to prevent the exposed surface of curd from drying during periods of twelve to twenty-four hours. This requires almost a saturated atmosphere. A room with special molding machinery is required and tables for wrapping, labeling and boxing the product are necessary. Box-making machinery is usually an economic necessity for work on a large scale.

[34] Sammis, J. L., Three creamery methods for making buttermilk cheese, Wis. Exp. Sta. Bul. 239, 1914.

[35] Matheson, K. J., C. Thom and J. N. Currie, Cheeses of the Neufchâtel group, Conn. (Storrs) Exp. Sta. Bul. 78, pages 313-329, 1914.

Adequate refrigeration is requisite both to chill the curd before molding and to preserve it after packaging.

Fig. 13.—Neufchâtel draining racks.

118. Cans.—For curdling, the "shot-gun" can, about nine inches in diameter and twenty inches deep, is generally used. This holds thirty to forty pounds of milk. Increased capacity is dependent, therefore, on the number of units installed, not on changes in the units themselves.

119. Draining racks.—A draining rack is required for each can of curd. These racks also are standardized units whose number limits the capacity of the factory. The design of these racks (Figs. 13, 14) and their arrangement in the draining room are taken from Bulletin 78 of the Storrs Agricultural Experiment Station: "The racks are rectangular, thirteen inches wide, thirty-six inches long and ten inches deep. The corner posts extend one and one-half inches beyond the strips at top and bottom with the tops rounded as a rule as seen in the photograph. The bottom slats fit loosely into notches, hence are removable for washing purposes. The materials required are four corner posts one and one-half by one and one-half inches; nine strips one by three-eighths by thirty-six inches; six strips one by three-eighths by thirteen inches, two strips one by three-eighths by twelve and a quarter inches, notched to receive the bottom slats; all made from pine."

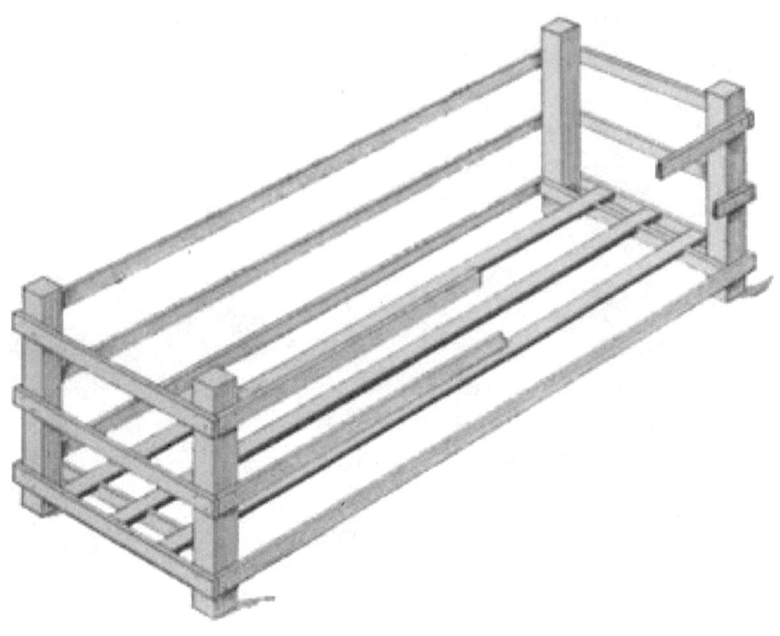

Fig. 14.—Detail of a Neufchâtel draining rack.

120. Cloths.—For each draining rack, a cloth one yard wide and one and one-half yards long is required. Cotton sheeting is satisfactory for the purpose; "even-count, round-thread, unmercerized voile" is suggested by Dahlberg.[36]

121. Molding machinery.—For work on a large scale, special power machines[37] are regularly used. These consist of a hopper and worm delivering a standard size stream of curd through a proper size and shape of delivery tube. This curd stream is cut by an automatic device into the proper lengths to form the standard cheese. In this way a uniform size of cheeses is obtained. Experimental work with hand apparatus showed that a worm six inches in diameter is required to deliver curd in a smooth column one and one-half inches square. If the pressure is not sufficient, the column will frill at the edges. Such irregular surfaces cannot be wrapped smoothly enough to delay spoilage.

---

[36] Dahlberg, A. O., The manufacture of cottage cheese in creameries and milk plants, U. S. Dept. Agr. Bul. 576, pages 1-16, 1917.

[37] Since the number of factories has continued small, the manufacture of this type of machine has remained a monopoly in which each machine is made to order by the Van Eyck Machine Co. of Holland, Mich.

Fig. 15.—Neufchâtel and cream cheese molds.

On a small scale, a fair grade of product can be molded through a tin tube (see Fig. 15) one and three-quarters inches in diameter and ten inches long in which the curd is compressed by a close fitting plunger operated by hand.

122. Milk for Neufchâtel should be clean, free from gas and taint. Such milk should preferably be not more than twelve hours old when received and in no case show higher than 0.20 per cent lactic acid by titration. Milk testing 4 per cent fat or higher will produce a higher quality of product than lower grade milk, although every grade from skimmed-milk to cream is used in producing some form of Neufchâtel. This milk should be pasteurized unless shown to be free from tuberculosis by proper test of the cattle. Evidence[38] that the organism of tuberculosis will withstand the regular handling process for cheeses of this group and retain its ability to cause disease in experimental animals makes the introduction of pasteurization necessary in this whole group of cheeses. Any effective pasteurization may be used, but temperatures of 140-145° F. for thirty minutes have been effective with less changes in the milk than higher temperatures for shorter periods. The

[38] Presented by Dr. E. C. Schroeder of the U. S. Dept. Agr. to the International Association of Dairy and Milk Inspectors, at Washington, Oct. 17, 1917, published Jour. Am. Vet. Med. Assoc'n 52, N. S. 5, no. 6, pages 674-685, 1918.

milk should be cooled to curdling temperature and the starter and rennet added and stirred into the milk in bulk. The milk may then be quickly distributed into the curdling cans with a hose or from the gate valve of the mixing vat.

123. Starter.—To insure the development of a clean acid flavor, a small amount of lactic starter should be used. The quantity to use depends on the quality of the milk. With skimmed-milk, a pint for each thirty-pound can is recommended by Matheson and Cammack[39] and by Dahlberg. (See page 98.) For whole-milk Neufchâtel, 2 c.c. to a thirty-pound can of milk commonly gives good results. On this basis 2 ounces of starter would be sufficient if properly stirred into about 1000 pounds of milk. Too slow development of acid is preferable to over-rapid souring.

124. Renneting or setting.—The milk should be cooled after pasteurizing to between 70° and 75° F. Rennet is added at the rate of ½ c.c. to a thirty-pound can (roughly ⅓ ounce to 1000 pounds). This will thicken the milk sufficiently in the first few hours to reduce the separation of the cream. For completion of the curdling and souring process, twelve to eighteen hours are required. Usually the cans stand overnight at uniform temperature. When ready to drain, the curd should be firm, smooth and mildly acid. Whey separating from it should not titrate above 0.35 per cent titrated as lactic acid.

125. Draining.—A cloth is spread over a draining rack and the contents of one "shot-gun" can poured upon the cloth with as little breaking as possible. In this way a large surface is exposed. The room must be kept wet to prevent the surface of the curd drying to form crusts which stop draining. A temperature of 60° F. is favorable to the maintenance of proper texture and humidity without the development of objectionable organisms, especially *Oidium lactis*, which tends to cover every exposed surface in such rooms. Draining may be hastened by turning the curd or changing the position of the cloth. In factory practice, the large draining surface reduces the necessity of handling the curd and reduces the loss of fat. About twelve hours are required upon the draining racks.

On a small scale with a few cans of curd in the home, any form of draining rack may be used, such as a potato or berry crate, or the corners of the cloth may be brought together, tied and the mass hung up. The curd must be turned by pulling up the corners of the cloth to prevent drying at the edges and stoppage of draining from the center of the mass. Such treatment produces much more rapid drainage than the factory practice and involves proportionately more labor and larger fat losses.

126. Cooling Neufchâtel.—When whey ceases to separate readily, the corners of the cloth are loosed from the rack, folded diagonally or tied, and the curd cooled on ice or in refrigerators. When thoroughly chilled the bags of curd are put into presses, where light but increasing pressure forces more whey out of the mass. Tests at this time should show about 0.60 per cent acid in the whey. With low-fat curd every step of the process may be hastened, but with high-fat care must be exercised to prevent loss of fat during pressing especially. Any pressing device

[39] Matheson, K. J., and F. R. Cammack, How to make cottage cheese on the farm, U. S. Dept. Agr., Farmers' Bul. 850, pages 1-15, 1917.

permitting continuous pressure with ease of manipulation may be used.

127. Pressing.—The ideals of the maker must determine the extent of pressing. A high yield is obtained by leaving whey in the curd. If immediate consumption is certain, such cheese may be satisfactory, but if the cheese is to be held some days the extra whey carrying more milk-sugar favors increased acid development. This produces very sour cheese with much more danger of other fermentations which cause objectionable flavor. Too much water favors more active bacterial growth as well as produces cheese too soft for the necessary handling in the market.

In the press, several bags of curd may be piled together. The press should be released and the bags turned from time to time to insure even drainage. Several hours of pressing are usually required. The danger of insufficient pressing is due to the difference of texture between the worked and unworked curd. Before working, curd carrying 10 per cent excess moisture resembles the finished product sufficiently to deceive any but the experienced maker. But if this curd is transferred to the worker and to the molding machine, it is found to become soft, pasty and sticky, to lack "body," hence to make very unsatisfactory packages and to spoil very quickly. The masses of curd should come out of the press as dry and hard flat cakes.

Fig. 16.—Working Neufchâtel.

128. Working and salting Neufchâtel. — The cakes of curd go from the press to the working table. Here they are broken by hand or by a butter-worker or kneading machine (Fig. 16). Salt at the rate of one and one-half pounds to 100 pounds of curd is added. If the curd is not sufficiently pressed, the masses become mushy or pasty during the working process. The working is continued until the whole mass is uniformly smooth and buttery.

129. Storage. — The draining and working processes permit the contamination of the curd with organisms from the air and from the apparatus. These are distributed throughout the mass. Air is also worked thoroughly into the curd. Such a product spoils quickly. Distributing houses find the Neufchâtel trade uncertain in volume from day to day, hence many of them store the cheese in bulk and package only fast enough to fill orders. This minimizes the loss due to spoilage. Such curd may be packed into tubs and kept for considerable time in cold storage. If molded for the retail trade, it is more quickly perishable. When packed solidly in mass, curd is largely protected from spoilage by the exclusion of air and perhaps the quick exhaustion of free oxygen through the respiration of the micro-organisms present and by its acidity. This must be supplemented by low temperature to reduce the loss to a minimum. Even when spoilage begins, it is easily confined to the slight growth of *Oidium lactis* or green mold and bacteria on exposed areas. These can be removed with minimum loss and damage to the mass. On the other hand, such curd molded into the commercial package of 3 to 6 ounces and wrapped in paper, with tin-foil or carton for protection, still presents enormously increased surface for the growth of aerobic forms — especially *Oidium lactis*, green mold (Roquefort mold is the usual green species) and accompanying bacteria. Curd in tubs may be kept some days; in commercial packages lowering of quality (flavor) begins almost at once.

130. Molding. — When the standard molding machine (Fig. 17) is provided, curd is brought directly from the refrigerator to the machine. If permitted to become warm, the mass becomes sticky; when cold it is more readily handled. The machine is fitted with the special delivery tube for the variety to be handled, cylindrical for Neufchâtel in its various forms, rectangular in section for cream. Enough workers should be provided to wrap and label the cheese without leaving it exposed to contamination or heat. Parchment paper and tin-foil cut the proper size for each variety and bearing printed labels are readily obtainable. Each cheese should be wrapped with paper and tin-foil and put directly into a flat box which holds a standard number (usually 12 or 24) of the special product.

Fig. 17.—Molding Neufchâtel.

In working with the hand molding tube (Fig. 15) the same care is required. Chilled curd is forced into a firm smooth mass with the plunger. It is removed and wrapped when it reaches the regular size of the variety.

All forms when molded go directly into the boxes and then back to the refrigerators until demanded for actual use. The details of the process differ according to the form made.

131. Skimmed-milk Neufchâtel.—Separator skimmed-milk is frequently made into curd by the Neufchâtel process. The absence of fat eliminates the largest element of loss in manufacture. Each stage of the making process, therefore, may be shortened. The demand that the curd shall be smooth and buttery in texture rather than rough or gritty requires the exercise of care in curdling of milk. The draining and pressing of the curd may be accomplished much more rapidly than in the fatty cheeses. The final product should differ from cottage cheese in smoother texture, milder acidity and, as a rule, cleaner flavor. In composition, the absence of fat must be largely compensated by leaving more water in the cheese. Such a product reaches the market with 65 to 75 per cent of water and perhaps 1.25 per cent of salt. Casein forms 20 to 30 per cent of the mass.

These cheeses are very perishable on account of their high water-content. The destructive effect of microorganisms both in the interior of the cheese and upon its surface is rapid.

Cheeses of this description may be found in the trade as cottage cheese, Neufchâtel style, and as Neufchâtel made from skimmed-milk; skimmed-milk Neufchâtel would be a strictly proper labeling.

132. Baker's cheese.—There is considerable market for skimmed-milk curd as Baker's cheese. This product is essentially skimmed-milk Neufchâtel curd, partially drained and sold in bulk. When the bakery is near by, the curd is frequently shoveled into milk-cans in very wet condition and sent directly from the factory to the bakery. If the distance is such as to require considerable time for transportation, the same care is frequently given as for Neufchâtel curd packed in bulk for storage and transportation.

Great variations in practice are found among the makers of this type of product. In some cases low grade skimmed-milk is handled on a large scale. Curdling is done quickly and little care is given to the details of flavor and texture in the curd. Working in this manner, two men are able to make a ton of such curd, and ship it out in milk-cans each day. The resulting product, although very deficient in flavor and texture, goes into manufactured specialties which conceal its deficiencies if considered as cheese.

133. Domestic Neufchâtel.—The name Neufchâtel, unless limited clearly by the label, should designate a cheese made from fresh whole milk. Cheeses of this group are produced in a small number of well-equipped factories scattered widely through the dairy states of the North and Northeast. Every factory uses one or more trade names for its product. The same product is frequently relabeled by the distributor who uses his own trade name instead of that of the maker.

The usual form of package is cylindrical, about 1¾ inches in diameter and 2½ inches long, or sometimes rectangular 2½ by 1½ by 1½ inches. The cheese is protected by wrapping in parchment paper closely surrounded by tin-foil. These packages vary from 2½ to 4 ounces. In some cases screw-topped glass jars are substituted for the tin-foil package. They are objectionable, first, because of cost and, second, because they are so commonly associated with less perishable products as to mislead either dealer or consumer into holding the product for too long a time. The paper or tin-foil package can be kept only at refrigerator temperature, hence automatically keeps its possessor reminded of the perishable nature of its contents.

Neufchâtel of the best quality made from whole milk testing about 4 per cent fat may be expected to fall within the following limits;[40] many grades contain more water than this at the expense of flavor and keeping quality:

Water	50-55 per cent
Fat	23-28 per cent
Casein	18-21 per cent
Salt	0.5-1.25 per cent

Yield 12-14 lb. per 100 lb. of milk.

134. Partially skim Neufchâtel.—Brands of Neufchâtel made from milk that would test every gradation from whole milk to separator skimmed-milk may be found. The quality of the product varies with the skill of the maker from brands no better than cottage cheese to products scarcely distinguishable from the best whole-milk Neufchâtel. Many factories that produce more than one quality of Neufchâtel use labels of different color, different design or both to separate them; for example, blue labels usually stand for whole milk, red labels represent lower

---

[40] Taken from Conn. (Storrs) Exp. Sta. Bul. 78, page 328.

grades. Sometimes the difference in material is indicated by a clear cut grade mark. Frequently color, a design of label or both are the only definite marks upon the cheese. The consumer unfamiliar with the trade practice commonly has no means of knowing the quality of the product offered. Such cheeses vary in water-content from 55 to 70 per cent; in fat from 10 to 25 per cent; in casein from 18 to 25 per cent.

135. Cream cheese.—The Neufchâtel process is also used to make cream cheese. The material utilized is commonly what has been called double cream. This is produced by separating about half of a given volume of milk and running the cream into the other half. Usually cream cheese is made in the same factory as various grades of Neufchâtel. No material is lost. In some instances, cream cheese is prepared by working thick cream into the Neufchâtel type of curd from practically skimmed-milk. In working with high percentages of fat in curd, care must be taken to avoid loss of fat in draining and pressing. The curd is carefully chilled before pressing to reduce this loss. This may be done under refrigeration or upon cracked ice. Otherwise the manipulations of the process are unchanged. The cheeses are commonly molded in the Neufchâtel machine into square cakes weighing about 4 ounces and measuring approximately 3 by 2¼ by ⅞ inches. These are wrapped in paper and tin-foil and handled exactly as Neufchâtel.

Cream cheese of high quality made from reënforced milk testing 7 to 9 per cent fat may be expected to test approximately as follows:[41]

Water	38-43 per cent
Fat	43-48 per cent
Protein	13-16 per cent
Salt	0.5-1.25 per cent

Yield 16-18 lb. per 100 lb. of cream.

Increases of water, hence greater yields, are very common but usually associated with loss in quality both as to flavor and texture, and in more rapid spoilage; certain brands regularly carry 50 to 60 per cent of fat but their increased cost of manufacture and sale restricts them to the rôle of specialties with closely limited distribution. Trade names such as Philadelphia Cream, Cow Brand, Eagle Brand, Square Cream, Blue Label and many other factory brands are on the market.

136. Neufchâtel specialties.—Neufchâtel or cream cheese curd is frequently mixed with some flavoring substance, such as pimiento (pickled Spanish peppers), olives, nuts, spices or other cheeses, such as Roquefort. These bear appropriate trade names and form a very attractive addition to our varieties of cheese. Among the names found are Pimiento, Olive, Nut, and Pim-olive or Olimento.

137. Gervais is a brand of cream cheese made in Paris and sold widely in France and even in other continental countries. It occasionally comes to America. As made in Paris, these cheeses are flat cakes containing approximately 40 per cent water and 35-45 per cent fat. It clearly differs only in detail from the square cream cheeses made in America. The name Gervais is the property of a particular

---

[41] Taken from Conn. (Storrs) Exp. Sta. Bul. 78, page 328.

company. Since the cheese differs in no essential feature from other cream cheeses, this name should not be applied to a domestic cream brand.

138. European forms occasionally imported.—Among the cheeses related to Neufchâtel as they reach the market are the "White" cheeses of southern Europe. These differ greatly in quality according to their source and to their content of cow, sheep, goat's milk or some combination of these. This texture and flavor link them with unripened Neufchâtel. The time required for importation puts a minimum possible period of ten to fifteen days between production and consumption with a probable period of at least one month for most samples. As they come to America, these forms usually show fermentive changes beyond those tolerated in the domestic product. This may take either of several forms: (1) intensification of acid flavor with the intensification of the characteristic flavors of the particular brand; (2) the development of old or rancid flavors; (3) the development of Oidium and partial softening of the mass through its agency; (4) the growth of Roquefort mold and development of the flavor associated with that organism. This last form was found in a shipment of Hungarian Briuse which showed about 40 per cent fat, 14 per cent protein and 43 per cent water.

CHAPTER VIII
SOFT CHEESES RIPENED BY MOLD

Hand cheese and its allies; Pennsylvania pot cheese; Appetitost (Appetite cheese); Ripened Neufchâtel, French process; The Camembert group; Camembert cheese; Description of Camembert; Conditions of making and ripening; Outline of making process; Acidity; Ripening the cheese; Composition; Factory; Economic factors; French Brie; Coulommiers.

The ripened soft cheeses include a series of groups of varieties which, in addition to initial souring, have been subjected to special ripening processes, and which in the ripened condition are soft in texture and mostly have high flavors. The varieties in each group have in common some essential principles of manufacture together with a ripening process dominated by a characteristic group of organisms. In certain groups, the ripening is dominated by a yellowish or orange viscid surface slime containing *Oidium lactis* and bacteria; in another series, the characteristic organism is a mold of the genus Penicillium (*P. Camemberti*). Referring to the analysis of groups (page 83), the ripened soft cheeses are found to fall into three well-marked groups, one of which may perhaps be subdivided as indicated. The series curdled by souring alone begins with approximately cottage cheese curd and develops high flavors by ripening, as in "hand" cheese. Ripened Neufchâtel curdled by souring and rennet together finds its basis in Neufchâtel curd also but modifies the final product until the familiar flavor and texture of the unripened form are no longer recognizable. Among the forms curdled by rennet alone the Camembert series contains one form, Coulommiers, which is occasionally used unripe, but represents in general a mold-ripened group of highly flavored forms. The series of soft rennet cheeses ripened by bacteria may be broadly designated the Limburger group.

139. Hand cheese and its allies.—Among skim cheeses, there is a series of forms largely German in origin in which curd not far removed from cottage cheese is the basis of the product. Harz cheese is one of the best-known of these forms as studied by Eckles and Rahn.[42] One of these forms, hand cheese,[43] is manufactured on a commercial basis in farm dairies among families of German descent principally in Pennsylvania, and on a factory basis in a few places in New York, northern Illinois and Wisconsin. On the small scale, curd is made by natural

[42] Eckles, C. H., and O. Rahn, Die Reifung des Harzkäses, Centralb. f. Bakt. etc. 2 abt. 14 (1905), pages 676-680.

[43] Monrad, J. H., Hand cheese, N. Y. Produce Rev. etc. 25 (1908), 16, page 644.

souring or by use of starter, heated to expel water, cooled and molded by hand into cakes two to three inches in diameter and one-half to three-quarters inch in thickness. The freshly formed cakes are placed upon a shelf to dry. There they are turned daily until fairly firm, then packed in rolls into wooden boxes and ripened in a cool damp room. In this ripening there is a prompt development of a heavy viscous slime, which consists of Oidium and bacteria. Other molds forming loose cottony mycelium are brushed off if they appear. The proper consistency of this slimy covering depends on a close adjustment of water-content in the cheese with temperature and relative humidity in the ripening room. If conditions are too dry, the cheeses harden quickly or if less dry they are attacked by green or blue-green molds. If too wet, the slimy covering becomes too soft and watery, or secondarily covered with loose shimmering masses of mold (Mucor sp.). Ripening should proceed slowly and occupy a period of six to eight weeks.

140. Pennsylvania pot cheese.—A form of "pot" cheese is made in certain counties of Pennsylvania, principally for local use. Production of this cheese on a factory basis is now being attempted. The steps in manufacture are about as follows:[44] (1) The home-made type of cottage cheese curd is prepared, put into a crock or pot and covered carefully; (2) kept in a warm place (in kitchen usually); (3) stirred from time to time, until it has ripened to a semi-liquid condition. This occurs very rapidly under the attack of *Oidium lactis* accompanied by bacteria. Within a period of three to seven days, according to the temperature and to the water-content of the mass, the granules of curd become covered with a wrinkled gelatinous almost viscid mass of mold mycelium beneath which is a layer of semi-liquid curd with a strong characteristic odor and taste. This ripened or semi-liquid part reaches about half the total mass in four or five days at favorable temperatures. (4) The vessel is then placed in a larger vessel of water and heated over the fire with constant stirring until the whole mass is melted and smooth. (5) Butter or cream, and salt or other flavor is finally added, stirred in and the liquid cheese poured into molds or jelly glasses to cool. If properly made and cooked, the resultant cheese has a soft buttery consistency with an agreeable flavor, which frequently resembles that of Camembert cheese.

141. Appetitost (Appetite cheese).—A Danish buttermilk cheese is made under this name. Sour buttermilk is heated, by some to boiling temperature but others (Monrad[45]) prefer 120° F., stirred thoroughly and allowed to settle. The whey is removed as far as possible. The semi-liquid mass is covered and set in a warm place. Fermentation becomes active. This tends to make the curd more viscous or sticky. It is then kneaded and allowed to ferment again. This process is repeated until the mass is yellowish and soft but tough or viscous. When thoroughly fermented, the mass is again heated to 120° F., and 6 per cent salt is added together with spice; both are worked in and the cheese is formed into fancy shapes for sale.

---

[44] The authors are under obligations to Mrs. E. E. Kiernan for her description of this process (in the Somerset County Leader, Jan. 10, 1908) and her letters concerning it. The statement of the process given here combines the published statement with the results of our own experiments.

[45] Monrad, J. H., Appetitost, N. Y. Produce Rev. etc. 25 (1908), 16, page 644.

142. Ripened Neufchâtel, French process.—Neufchâtel as a ripened cheese is made rather widely in France but it is produced on an especially large scale in Seine-Inferieure.[46] Some factories use whole milk, or milk with added cream, others skimmed-milk.[47] The whole-milk brands of Neufchâtel are those which have the widest reputation. For making this cheese, the working room is held as closely as possible at 15-16° C. (58-60° F.). The milk is strained into earthen vessels holding twenty liters. Rennet is added to the freshly drawn milk at about 30° C. (86° F.) in amount sufficient to produce coagulation in about twenty-four hours. Draining racks of various forms are covered with cloth. The vessels of curd are dumped upon the racks. The whey separates slowly and drains off through the cloth. About twelve hours are allowed for this process. The corners of the cloth are then brought together and folded in or tied and the mass pressed to complete the drainage. The finished curd is worked or kneaded to produce a smooth and uniform texture. This process of curd-making is essentially the same as the American factory process of making Neufchâtel. The ripening process has been entirely dropped in America. The curd is finally molded in metal forms 5 cm. (2 inches) in diameter and about 6.7 cm. (about 3 inches) high, open at both ends. These molds are filled, the freshly formed cheeses are pressed out with a plunger or piston and their surfaces smoothed with a wooden knife.

After molding is completed, the cheeses are salted by sprinkling the entire surface with fine dry salt as the cheese is held in the hand. In this way each cheese receives and absorbs 3 to 4 per cent salt. After salting, the cheeses are arranged upon boards and allowed to drain twenty-four hours. They are then removed to the first or drying room. The frames of the drying room (secherie) are covered with straw and the cheeses are placed carefully upon the straw to avoid contact with each other. They are turned each day to present a fresh surface to the straw during a period of two to three weeks in the drying room (secherie). Mold begins to show as white cottony mycelium after five to six days, and slowly turns to "blue" (bluish green). When the cheeses are well covered with this moldy rind, they are removed to the ripening cellar. In the ripening cellar also the cheeses stand upon straw. They are turned over every three or four days at first, then allowed to stand for a longer period.

When ripe, a Neufchâtel cheese so made weighs about 125 grams. One liter of milk makes 225 grams of such cheese. The ripening of Neufchâtel has never been fully studied, but a series of these cheeses were obtained by one of the authors; cultures were made and examined.[48] The salt-content in the first place was found to be so high that *Oidium lactis* was eliminated as an active factor in the ripening. The mold proved to be on some cheeses *Penicillium Camemberti*, the typical mold of Camembert as it is made in Normandy, on others *P. Camemberti* var. *Rogeri*, the

---

[46] Pouriau, A. F., La Laiterie, sixième ed. par Marcel Monteran, page 453, Paris, 1908.

[47] Among the varietal names for Neufchâtel cheese from whole milk or with added cream are Petits Bondons, Malakoffs, Carrés affinés. Among low fat or skim forms, Petit Suisse, Gournay.

[48] Thom, C., J. N. Currie and K. J. Matheson, Studies relating to the Roquefort and Camembert types of cheese, Conn. (Storrs) Exp. Sta. Bul. 79, page 392.

pure white form as used under the patents of M. Georges Roger in the region of Seine-et-Marne to the eastward of Paris and called by him and by Mazé *P. candidum.* The physical condition of the ripened curd and the flavors encountered were those associated with these two species by many hundreds of experiments during the Camembert investigation in Connecticut.[49] These facts justify the conclusion that ripened Neufchâtel is first soured by lactic organisms, then so salted as to eliminate or reduce to a minimum the characteristic activities of *Oidium lactis,* while the proteolytic action and the physical changes are closely similar to those of Camembert which is ripened primarily by the same molds.

143. The Camembert group.—The soft cheeses ripened by molds are French in origin. Their manufacture has spread into Germany, Italy and America. Of the series, the most widely known is Camembert, which will be described as typical for the group. Brie, Coulommiers, Robbiola and Ripened Neufchâtel belong to this series.

144. Camembert cheese.—The origin of Camembert is given by French authorities as 1791 in the Commune of Camembert near Vimoutiers in Orne, France. From a very restricted production at first, Camembert-making has spread through the region from Caen in the west to Havre, Rouen and a considerable area east of Paris. In America Camembert began to be made in one factory about 1900. Several other factories followed by 1906. The difficulties and losses encountered led to the abandonment of these undertakings, until at the outbreak of the European war in 1914 but one factory was making Camembert and that only on an experimental scale. Meanwhile the United States Department of Agriculture and the Storrs Experiment Station had taken up and solved, on an experimental basis, most of the problems arising in these commercial failures. A shortage of product at the outbreak of the war brought about the re-establishment of a series of factories. The product as put on the market indicates that a permanent establishment of Camembert-making is entirely practicable.

Camembert cheese is made from cow's milk either whole or very slightly skimmed; the removal of about 0.5 per cent of fat has been found to be desirable if not actually necessary.

145. Description of Camembert.[50]—These cheeses are made in sizes 2½ to 4½ inches in diameter and 1¼ to 1½ inches in thickness. They are ripened by the agency of molds and bacteria which form a felt-like rind over their whole surface, 1/16 to 1/8 of an inch in thickness. This rind may be dry and gray or grayish-green, consisting of a felt-like surface of mold on the outside, below which a harder portion consists of mold embedded in partially dried cheese, or the moldy part may be more or less completely overgrown or displaced by yellowish or reddish slime composed mainly of bacteria. Good cheeses may have either appearance.

Inside the rind, the cheese is softened progressively from the rind toward the

---

[49] Full discussion of this product is found in U. S. Dept. Agr. Bur. An. Ind. Bul. 115. Camembert cheese problems in the U. S. also published as Storrs Exp. Sta. Bul. 58 with the same title. Also a supplementary paper in Bul. 79 of Storrs Exp. Sta.

[50] Thom, C., U. S. Dept. Agr. Bur. An. Ind. Circ. 145 (1909), page 339.

center from all sides, so that a fully ripe cheese has no hard sour curd in the center, but is completely softened. No mold should be visible inside the rind, but the moldy rind itself is necessary because the ripening is caused by the enzymes secreted by the organisms of the rind into the cheese. As the curd ripens, the changed portion assumes a slightly deeper color than the unripe curd as a result of chemical changes. Well-ripened cheeses vary from nearly a fluid texture to the consistency of moderately soft butter. The ripening of Camembert is finished in wooden boxes which protect the cheeses from breaking after they become soft and during the market period.

146. Conditions of making and ripening. — These processes depend on a very close adjustment between the composition of the freshly made cheese and the temperature and humidity of the rooms in which the cheeses are made and ripened. Very slight failures in control bring loss in ultimate results. The room for making Camembert should be maintained between 60° and 70° F. and should be wet enough to reduce drying to a minimum. The essentials of apparatus are comparatively inexpensive. Work on a factory basis calls, however, for the installation of special tables and other apparatus to utilize space and labor to advantage. Rooms are protected from change of weather by double sash in the windows. Flies must be excluded by close-meshed screens for all doors and windows with movable sash. The equipment installed in such a room is shown in Fig. 18. Curdling cans are ranged on a shelf a few inches above the floor along one side of the room below an open tin trough with side branches. This open trough brings the milk from the mixing vat to the curdling cans. (The open tin trough offers no lodgment for dirt.) The cans hold about 200 pounds of milk, are about 12 inches in diameter at bottom, and 20 to 24 inches at top. They are heavily tinned. Iron trucks as high as the shelf and with tops the same diameter as the bottoms of the cans form a convenient method of bringing cans of curd to the very edge of the draining tables.

Fig. 18.—Camembert cheese-making room in an American factory.

The wooden draining tables are placed about 32 inches above the floor; they are usually made of 2-inch lumber, have raised edges and slope slightly toward the wall. Whey and wash water are thus carried to a draining trough along the wall. For cheese-making, each is covered with a strip of matting consisting of wooden strips held together by thread (Fig. 19). The strip of matting should be exactly the width and length of the table. The hoops used are heavy tin, with edges turned and soldered, about 5 inches high, 4⅝ inches in diameter with three rows of holes about 1/12 inch in diameter and 2 inches apart in the row. These hoops are placed as thickly as possible upon the mats.

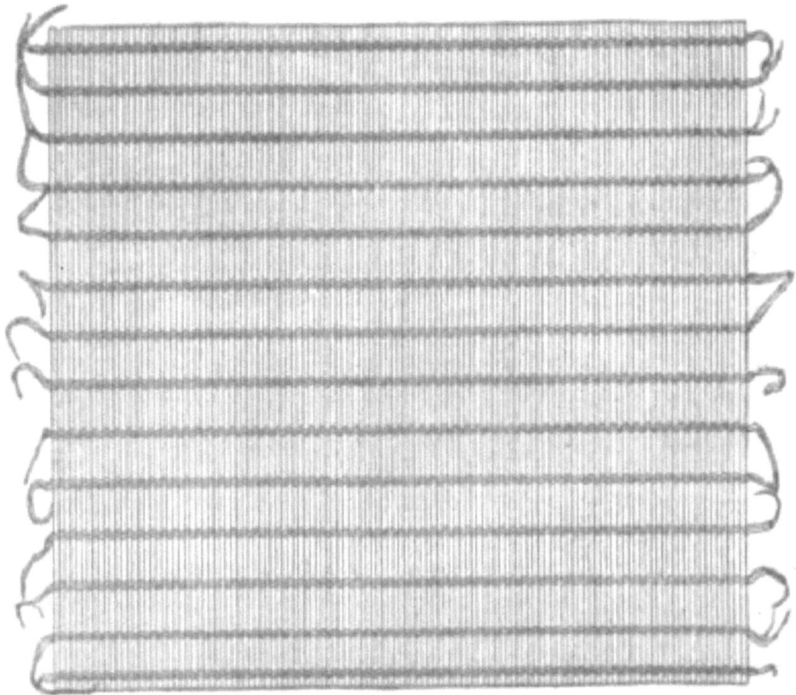

Fig. 19.—Draining mat for Camembert cheese.

147. Outline of making process.—The making process[51] is summarized as follows (Thom, 1909):

Starter.—From 0.5 to 1.0 per cent of active starter is added to milk kept overnight below 60°F.

Acidity at renneting.—Milk titrated to phenolphthalein should test 0.20 to 0.23 per cent calculated as lactic acid.

Temperance of renneting.—84°-86° F. is used for Camembert.

Rennet.—From 3 to 5 oz. of standard rennet extract to 1000 lb. milk (10-15 c.c. per 100 lb. milk) produces a curd of proper texture.

Curdling time.—To reach the proper condition for handling, 1¼ to 1½ hours or longer is required. This is indicated by the onset of "sweating" or the separation of large drops of whey on the surface of the solid curd.

Dipping.—A long-handled dipper is used to transfer curd from cans to hoops. This can be lowered into the hoop. This transfer is to be done with the least possible breaking. One dipperful is transferred at a time to each of a series of hoops. By the time the series is covered, some drainage has occurred and a second dipperful

[51] Lot record cards for the making and ripening of Camembert are given on pages 124 and 125.

is added to the contents of the hoop. In this way the hoop is filled within a period of two to four hours.

Draining.—Hoops when properly filled have taken in approximately 2 quarts of milk each. No pressure is used. Cheeses drain by gravity. They stand unturned until the following morning when they should be firm enough to permit turning without removing the hoops. The cheeses when firm enough to handle (usually on the third morning) are salted by dusting the entire surface with coarse salt and permitting all that adheres to remain. The cheeses should then be removed to a room at about 58°F. to prevent too rapid leakage of water and salt from their surfaces. Ripe cheeses of good quality show a total salt-content varying from 2.25 to 3 per cent with an average of about 2.5 per cent. When so handled there is slight, if any, loss of water and salt in the salting period of twenty-four to forty-eight hours. At the end of the salting period such cheeses should carry 55 to 57 per cent water or slightly more.

148. Acidity.—The essential biological factor in the making period of Camembert is proper souring. The milk should be free from gassy organisms. The lactic starter required should introduce the typical lactic organism (*Streptococcus lacticus*) in numbers sufficient to suppress all other forms during the next twenty-four hours. The amount of acid starter introduced, however, plus the acid resulting from growth during the curdling period, should not produce a grainy acid curd. The temperatures of handling are such as to favor this group of organisms if properly introduced and permit the development of nearly 1 per cent of acid (estimated as lactic) by the second morning. Cheeses with such acid are fairly free from further danger from bacterial activity. Members of the high-acid group (*B. Bulgaricus* and allies) may be found in these cheeses but do not appear to develop in numbers sufficient to affect the cheese to any marked degree.

Fig. 20.—Halloir, the first ripening room for Camembert in an American facto-ry.

CAMEMBERT CHEESE RECORD

Date..........................   Set............No.

Amt. milk................. No. cheese................. Milk per cheese..............

Producer of milk..........................

Apparent cleanliness of milk..........................

Acidity:

     Before adding starter....................................

     After adding starter...............................

     After acidity period..................................

     Whey at dipping.................................

Starter:

     Kind...........................   Age.....................   Amt................

Color:

     Amount..........................

Curdling:

     Temperature used..................................

     Amount of rennet.................................

     Time at which rennet is added..................

     Time at which milk is curdled.....................

     Time of curdling...

     Quality of curd...

Dipping:

     Cut or uncut.................................

     Amt. of cutting...............................

Draining:

     Temperature of room during...........................

     Condition of cheese after...............................

Salting:

     Time of......... Total amt. of salt used......... Kind of salt.......

                Amt. of salt per cheese...........

Mold inoculation:

     Form of culture used...............................

     Method of inoculation...................................

     Time of inoculation....................................

Remarks on making:

Curing:

     Transfer of curing rooms.............................

     Condition of cheese......................................

     Rooms...

     Dates..

Mold growth:

Date of first appearance..............................

Purity and vigor..............................

Date of changing color..............................

Surface of slimy growth:

Extent of..............................

General character of..............................

Surface contamination:

Mold..............................

Oidium..............................

Yeast..............................

Bacterial..............................

Wrapping:

Date ....   Material..........................

Condition of cheese..........................

Ripening:

Rapidity of..............................

Texture..............................

Flavor:

Ripened curd..............................

Unripened curd..............................

Special treatment and reasons for same:

Record of treatment by days..............................

Room.............. Date.............. Observations.

1 D........	16 D........
2 D........	17 D........
3 D........	18 D........
4 D........	19 D........
5 D........	20 D........
6 D........	21 D........
7 D........	22 D........
8 D........	23 D........
9 D........	24 D........
10 D........	25 D........
11 D........	26 D........
12 D........	27 D........
13 D........	28 D........
14 D........	29 D........
15 D........	30 D........
	31 D........

149. Ripening the cheese.—The cheese is now ready for the ripening rooms (Fig. 20). For this process temperatures between 52° and 58°F. are desirable; lower temperatures only delay the process; higher temperatures favor undesirable fermentations. The cheeses rest upon coarse matting (Fr. clayons) consisting of round wooden rods about the size of a pencil separated 1-1¼ inches and held in position by wire strands. Assuming cheeses of optimum composition as indicated above, the relative humidity of the ripening rooms should be 86 to 88 per cent. Higher humidities produce too rapid development of slimy coatings; too low humidity is indicated by drying, shrinkage and the growth of green molds on the surface. A slight and very slow evaporation is demanded; by this the water-content of the cheeses is reduced 3 to 6 per cent in two weeks. During the first two weeks of ripening, the cheeses commonly show some growth of yeast and *Oidium lactis* first, followed by cottony white areas of Camembert mold (*Penicillium Camemberti*). This mold must be introduced by inoculation in new factories but once firmly established in the factory will propagate itself if conditions are kept favorable. Climatic conditions in most dairy sections of America have been sufficiently unfavorable to make more or less continuous use of pure cultures desirable. At the end of two weeks, Camembert cheeses should show a well-established rind, consisting of a well-matted felt work of mold hyphæ through the outer 2 mm. (¹⁄₁₂ inch) of the whole surface of the cheese. More or less of the pale gray-green fruit of the characteristic *Penicillium Camemberti* can usually be seen. Beginning at about twelve to fourteen days,[52] a softening of the curd is first directly detectable under the rind. This is preceded by the disappearance of the acidity of the curd, which progresses inward. The softening of the curd follows closely the lowering of the acidity. Thus a litmus test taken along the cut face of a Camembert cheese at any stage of softening will always show a sharp acid reaction in the solid sour portion which changes to alkaline just before the softening due to proteolytic action becomes noticeable. These two changes appear to be due to enzymes secreted by the mycelium of the *Penicillium Camemberti* and *Oidium lactis* which constitute the most active factors in the ripening. Some accessory bacterial action is indicated but of minor importance in the changes found.

To avoid loss from breaking, after the softening of the curd has fairly begun, the cheeses must be removed from the coarse matting to smooth boards where they are watched and turned repeatedly, or as in the more common practice, wrapped at once in parchment paper and boxed. The ripening may be completed in either way. The conditions necessary are such as to favor the extension of slimy areas of bacteria over part or all of the rind to the exclusion of further development of gray-green fruiting areas of mold.

Complete softening may occur in three weeks in cheeses in which evaporation has gone on too slowly. Such cheeses are found to contain 51 to 55 per cent of water when ripe and decay very quickly. If handled properly, the water-content

---

[52] Bosworth, A. W., Chemical studies of Camembert cheese, N. Y. (Geneva) Exp. Sta. Tech. Bul. 5, pages 23-39, 1907.

Dox, A. W., Proteolytic changes in the ripening of Camembert cheese, U. S. Dept. Agr. Bur. An. Ind. Bul. 109, pages 1-24, 1908.

should fall from about 57 per cent at the beginning of ripening to 48 per cent at its completion which should require a minimum period of about four weeks. It is more desirable that a cheese four weeks old show a thin core of sour curd in the center than that it be entirely liquid at that age.

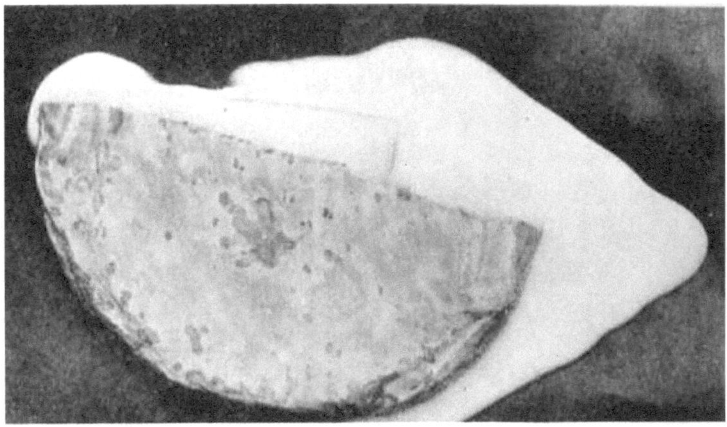

Fig. 21.—Very soft Camembert cheese.

150. Composition.—Properly ripe Camembert shows about the following range of composition: Water 47 to 49 per cent; fat 25 to 28 per cent; protein 18 to 21 per cent; salt 2.2 per cent to 2.8 per cent. Variations outside these limits are usually associated with less desirable qualities. The approximate limits and characters outlined for Camembert still leave a considerable latitude for variations in practice which characterize the output of particular factories in a producing group. At one extreme are brands of Camembert cheese which are very soft (Fig. 21), some of them actually liquid when ripe, and which have very strong odor and taste; one such brand has held first place in the trade of certain American cities for years. Another popular brand when fully ripe is well covered with yellow-orange viscid slime[53] but is fairly firm in texture with high flavor; still others show dry moldy surfaces and mild flavors. The product of certain factories is always characterized by the presence and characteristic ammoniacal odor of *Penicillium brevicaule.*

Each of these forms seems to appeal to some classes of consumers, so that in handling imported Camembert the trade comes to assign the product to specific groups of purchasers according to the conditions observed at its arrival from Europe.

151. Factory.—The type of factory to be used in making and ripening Camembert must be adjusted to the climate. This product originated in the Normandy section of France which is but a few feet above sea level, is swept by winds from the Gulf Stream, and has a narrow range of temperature, with highly humid conditions. In that region, every effort must be made to secure ventilation to carry off the necessary amount of evaporation water. In contrast, most of the dairy sections

[53] Esten, W. M., and C. J. Mason, Bact. Stud. of Camembert cheese, Storrs Exp. Sta. Bul. 83 (1915), pages 103-111.

of America have land instead of sea breezes, much higher altitudes, much greater extremes of temperature and a lower range of relative humidities. The conditions of an upstairs room full of windows in Normandy (Fig. 22) are most readily reproduced in rooms partly or completely below ground in this country. The industry calls for the production and maintenance of a specific set of working conditions. These are furnished by nature in northern France, probably also in certain Pacific coast areas, but must be artificially obtained where the climate is unfavorable.

Fig. 22.—Camembert cheese factory at Lisieux, France. The square windows are seen in the second-floor rooms.

152. Economic factors.—Camembert cheeses show a yield of about 13 pounds to 100 pounds of milk testing 4 per cent fat. At roughly one-half pound each, the number of cheeses will be approximately twenty-six. Assuming no losses and a wholesale price of 15 cents each, the wholesale value of 100 pounds of milk would be $3.90. The labor cost of production is high, the package represents (box, wrapping and label) at least 1½ cents a cheese. The time between the purchase and the consumption of the cheese will average about one month. Few cheeses actually remain this length of time in the possession of the maker. This short investment period, therefore, is a distinct advantage of Camembert. Among disadvantages, however, the extremely perishable character of the fully ripe cheese makes provision of an adequate and constant market essential. Losses due to failures in manufacturing or ripening conditions are also frequent. Excessive heat in summer and very cold periods in winter are both unfavorable. The Camembert-maker cannot, therefore, use the cheapest milk of the summer months at all and the losses entailed by failure of control in winter fall on the most costly milk of the year. Camembert requires, therefore, careful selection of the location for manufacture and ripening, effective control of conditions throughout the period and adequate marketing facilities. Camembert at its best is one of the finest of all cheeses; when bad, it becomes quickly inedible and is a total loss.

153. French Brie.[54]—Brie cheese has its center of production in Seine-et-Marne, east of Paris in northern France. The apparatus, arrangement of the factories and details of manipulation differ from those described for Camembert, but the final product is in flavor and texture closely related to Camembert. Brie cheeses are the same thickness as Camembert, 1 to 1¼ inches; in diameter, however, there are three or more sizes varying from 8 to 16 inches, or even greater. The largest cheeses weigh 5 to 6 pounds. As in Camembert, practices of making and ripening vary to such a degree as to produce various qualities of product. These run from whole milk through all shades of skimming. Perhaps the best established practice puts the cheese-making room next to the stalls of the cows. The milk is drawn, strained directly into the curdling cans and renneted while still warm,—86-92° F. (30-33° C.). No lactic starter is added and no ripening period is given to the milk. The other manipulations differ only in detail from Camembert. Ripening of Brie follows the same course with the same organic agents, namely, Camembert mold (*Penicillium Camemberti*) and *Oidium lactis* with the accompaniment of a mixture of slimy organisms upon the surface of the cheese. The process admits of many minor modifications each capable of affecting the product in a characteristic way. The judgment and skill of the maker is given a wide opportunity to establish and work toward a particular ideal of appearance and texture and flavor. Brands with characteristic qualities, therefore, command their own market.

Brie as known in France must not be confused with the American "d'Isigny," or with the particular sizes of that type which have been called Brie on account of diameter only. Very little Brie as known in France has been made in America and only a limited amount has been imported for very restricted trade.

154. Coulommiers.—Another member of the Camembert group is called, from its place of origin, Coulommiers. This form is made at the same thickness as Camembert and about 5¼ inches in diameter. It appears as either a ripened or unripe cheese. As a ripened cheese, Coulommiers is not essentially different from Camembert except that some brands are made without salting. As a cheese eaten unripe, it has certain advantages over the other cheeses with the flavor of sour milk only. The cottage and (American) Neufchâtel group of cheeses comprises the best known forms with the acid flavor. These cheeses are very perishable in nature. On the other hand, Coulommiers as eaten fresh can be held and used over a much longer time without loss. Coulommiers[55] in this sense is simply a fresh Camembert. Such a cheese, when ready for the salting process, is a firm sour mass, close textured, almost impervious to air and but slowly permeable to liquids. Spoilage in such a cheese begins only on the outside, and not throughout the mass as in cottage cheese or Neufchâtel. Successive portions of such a cheese can be removed daily over a considerable period with no loss of substance aside from slight scraping at times and little or no change in flavor. This product has very tangible merit for manufacture and use on the farm in many sections of America.

[54] See page 134 for domestic or American use of the name Brie.

[55] McNaughton, J., Coulommier cheese, Dept. Agr. Ottawa, Canada, Dairy and Cold Storage Ser. Bul. 25, 1910.

CHAPTER IX

SOFT CHEESES RIPENED BY BACTERIA

The Isigny group; Raffiné; Liederkranz cheese; Limburger cheese; The milk; Making the cheese; Draining and salting; Ripening; Marketing and qualities of Limburger; Yield and composition of Limburger; Münster cheese;.

A bacterially-ripened series of cheeses parallels the mold-ripened group as typified by Camembert. Although the varieties overlap, these may be roughly grouped as: (1) those made from friable or soft curd; (2) those made from firm or rubbery curd. In the first group, the curd is set at 86° F., or below; in the second, the rennet is added at 90° F. or above. In the first, the lower temperature and long curdling time with ripened milk gives a soft friable curd which may be toughened somewhat by cutting and stirring in the whey. This section is typified by d'Isigny, American Brie, Liederkranz. In the second, curdling of unripened milk at temperatures of 90° F. or above insures a smooth elastic curd which fuses more or less completely into the firm rubbery mass typified by freshly made Limburger.

155. The Isigny group.—A series of names, d'Isigny, Brie, Brie d'Isigny, combined with trade names, are used for a domestic cheese, made in a small number of factories distributed over New York, Pennsylvania, Michigan, Illinois, Wisconsin, Iowa and California. The cheeses sold under the separate varietal names differ only in diameter; their thickness is fairly uniform; the process of manufacture and ripening with resultant textures and flavors furnishes no fundamental varietal characters, although the products of the several factories show noticeable differences in market quality. D'Isigny, while the name of a French town famous for butter production, is not used to designate a cheese in France. It may, therefore, be accepted as a French name arbitrarily applied to a domestic product. Brie as used in France is a markedly different cheese (p. 131), and the name should be dropped from this form as made in America. As used for a member of this series made in America, it merely means cheese 7 to 15 inches in diameter. The cheese partakes of the characters of French Livarot, and of Pont l'Eveque without exactly reproducing either form.

The milk varies from separator skim to whole milk, with resultant differences in quality. Freedom from gas is essential to the best results. The milk is curdled at 85° to 86° F. with sufficient rennet to produce a very firm curd within a period of one and one-half hours. Curd is then cut in two directions, allowed to stand a few minutes or gently agitated to produce a very slight toughness or "worked" condition, then scooped into hoops 4½ to 5 inches in height and varying in diameter from 2½ to 15 inches according to the size selected for manufacture. To aid in the escape of whey, three rows of holes 1/12 inch in diameter and 2 inches apart in the row are made in each hoop. The hoops are arranged upon draining tables with more or less corrugated surface, which for best drainage should be covered with matting. The cheeses are allowed to drain without pressure. They are commonly turned the second morning, although they are sometimes solid enough to turn within the first day. When fully drained, the cheeses are salted by rubbing coarse salt on the surface, after which they stand an extra day. They are then arranged upon shelves in a ripening room held between 50° and 60° F. with humidity so high that evaporation is kept at a minimum. In this room, a surface slime develops quickly. This consists of bacteria of several forms, yeasts, *Oidium lactis* and accidental species of other molds. During this ripening, the cheeses are turned, rubbed with the hands, washed with salt water and scraped if infected with molds which produce colored colonies. In the course of ripening, the slimy surface layer acquires a yellowish orange color with the strong odor and taste characteristic of the series.

Brands of d'Isigny are made from every grade between separator skim and whole milk. They reach the market in condition all the way from "Kosher" forms[56] which are eaten entirely unripe, to brands which approximate the qualities of Limburger and others which approach Port du Salut.

The biology and chemistry of the ripening of this type of cheese have not been completely followed. An initial souring process always takes place quickly. *Oidium lactis* is always present in some degree on the surface, but the organisms in the yellowish to orange slime on the surface of the cheese appear to produce the characteristic odor and taste. These appear to be due to the development of volatile fatty acids, such as valerianic and caproic, which diffuse throughout the cheese, even penetrating the unripened sour portions. The same odor and taste in varying intensity are present in Limburger, Brick, and a long series of German varieties not handled in America.

High-flavored cheeses such as these, form an acceptable part of the meal in cases in which the intensity of other flavors is such as to mask entirely the milder flavors of Camembert or cream cheese.

In composition, a characteristic whole-milk brand of this group showed the following analysis:[57] water, 45.5 per cent; fat, 25.28 per cent; protein, 18.22 per cent.

156. Raffiné.[58]—This cheese is made in the French settlement of the Isle of Orleans in the St. Lawrence River. The practice seems to have been brought from France and represents an intermediate product between Camembert and perhaps

---

[56] Kosher forms are prepared in compliance with the Mosaic law as demanded by the Jewish trade.

[57] Unpublished analysis of the Storrs Exp. Sta.

[58] Chapais, J. C., Monographie, Le Fromage Raffiné de L'Isle d'Orléans. Quebec, 1911. Published by Ministry of Agriculture, pages 1-31.

Livarot, a cheese on the borderline between Camembert and Isigny as made in America. The outline of the making process as given follows: Milk freshly drawn is curdled without cooling, at approximately 90° F. The rennet is prepared on the farm. About one-half hour is required for curdling. The curd is cut into 2-inch cubes. Whey is removed as fast as it separates. About two hours are required for draining. The curd then goes into the hoops. The metal hoops, which are closed at one end, are 6 inches high, 4½ inches in diameter, with holes about ⅟16 inch at intervals of about ½ inch, and stand upon three legs about 1 inch in height. When filled, the cheeses are left on a draining table. Some salt is put on top while draining. When the volume is reduced to one-half, the cheese is turned. The draining room is kept at about 70° F. After they are firm enough to handle, drainage is completed on racks covered with rush matting. These are arranged on special racks. The cheeses are turned twice a day, and washed in slightly salted water every two days. After each washing, they are drained for two hours on cloth, and placed on clean matting. This treatment continues about fifteen days.

After fifteen days on the matting, the cheeses are ready for ripening. They are first covered with cold brine and let stand twenty-four hours. The cheeses are packed in rolls or tiers in boxes, covered with cloth and ripened at 45° F. They must be kept moist; if signs of drying appear, moisture must be added. If the cheeses develop yellow slime, they are washed with clear water and rinsed in water with salt added. After a ripening period of three weeks, the cheeses should begin to be soft when pressed with the finger. The growth of molds must be prevented by washing the boxes, cloths, and washing and scraping the cheeses if necessary. When the cheeses are ready for the market, they are scraped clean and white, wrapped separately in cheese-cloth or parchment paper and packed into the boxes. Ripe cheeses are about 5 inches in diameter, 1 inch thick and weigh a little over 5 ounces.

The outline of the Raffiné process follows:

Coagulation by rennet	30 minutes
Cutting and draining curd	2 hours
Draining in hoops	10 hours
Stand on mats	15 days
Ripening in boxes	21 days
Total period	36 days

The treatment described closely resembles the handling of Livarot cheese in the department of Calvados, France.

157. Liederkranz cheese. — Among the specialties in the bacterial group is Liederkranz, made from curd with the soft friable texture of a Camembert, molded in rectangular blocks of about 4 ounces in weight and ripened very completely. Although this name is the private brand of a single factory, it has become widely known with the effect of creating a type name in the American market. Analysis of this brand of cheese gives about 55 per cent water, 25 per cent fat, 17 per cent protein, which indicates a whole milk cheese.

158. Limburger cheese[59] derives its name from the town of Limburg in Belgium. The manufacture of this cheese is now widely practiced in Europe and in certain parts of the United States, especially in New York and Wisconsin. Practically no cheese of this name is at present imported, and the practices described are limited to those in American factories.

159. The milk.—Limburger cheese is probably best known on account of its pronounced odor. Because of this characteristic pungent smell, it is often thought that the cheese is made in dirty or unsanitary places. On the contrary, Limburger cheese is usually made in small factories which are clean and sanitary. Because of the constant attention required, a cheese-maker can handle only about 2000-2500 pounds of milk a day, and then some help is necessary to care for the cheeses in the curing room.[60] The discussion of the milk given in Chapter II applies to that to be made into Limburger cheese; however, Limburger requires sweeter milk than do some of the other types. To be sure of obtaining very sweet milk, it is the usual practice for the milk to be delivered without cooling morning and evening at the cheese factory. The cheese is made twice a day. Because the milk must be delivered twice daily, it is obtained from only a few producers near the factory. A factory usually does not have more than eight to twelve patrons. Because of the small number of patrons, it is comparatively easy to obtain a supply of fresh clean milk.

Fig. 23.—A common type of Limburger cheese factory.

The factories are variously built. A common type takes advantage of sloping ground so that the floor at one end may be on the ground level and run backward into a hillside until the other end is a cellar with small windows at the ceiling opening at the ground level (Fig. 23). The family of the cheese-maker often lives in the same building above the factory.

160. Making the cheese.—Limburger cheese is made from the whole milk.

[59] The authors acknowledge the assistance of Mr. Louis Getman in preparing this description.

[60] Zumkehr, P., Limburger cheesemaking, Wis. Cheese-makers Association, 15th Annual Meeting, 1907, page 62.

When the milk is received at the factory, it is placed in the cheese vat. As the milk is delivered both morning and evening without cooling, it reaches the factory at a temperature of 90 to 96° F. In some cases the night's and morning's milk is mixed and then warmed to about 94° F. This practice is not recommended but is frequently adopted, when the supply of milk becomes too small to work in two lots. As soon as all of the milk has been delivered, the cheese-making process begins. No starter is used. The milk is not ripened because no acid development during the making process is desired. The milk is set or curdled at the temperature at which it is received at the factory, usually from 90 to 96° F. Sufficient rennet extract is used to give a firm coagulation in twenty to thirty minutes. This usually requires 2½ to 3 ounces of rennet extract for each 1000 pounds of milk: This is diluted in about forty times its own volume of cold water and added to the milk. (For method of adding rennet extract to milk, see Chapter V.) When the coagulum has become firm so that it will split clean over the finger, the curd is ready to cut. Coarse Cheddar cheese knives are used. Sometimes only the perpendicular knife is employed, and the curd is broken up while being stirred with the hands and rake. This usually causes a large fat loss. After cutting, the curd is stirred first by hand and later with an ordinary wooden hay rake. Usually the curd is not "cooked" or heated after setting, though occasionally it is brought up as high as 96° F. to 98° F. If the curd does not firm up, the temperature may be raised to 98° to 100° F. to aid in expelling the moisture.

When ready to dip, the curd should still be in large soft shiny pieces. It requires from one hour to an hour and thirty minutes from the time the rennet extract is added until the curd is ready to dip. When, in the judgment of the cheese-maker, the curd has become sufficiently firmed in the whey, the whey is drawn down to the surface of the curd. The curd is then dipped into the Limburger molds. These molds are 5 inches square by 8 inches deep without top or bottom. Usually there are five or six of these molds built together into a section. These molds are placed on a draining table beside the vat and the curd is ladled into them with a large tin ladle. The draining table has strips on both sides and one end and slants toward the other end so that the whey will drain from the curd and yet not go on the floor except at the one end. This makes it easy to save and catch the whey for stock feed.

161. Draining and salting Limburger.—In some factories, a clean piece of burlap is put on the draining table and the molds and curd placed on the burlap. This aids in the rapid draining of the whey from the curd and prevents the loss of curd particles. The curd should be turned frequently in the mold to obtain uniform draining. The molds are transferred to the salting room as soon as well drained, usually in about twelve hours, but sometimes they are left until the following morning. Here they are placed on another draining table, which has strips about 5 inches high on the sides and one end. The cheeses are placed along this board, each cheese being separated by a piece of board 4 inches high and 5 inches wide. When the row is filled, a long strip the length of the table is placed against the row. Another row is laid down against this strip in the same manner as the first, and so on until several rows are on the table. The last long strip is held firmly in place by sticks wedged between it and the opposite side of the table. These strips and pieces form a mold for each cheese while draining. Usually the cheeses are turned several times in this period to obtain a uniform expulsion of whey. In about twenty-four hours the cheeses are ready to be salted. This is done by applying the salt to the outside of the cheese. The edges are rolled in a box of salt and the salt then rubbed on the two broad surfaces. Any excess salt is brushed from the cheese with the hand. The cheeses are then laid on a draining table in single layers. The second day, they are salted again in the same way and piled two deep; they are salted again the third day and piled three or four layers deep. The salting room or cellar should have a temperature of 60° F. and be fairly damp. The amount of salt used is very important. The tendency is to use too much salt. This retards the ripening process and in extreme cases gives the cheese a salty taste. If not enough salt is used, the cheese will deteriorate very rapidly on account of the development of undesirable types of fermentation. The cheeses when salted are then placed in the curing room, which is a cellar, usually beyond the salting room. This cellar should have a temperature of 58° to 64° F. and a relative humidity of 95 per cent of saturation. In winter it is necessary to have a fire to keep the rooms warm, otherwise the cheese would cure very slowly or not at all. In some factories the curing and salting cellars are a single room.

162. Ripening Limburger. — When first placed in the curing cellar, the cheeses are put on edge close together, and as they cure are gradually separated. While in the curing cellar, the cheese must be rubbed frequently by hand and washed, usually with salt water. The object of the rubbing is to keep the surface of the cheese moist and prevent the growth of molds. The drier the cheese and the more mold, the oftener the cheeses must be rubbed. The drying or the evaporation from the cheese can be retarded by sprinkling the floor of the cellar with water. When first placed in the curing cellar, they are usually rubbed daily; after a few days they are rubbed every other day and finally as often as the cheese-maker can find time to work at them. The more the cheeses are rubbed, the better the rind.

In the curing of Limburger cheese, protein compounds are attacked by the micro-organisms. Certain highly-flavored fatty acids are commonly produced.[61] This change works most rapidly near the outside and more slowly toward the center of the cheese. The stage of ripening can be determined by examining the cheese. When first made, a cheese is harsh and hard and the outside is more or less white: as the curing changes take place, the cheese becomes soft and pasty or buttery. The outside color changes from a whitish to a yellowish and finally even a reddish brown. It requires considerable time for the ripening agents to work from the outside to the center of the cheese. As ripening progresses, Limburger cheeses tend to become soft enough to break in handling. If such cheeses are wrapped in manila paper after three to four weeks of ripening and packed in boxes, losses from handling are eliminated. One loose board is left on each box and the boxes remain in the ripening cellar until the cheese-maker decides by removal and examination of cheeses from time to time that they are ready for shipment. When fully ripe, the cheese spoils very quickly. Unless handled very carefully, the outer part

---

[61] Currie, J. N., Flavor of Roquefort cheese, Jour. Agr. Research 2 (1914), no. 1, pages 1-14.

may actually rot before the interior is fully ripe. The cheeses are shipped from the factory when they are eight to ten weeks old. They are then placed in cold storage, which checks the action of the ripening agents and so lengthens the commercial life of the cheese.

163. Marketing and qualities of Limburger.—As shipped from the factory, each cheese is wrapped in heavy manila paper and frequently also in tin-foil. The cheeses are packed in boxes which hold forty-eight. Each cheese weighs about two pounds.

Limburger cheese should be regular in shape. The rind should not be cracked or broken nor the sides bulged, nor should it be lopsided. It should have the pronounced characteristic flavor, without other objectionable flavors due to undesirable fermentations. The body should be uniform throughout. It is common to find cheeses that have not a uniform body, due to lack of curing; a small part of the interior at the center will be hard and not cured, while the remainder of the cheese will be soft and buttery. The color should be uniform. When not entirely cured, the uncured part at the center is usually of a lighter color.

The cheese should contain the proper amount of salt. The most common defect is in the flavor. If the milk is not free from bad odors and flavors, these are apt to be more pronounced in the cheese than in the milk. (For care of milk see Chapter II.) Gas-forming fermentations are very bad in this variety of cheese as they cannot be controlled and give the cheese a bad flavor and a "gassy body." When a cheese is gassy, the sides are most liable to be bulged and the body is full of gas holes or pockets. Another defect is a sour cheese. This is caused by the development of too much acid in the milk or during the manufacturing process. A sour cheese usually cures slowly and has a pronounced sour taste. The body is hard and bitter.

If the cheese contains too much moisture, it will cure rapidly and the body will be very soft and pasty. In extreme cases it will be so soft that it will run when the rind is broken. On the other hand if the cheese does not contain sufficient moisture, it will cure very slowly and the body will be hard and dry and sometimes crumbly. There is no standard score-card for judging Limburger cheese. The Wisconsin Cheese-makers Association[62] uses the following score-card for Limburger:

Flavor	40
Texture	40
Color	10
Salt	5
Style	5
	— —
Total	100

164. Yield and composition of Limburger.—The yield of cheese depends on: (1) the amount of fat and other solids in the milk from which it is made; (2) the amount of moisture incorporated into cheese; (3) the loss of solids during the man-

---

[62] Wis. Cheese-makers Assoc., 12th Annual Meeting and Report, 1906, page xxviii.

ufacturing process.

The yield varies from 12 to 14 pounds of cheese from 100 pounds of milk. The more fat and other solids in the milk, the more cheese can be made from 100 pounds of the milk. The more moisture incorporated into the cheese, the larger the yield. The quality of the cheese and the amount of solids determine the amount of moisture that can be incorporated into the cheese. The greater the losses during the manufacturing process, the less is the yield. The composition of Limburger cheese is affected by the same factors as the yield. The average cheese probably carries from 40 to 42 per cent of moisture. Limburger cheeses will vary in composition from this analysis about as follows: water 38 to 44 percent, protein 21 to 25 percent, fat 25 to 30 percent. The differences in practice in factory groups are considerable. Certain markets call for more solid brands, others for the very soft forms.

165. Münster cheese originated in Germany near the city whose name it bears. There is a limited demand for this variety in America; therefore it is not extensively made. It is usually manufactured from whole milk in a Limburger or Brick cheese factory. The process of manufacture is between that of these two varieties in temperatures used, firmness of curd and amount of moisture in the curd and cheese. The process is probably more like that of Limburger. The curd is firmed more in the whey than for Limburger, and more acid is developed. The cheeses are pressed or drained in round forms 7 inches in diameter and 6 inches high. The hoops are lined with cloth to prevent the loss of curd particles while draining. When the cheeses are sufficiently drained, until they are firm enough to hold their shape, the cloths are removed. The cheese is salted by rubbing dry salt on the surface or soaking the cheese in brine. The product is handled in the curing room very much the same as Limburger or Brick cheese. When sufficiently ripe, each cheese is wrapped in parchment paper and placed in a separate wooden box. This cheese, when cured, has a characteristic flavor which is between that of Limburger and Brick. The body is more or less open. The essential factor in the manufacture of Münster cheese is clean milk. Bad fermentations, such as produce gas and bad flavors, seriously interfere with the manufacture and sale of the product. The cheese is usually made in the late fall and winter, when it is difficult to manufacture Limburger.

CHAPTER X

SEMI-HARD CHEESES

The green mold group; Roquefort cheese; Cow's milk or Façons
Roquefort; Outline of making Roquefort; Ripening of Roquefort;
Gorgonzola; Stilton cheese; Gex; Bacterially-ripened series; Brick
cheese; Making of brick cheese; Ripening brick cheese; Qualities
of brick cheese; Composition and yield; Port du Salut cheese.

Between the quickly perishable soft cheeses and the typical hard group, are
two series of varieties, one ripened by green mold and best known by Roquefort,
the other ripened by bacteria and typified by Brick cheese. These cheeses are fairly
firm, hold their shape well, ripen over a period varying from a few weeks to several months and their marketable period is comparatively long. In texture they are
intermediate between the conditions known as "soft" and "hard." In water-content, they range at their best from 37 to 45 percent. Outside these limits, the cheeses
are often marketable but they lose in quality[63] and trueness to type.

166. The green mold group.—There are three well-known semi-hard cheeses
ripened by green or blue-green mold.[64] The mold is an incidental factor in certain
other forms but none of these forms has won larger than local or purely national recognition. French Roquefort, on the contrary, is probably the most widely
known of all cheeses. Stilton, to a small degree at least, has followed the English
to the many lands they inhabit. Gorgonzola, although made in Italy alone, has
a large market in other parts of Europe and in America. In the manipulations of
manufacture, these forms are not closely related but they resemble each other in
that each becomes streaked or marbled by the growth of green mold (*Penicillium
Roqueforti*) through open spaces within the cheese. The "blue-veined" or marbled
cheeses have a characteristic taste which is developed in its most typical form in
Roquefort.

167.—This is a rennet cheese made from sheep's milk (with occasional and minor admixture of goat's and cow's milk) in the section of southern France center-
ing about Roquefort in Aveyron. The practices are standardized and controlled by
a few companies, thus reaching exceptional uniformity. Roquefort is uncolored,

---

[63] Currie, J. N., The relation of composition to quality in cheese, American Food Jour.
11 (1916), no. 9, page 458. See also Dox on the True Composition of Roquefort Cheese, Ztsch.
Untersuch. Nahr. u. Genussmtl. 22 (1911), pages 239-242.

[64] Thom, C., and Matheson, K. J., Biology of Roquefort cheese, Storrs Exp. Sta. Bul.
79, pages 335-347, 1914.

open, made from firm but brittle or crumbly, not tough or waxy curd. Each cheese is about 7¼ inches (20 cm.) in diameter and 3¼ inches (9 cm.) in thickness without a definite rind, and when ripe enough for market is scraped carefully, closely covered with tin-foil and kept in refrigerators. The cut cheese shows extensive open spaces which are lined with green mold. This cheese, in addition to a strong cheesy odor and taste, has a peppery or burning quality which according to Currie[65] is due to the formation of volatile fatty acids such as caproic, caprylic and capric from the butter-fat of the sheep's milk used. A series for Roquefort cheeses selected for excellent quality was found by Dox[66] to show the following composition:

TABLE IV

COMPOSITION OF ROQUEFORT CHEESE

	WATER PER CENT	FAT PER CENT	PROTEIN PER CENT	ASH PER CENT	SALT PER CENT
Fat	38.69	32.31	21.39	6.14	4.14
Minimum	37.49	31.50	19.14	5.18	3.64
Maximum	40.10	33.53	23.06	6.81	4.88

The composition of the sheep's milk of the Roquefort producing region is reported by Marre:[67]

TABLE V

COMPOSITION OF SHEEP'S MILK

	WATER PER CENT	CASEIN PER CENT	FAT PER CENT	LACTOSE PER CENT	ASH PER CENT
Range	76-83	5-8	5.5-10.5	4 to 5	.8-1.2
Average	79.5	6.5	8.0	4.5	1.0

The cheeses when properly made in the local factories are transported to Roquefort for ripening in the famous caves which have made possible the development of a great industry.

The Roquefort caves were originally natural openings leading back into the face of a cliff until they reached a deep, narrow fault or crack in the rock leading to the plains above. The cooler air from the plains came down this crack over moist and dripping rocks and issued through these clefts in a cold moisture-laden current which kept the caves about 50 to 55° F. and moist enough to ripen the cheeses without shrinkage. As the business outgrew the natural caves, great cellars, some of them five or six floors deep, were excavated and tunnels were dug back to the crack so that the strong ventilating current reaches every part of the cellars and

[65] Currie, J. N., Flavor of Roquefort cheese, Jour. Agr. Research, 2 (1914), 1, pages 1-14, Washington.

[66] Dox, A. W., Die Zusammensetzung des echten Roquefort-Käses, in Ztschr. Untersuch. Nahr. u. Genussmtl. Bd. 22, Heft. 4, pages 239-242, 1911.

[67] Marre, E., Le Roquefort, Rodez, 1906. This is the authoritative monograph on Roquefort cheese problems.

keeps both temperature and relative humidity favorable to the ripening of the cheeses.

168. Cow's milk or Façons Roquefort.—The supply of Roquefort is automatically limited by the supply of sheep's milk. The sheep gives milk only about five months in the year and at best a scant average of about a pint a day to a sheep. Sheep's milk for cheese-making is not produced, therefore, outside of very limited regions. Some cow's and goat's milk unavoidably finds its way regularly into the industry itself. Attempts were naturally made to substitute cow's milk. Outside the controlled area, factories were established for this purpose. The quality of the product did not equal that of the Roquefort factories, and French courts decreed that the name Roquefort should not be used for such products. Although some local success was obtained, not much progress was made against the intrenched Roquefort industry. Similar attempts to make such a product in Germany[68] were tried on an extensive scale but failed. More recently, under the inspiration of Conn, the United States Department of Agriculture and the Storrs Experiment Station have studied the possibilities of such an industry. Although the work is not completed, the preliminary reports[69] have indicated the fundamental principles which must underlie such development.

169. Outline of making Roquefort.—Some of the results of these experiments are summarized in the following paragraphs:

Milk.—Clean-flavored fresh milk testing 4-4.2 per cent fat and up to 2.8 per cent casein gives the best results. The milk with a high percentage of cheese-making solids forms a firmer curd, hence works up better in the process than milk of lower quality.

Acidity.—The milk is ripened by lactic starter up to an acidity of 0.23 per cent titrated as lactic acid at the time rennet is added. This gives a firm curd, which drains to the desired water-content but is low enough to prevent the toughening effect of too high acid. A very slight increase in initial acid—1 to 2 hundredths per cent—combined with the rate at which acidity is developing introduces such physical changes in texture as to make the final texture of Roquefort impossible.

Temperature.—Rennet is added at or below 84° F. Every degree of heat adds definitely to the efficiency of rennet. Below 82° F., curdling becomes slower and the coagulum softer and more difficult to drain. The sheep's milk curd is made from 76° to 84° F. but sheep's milk has about twice the cheese solids found in cow's milk. It was found necessary to raise the temperature as high as texture would permit. However, at 86° F. the physical character of the curd tends to become tough or waxy in handling. At 84° F. the curd remains brittle and crumbly. It was, therefore, necessary to keep the curdling temperature down to 84° F.

Renneting or setting.—Rennet at a rate of 3 to 4 ounces of standard liquid rennet to 1000 pounds (10 to 12 c.c. to 100 pounds) was found to give the best curd under experimental conditions.

---

[68] Reported on the word of Prof. Fleischmann.

[69] Thom, C., J. N. Currie and K. J. Matheson, Studies relating to the Roquefort and Camembert types of cheese, Storrs Exp. Sta. Bul. 79, pages 335-394, 1914.

Curdling time.—One and one-half to two hours gave most satisfactory results in forming curd. This should be very firm and stand until it begins to "sweat," until beads of whey have begun to collect upon its surface.

Cutting.—The cow's milk curd gave best results when cut in two directions with the half-inch curd knife. The resulting columns, a half inch square in cross-section, may be handled without excessive losses.

Draining.—The cut curd is dipped to a draining rack covered with cloth with as little breaking as possible. During the draining process, a certain amount of turning is necessary to facilitate the separation and escape of the whey. If handled too much, losses of fat are increased and the curd becomes tough or waxy instead of remaining brittle or crumbly. When properly handled, not over 0.35 per cent of fat is lost. Under favorable conditions, four-ninths to two-thirds of the original weight of curd will separate and run off as whey in twenty to thirty minutes. The curd meanwhile is exposed to the air of the room and cools toward room temperature. If cooling goes too far, further drainage is interfered with. Hence the curd is put into the hoop and the drainage completed while the cheese is reaching its final form.

Hoop.—Hoops for cow's milk Roquefort must be 7½ inches in diameter and about 5¾ inches high to hold curd enough to produce a cheese the size of the standard Roquefort when completely drained. Sheep's milk with its higher percentage of solids does not require such high hoops. The curd as it goes into the hoop should be a soft, pulpy mass with no suggestion of toughness.

Inoculation with mold.—The mold for Roquefort cheese (*Penicillium Roqueforti*[70]) is readily grown in pure culture in ordinary loaves of bread. For this purpose loaves hot from the oven are quickly drenched with or immersed in hot paraffine to form an impervious crust to retain moisture as well as to keep out contaminations. It is then allowed to cool. The interior of each loaf is inoculated by drawing a suspension of *P. Roqueforti* spores in water into a sterile pipette (10 c.c.) which is then thrust through the paraffined crust to the center of the loaf of bread and allowed to empty there. The hole is sealed up with paraffine. These loaves are incubated for about a month at room temperature. When cut, every open space should be found lined with the green spores of the mold. When dry enough, the mass may be powdered, and put into an ordinary pepper box. When the curd is ready to go into the hoop, this mold powder is sprinkled upon it from the pepper box.

Handling.—Freshly made cheeses are turned within the first hour to insure the proper smoothness of both sides. Further draining is best accomplished in a room at about 64° F. with a relative humidity of 85 to 90 per cent. If the surface of the cheese becomes too dry, a rind is formed. No real rind is permitted on Roquefort. If the temperature is too high, slime forms quickly and unfavorable fermentation may occur. Slime (bacteria and *Oidium lactis* usually) must be scraped when it becomes too heavy.

Salting.[71]—Experimental cheeses were found to give the best results when

[70] Thom, C., U. S. Dept. Agr. Bur. An. Ind. Bul. 82, 1905.
[71] Thom, C., The salt factor in the mold ripened cheeses, Storrs Exp. Sta. Bul. 79,

at the end of about three days' drainage they contained about 50 per cent water. Such cheeses were salted by sprinkling the entire surface lightly, replaced upon the drain boards for one day, salted again and piled in two's. After another day they received the third salting and were piled in three's for two days longer. A total of about 10 per cent by weight of salt was used to secure an absorption of 4 per cent. At the same time the water-content dropped to 40 to 43 per cent. After salting is completed, the cheeses are brushed and punched with holes to permit oxygen to enter.[72] They are then ready for ripening.

170. Ripening of Roquefort. — The ripening of experimental Roquefort has required four to six months at a relative humidity of 85 to 90 per cent. This relative humidity is just below the equilibrium relative humidity of the cheese, hence permits a shrinkage of 2 to 4 per cent in the water-content of the cheese. This makes it possible to control the amount of surface slime developed.

If the relative humidity goes too high, the surface slime of bacteria and yeasts becomes very heavy, soft and almost liquid, and follows the openings into the cheese with resultant damage to appearance and flavor. Even under the conditions at Roquefort, this slime must be removed by rubbing or scraping several times to avoid injury to the cheeses, together with the production of bad odor and taste. If the humidity becomes too low, the surface becomes dry, hard and cracks open, the friable crumbly texture is injured, and there is considerable loss in weight. Salt forms about 4 per cent of the cheese. This is in solution in the water present, which is about 40 per cent, and makes a brine of about 10 per cent strength. This strength of brine does not prevent the growth of the Roquefort mold (*Penicillium Roqueforti*) but does hinder the development of *Oidium lactis* in the open spaces within the cheese. Accurate adjustment of temperature and relative humidity in the ripening rooms to salt and water-content in the cheese is essential to proper ripening. These conditions are furnished by the unique natural conditions of the caves of Roquefort. The production of such cheeses elsewhere depends either on the discovery of another locality with closely similar conditions or on the artificial production and control of the necessary temperature and relative humidity. This has been done on an experimental basis by the use of cold storage apparatus combined with proper humidifiers.

The differences between working with sheep's and with cow's milk lie in the making process rather than in the ripening. Sheep's milk freshly drawn shows a higher acidity than cow's milk, probably on account of the acid reaction of its greater casein content. With nearly double the total solids of cow's milk, the yield to one hundred pounds is much greater, consequently the drainage of the curd is much more easily handled.

Once made and salted, the cheeses require very nearly the same conditions of ripening. The resultant products are alike in appearance and texture. In flavor, cow's milk Roquefort differs in character from sheep's milk cheese to such a de-

pages 387-394, 1914.

[72] Thom, C., and Currie, J. N., The dominance of Roquefort mold in cheese, Jour. Biol. Chem. 15 (1913), no. 2, pages 247-258.

gree as to be recognized by taste. The difference was found by Currie[73] to be due to an actual difference in the combination of fatty acids present.

Although these differences in character are recognizable by the expert in testing the cheese, as well as by chemical analysis, cow's milk Roquefort would satisfy that large proportion of consumers who use such cheese only in connection with other fairly high flavored foods. The demands for technical skill and factory equipment are not naturally greater than for many other lines of cheese-making. The gradual development of a cow's milk Roquefort may be anticipated.

Fig. 24.—Gorgonzola ripening establishment in valley near Lecco.

171. Gorgonzola[74] is a rennet cheese made from fresh whole cow's milk, in northern Italy. It takes its name from the village of Gorgonzola, a few miles from Milan, but the manufacture of the cheese has spread over a wide area. The cheeses are made on farms and in factories from which they are transported for ripening to cool valleys of the Alps, principally near Lecco (Fig. 24). Boeggild introduced the making of a cheese after the Gorgonzola process into Denmark about 1885. This industry has been successful on a small scale since that time. Gorgonzola cheeses are about 30 cm. (12 inches) in diameter and 18 cm. (7 inches) thick and weigh 15 to 20 pounds. As exported they are usually heavily coated[75] with a mixture usually barite, tallow and lard colored with annatto or other cheese color. This coating prevents shrinkage or mold on the surface of the cheese in transit. When cut these cheeses vary greatly. All show marbling with mold (Roquefort mold). During their ripening they become very slimy at the surface. To open up air spaces

[73] Currie, J. N., The composition of Roquefort cheese fat, Jour. Agr. Research, 2 (1914), 6, pages 429-434.

[74] Thom, C., Soft cheese studies in Europe, U. S. Dept. Agr. Bur. An. Ind. Rept. 22, pages 79-109, 1905.

[75] Frestadius, A., Nord. Mejeri Tid. 17 (1912), 14, page 159, Abs. N. Y. Produce Rev. 34 (1912), 2, page 54, and Cutting, W. B., The use of baritine in cheese rinds, Mo. Commerce and Trade Repts. 1908, 337, page 144, also in Practical Dairyman, 2 (1908), 7, page 76.

for mold growth, this slime is scraped off and holes are punched into the cheeses. These holes are readily seen in the final product. Some show crumbly texture, well distributed mold, as in Roquefort, with flavor approaching that cheese; in others the texture is waxy rather than crumbly, a condition correlated regularly with different character in the flavor. Frequently in whole areas or in small pockets, slime consisting of bacteria and Oidium has followed the openings into the cheese and affects its odor and taste.

Experimental Gorgonzola cheeses comparable with the Italian product were made with cow's milk ripened as for Roquefort or higher, to 0.25-0.30 per cent (titrated as lactic acid), curdled at 86° F. (30° C.), cut into cubes and slightly stirred, then dipped to a draining board for about one-half hour, and put into the hoop. The cheeses drained quickly to about 50 percent water and developed a surface rind as in the harder cheeses. Cut surfaces showed a fairly open cheese in which mold grew readily. These cheeses were salted to taste, not to a specified percentage. They ripened with the same irregular results and the characteristic range of flavors found in Gorgonzola. To avoid the rotting of the cheese by surface growths, they were exposed to low humidities for a time and cracks opened at the surfaces, as seen in the ripening rooms at Lecco (Fig. 24). The texture was more or less waxy or tough, which was correlated with the slightly higher heat at renneting together with the stirring or "working" of the curd. Comparative analyses of a series of imported cheeses confirm the interpretation that the salt-content of Roquefort, 4 per cent approximately, prevents the invasion of the interior of the cheese by Oidium. No complete study of the ripening of Gorgonzola has been made. As far as followed, it consists in an initial souring process followed by ripening by molds and slime organisms. At its best, Gorgonzola is nearly equal to Roquefort but the percentage of such quality is low. In spite of its irregular quality, England has used larger amounts of Gorgonzola than of Roquefort. Considerable quantities have been imported for the Italian trade in the United States.

Fig. 25.—Gorgonzola cheese curing-room.

172. Stilton cheese bears the name of an English village[76] in which it was first sold. It is made from cow's milk and is typically a whole milk cheese, although part skim cheeses are regularly made and sold as lower grades. In the Stilton-making counties, the milk from Shorthorn cattle testing about 3.5 to 4.0 per cent fat is preferred to richer or poorer grades. Such milk is curdled with rennet at about 86° F. in about one hour; the curd is cut, dipped to a draining table covered with cloth and drained slowly over a period of several hours, commonly overnight. During this period considerable acidity is developed. The curd is then milled or broken by hand, salted, packed into hoops 15 to 16 inches high and 7 inches in diameter. These hoops are made from heavy tin (Fig. 26) with four rows of holes about 3/10 inch in diameter. The freshly filled hoops are allowed to stand and drain without pressure in a room at about 70° F. (Fig. 26). Such cheeses are turned every day for several days. When solid enough to stand the hoops are removed, the cheeses are scraped or rubbed with a knife until the surface is smooth, and commonly wrapped with a cloth bandage to maintain the shape, if the cheese is still too soft to stand firmly. In the factories, several rooms are used with varying temperature and relative humidities, which makes it possible to place each cheese under the condition best suited to its texture and condition of ripeness. In general, the dairy

[76] Stilton Cheese—J. P. Sheldon—from abs. by New York Produce Rev. 28 (June 16, 1909), no. 8, pages 362-363. Stilton is said to have originated with Mrs. Paulet, Wymondham, Co. of Leicester, and to have been sold by her brother—Host of the "Bill" at Stilton from which village it derived its name.

sections of England are much more humid than those of America and there are less violent changes in temperature. Stilton cheese-making has grown up to take advantage of this climatic factor in handling the product. Transplantation of such an industry necessitates a mastery not only of the manipulations but a grasp of the fundamental principles underlying the process and a readjustment of practices to preserve those principles.

Fig. 26.—Stilton cheeses in hoops, draining.

Stilton is, then, a soured curd cheese in whose ripening a very prominent part is played by the green mold (usually some strain of *P. Roqueforti*) which grows throughout the cavities of its mass[77]. At its best, it has attractive texture and flavor. Much of it fails to reach high quality on account of the invasion of bacteria, *Oidium lactis*, and very frequently myriads of cheese mites. The following analysis

[77] Percival, J., and G. Heather Mason, The microflora of Stilton cheese, Jour. Agr. Sci. 5 (1913), part 2, pages 222-229. See also Thom, C., Soft cheese studies in Europe, U. S. Dept. Agr. Bur. An. Ind. Rept. 22 (1905), pages 79-109.

was furnished as typical for ripe cheese by Miles Benson,[78] late professor of dairying at Reading, England: Water 31 per cent, fat 36 per cent, casein 29 per cent, mineral constituents including salt about 4 per cent. Approximately the same figures are given by Primrose McConnell (Agricultural Note Book). The low percentage of salt is another factor of uncertainty in the control of this Stilton product, as in Gorgonzola, since these cheeses are commonly high in water-content at first and are thus subject to invasion by Oidium.

Stilton has been made on a small scale in Canada[79] and occasionally attempted in the United States. No serious effort to develop an industry of commercial importance has been made in America. Comparative study of the cheeses ripened by green mold tends to the conviction that the adaptation of the Roquefort practice to the use of cow's milk offers a more satisfactory basis for experiment than efforts to establish a Stilton or a Gorgonzola industry.

173. Gex.—A cheese under this name made in southern France resembles, in its general character as a ripened cheese, the English Stilton and Italian Gorgonzola. Although it has no commercial importance, reference is made to this cheese to show that mold-ripened cheeses have been developed entirely independently in different countries to bring about the same general character of product.

174. Bacterially ripened series.—The semi-hard cheeses ripened by bacteria stand half-way between true Limburger and the hard forms. In fact, brands of Limburger are readily found which approach the texture and ripening of Brick cheese. In the same way, Brick cheeses are often found which have the appearance, texture and much of the flavor of the Cheddars with only a trace of the taste of Limburger. Port du Salut, Oka, Münster, in France Livarot, in the Balkan regions Kascoval, belong in this series.

175. Brick cheese.—The name of this cheese is probably due to the finished product being about the size and shape of a brick. It is similar to the German cheese Bäckstein and may have been developed from it. It is typically a sweet-curd cheese, made from milk freshly drawn, without permitting the development of appreciable quantities of acidity until after the curd has been put into the hoop. In the making process, it is intermediate between Limburger and the cheeses of the Cheddar group. Some cheese-makers use an ordinary cheese vat, others a copper kettle in manufacturing.

It is the usual practice to deliver the milk to the cheese factory both morning and evening, without cooling. Cheese is made twice a day. In some cases the milk is delivered only once a day, and extra precautions must then be taken to care for the milk properly.

The discussion of the care of milk in Chapter II applies to that for Brick cheese. For the best quality of cheese, the milk in the vat should show about 0.15 of 1 per cent acidity and never above 0.18 of 1 per cent.[80]

---

[78] Benson, Miles, in personal letter from analyses of cheeses selected for the purpose.
[79] Dean, H. H., The Creamery Journal, Nov. 1904.
[80] N. Y. Produce Rev. etc., Vol. 32, no. 14, page 536.

176. Making of Brick cheese.[81]—The milk is received at the cheese factory at a temperature of about 92° to 96° F. For the best results, the acidity should be determined (by the acid test) to decide on the amount of starter to use. Few Brick cheese-makers use an acid test or a starter but these precautions would improve the product of many factories. For method of using the acid test, see Chapter V. Chapter IV discusses the preparation and use of starter. Usually 0.25 to 0.50 of 1 per cent of starter is the amount required. A small amount of starter is used to aid the development of lactic acid and for the beneficial effect it has on the flavor. A very small development of acid is desired after adding the starter; therefore the change in acidity should be very carefully watched with the acid test. The vat is usually set when the acid test shows 0.16 of 1 per cent acidity. The more acid in the milk, the less starter should be employed. Sufficient rennet extract should be used to give a coagulation suitable for cutting in thirty to thirty-five minutes. For method of adding the rennet extract, see Chapter V. When the coagulum is firm enough for the curd to break clean over the finger, it is ready to cut. The curd is cut with coarse knives into ⅜- or ½-inch cubes. After cutting, the curd is let stand three to five minutes, then stirred with the hands for a few minutes until the whey begins to separate and then stirred with the rake. Some makers do not stir by hand but use the rake directly after cutting. When this is done, great care must be exercised to stir the curd without breaking up the pieces, because this causes a loss of fat. After cutting the curd is stirred for twenty to thirty minutes before the steam is turned on. The curd is heated very slowly at first and more rapidly during the last stages of cooking. The curd is cooked to a temperature of 110° to 115° F. The lower the temperature that can be used to produce firm curd, the better the texture of the cheese. After cutting and during the cooking, the curd must be constantly stirred so that lumps will not form. When the curd forms lumps, the moisture is not evenly expelled. This results in uneven texture and curing. Sometimes some salt is added to the curd in the vat to restrain souring. The curd is stirred after cooking until it is sufficiently firm. It remains usually in the whey for a total period of one and one-fourth to one and one-half hours from the time of cutting. It is then dipped into forms 10 inches long by 5 inches wide by 8 inches deep. The forms are without top or bottom and are placed on a draining table. This table is so constructed that the whey can be saved for stock feed. When ready to "dip," the whey is drawn down to the surface of the curd in the vat, then the curd is dipped into the forms or hoops. Care must be taken to get the same amount of curd into each form to produce the cheeses of uniform size. Each cheese is turned several times to insure even draining and even reduction of the temperature. While draining, a follower is placed in each hoop and a weight placed on each cheese. Usually a brick is used

[81] N. Y. Produce Rev. etc., Vol. 30, no. 5, page 188; Vol. 30, no. 14, page 534; Vol. 31, no. 5, page 182.

Marty, G., Brick cheesemaking, Wis. Cheese-makers Assoc., 15th Annual Meeting, 1907, page 66.

Wuethrich, F., The manufacture of Brick cheese, Wis. Cheese-makers Assoc., 14th Annual Meeting, 1906, page 50.

Schenk, C., Brick cheesemaking, Wis. Cheese-makers Assoc., 13th Annual Meeting, 1905, page 38.

for this weight. A cheese is allowed to drain or press for ten to fifteen hours. It is then placed on the salting table and rubbed with coarse salt. While on the salting table, a cheese is placed on its broad side. Some cheese-makers prefer to salt their cheeses by soaking them in a salt brine. This brine should be strong enough to float an egg. Salting requires three days. The cheeses are then brushed free from excess salt and taken to the cellar to cure or ripen.

177. Ripening Brick cheese.—For this process, the cellars are kept at about 90 percent relative humidity and a temperature of 60° to 65° F. Some prefer a temperature for curing as high as 68° F. During the curing, the surfaces of the cheese are kept moist and mold growths kept down by rubbing or brushing the cheese with pure water or salt and water. In the curing cellars the cheeses are placed on shelves; at first they are set close together and as they cure, they are separated. During curing, the color changes from a whitish to a reddish brown. The cheese cures from the outside toward the center. When first made, the product is harsh and hard in texture but during the ripening process it becomes mellow and smooth. The cheeses remain on the curing shelves for four to six weeks, after which they are wrapped in heavy waxed paper and boxed. A cheese ready for market usually weighs about five pounds. A Brick cheese box is 5 inches deep by 20 inches wide by 3 feet long, and holds 110 to 115 pounds of cheese.

178. Qualities of Brick cheese.—The cheeses should be neat and attractive and the rind not cracked or broken. The sides should be square and not bulged. The cheese should have a clean, characteristic Brick cheese flavor. The body and texture should be mellow and smooth and when rubbed between the thumb and forefinger, should break down like cold butter. The color should be uniform. The cheese should contain the proper amount of salt and moisture. One of the worst faults with Brick cheese is bad flavor. This is many times due to the cheese-maker not using clean flavored starter. It may also be due to bad flavored milk. A Brick cheese-maker has no means of controlling gassy fermentations. These show themselves in the bad flavor of the cheese and in the porous body. They also cause the cheese to bulge. If detected, gassy milk should be rejected. If too much acid is developed, a sour cheese is the result. This will not cure normally and usually has a sour flavor. The body will be brittle and mealy. If too much salt is used, the cheese may have a salty taste and it will cure very slowly. If not enough salt is used, the cheese may cure too rapidly and undesirable flavors and fermentations develop. The cheese must have the proper moisture-content; if too much moisture is present, the cheese cures too fast and is soft and pasty in body; if not enough moisture, then the reverse is true. Tabulation of cheeses of special quality, as submitted in scoring contests, show an average water-content of 37 to 38 per cent, with occasional cheeses verging toward Limburger in texture and flavor with 40 to 42 per cent water, and others indistinguishable from Cheddar, with water-content as low as 34 per cent.

The Wisconsin Cheese-makers Association uses the following score-card for the judging of Brick cheese on a scale of 100:

Flavor	40
Texture	40
Color	10
Salt	5
Style	5
	— —
Total	100

179. Composition and yield.—The composition of Brick cheese varies within wide limits. The average cheese probably contains from 37 to 39 per cent of water, although many cheeses are above and below this average; Doane and Lawson[82] give the fat as 28.86 per cent, proteins 23.8 per cent and total ash 4.20 per cent.

The composition and yield are both affected by: (1) the moisture-content of the cheese; (2) composition of the milk from which made; and (3) losses during the manufacturing process. The average yield of Brick cheese is 11 to 13 pounds to 100 pounds of milk.

180. Port du Salut cheese.—The Trappist monks originated this type of cheese in their monasteries in France. Under the name of their community Oka, it has been made and sold widely by the Trappist Fathers of Quebec. In recent years, factories independent of the order have made such cheese both in America and in Europe.

The following outline of the making process indicates the close relationship between Port du Salut and Brick cheeses. Whole milk or milk not over one-fifth skimmed is ripened to medium acidity, then heated to 90° to 95° F. according to season and acidity. Rennet enough is added (see Chapter V) to curdle in thirty to forty minutes, although some makers shorten the time to twenty minutes. When formed, the curd is cut into small cubes and excess of whey is dipped away. The constantly stirred mass is then heated or cooked to 100° to 105° F. within a period of ten to twelve minutes or according to some makers twenty to thirty minutes. It is allowed to stand a few minutes to settle. Most of the whey is then drawn and the mass is stirred vigorously to prevent fusion of the curd granules. The curd is ready for the hoop when the particles are about the size of grains of wheat and do not stick together when squeezed with the hand. The individual grains of curd should crumble easily between the fingers. The hot curd is transferred directly to the hoops without cooling. For this purpose, a hoop is set upon the table covered with a cloth and the curd dipped into the cloth. The edges of the cloth are then folded over. In this condition the cheese is transferred to the press where gradually increasing pressure begins with 3 to 4 pounds and reaches about 70 pounds. To insure proper shape, cheeses are turned and put into fresh cloths at the end of the first hour and turned subsequently several times during the pressing period of about twelve hours.[83]

---

[82] Doane, C. F., and H. W. Lawson, Varieties of cheese, descriptions and analysis, U. S. Dept. Agr. Bur. of An. Ind. Bul. 146, 1911.

[83] Ligeon, X., Herstellung des Port Salut Käses, Milchztg. 38 (1909), no. 39, pages

Port du Salut cheeses are salted by rubbing fine salt on the surface by hand at the rate of 1.2 to 2 per cent of the weight of the cheese. After about two days in the salting process, they are put into the ripening cellars. The cellars are wet, since they reach 90 to 95 per cent relative humidity at a temperature of about 55° F. After two days in the cellar, the cheeses are plungedto the shelves where they are rubbed every day into a tank of saturated brine to which a trace of cheese color has been added. As they come out of these tanks, they are yellowish and greasy or slimy. They are returned with a cloth or by hands wet in brine. After about one week they are again plunged in the brine. Treatment with brine tends to insure a firm rind. The cheeses are rubbed more or less regularly with brine through the whole ripening period.

After six weeks, such cheese may be eaten. The cut surface of Port du Salut is creamy in color, may or may not show small holes. In texture it is soft enough to spread readily under pressure without losing its shape in handling. In flavor the cheese is a mild form belonging to the Limburger group.

Port du Salut cheeses as imported from France usually are firm round cakes about 1½ inches thick, weighing about 3 pounds.

CHAPTER XI

THE HARD CHEESES

The Danish group; The Dutch group; Edam cheese; Method of manufacture; Salting and curing Edam; Equipment for making Edam cheese; Qualities and yield of Edam cheese; Gouda cheese; Method of manufacture; Equipment for Gouda cheese; Composition and yield.

The hard cheeses form a great series of groups, whose most prominent physical character is their firm or hard texture. This is correlated with comparatively low water-content, which is usually between 30 and 40 per cent. Although certain varieties occasionally test above 40 per cent water, this deviation is accompanied by quick ripening and rapid spoilage. These varieties of cheese are staple products with long marketable periods; therefore they may be handled in large lots, shipped, carted and stored freely without the losses such treatment would entail in soft cheese. The retailer frequently buys hard cheese by the ton, not by the cheese or by the box.

In making, these varieties are characterized as cooked and pressed cheeses. Although both the heating of a curd and the pressing of a newly made cheese occur among semi-hard forms, these practices appear in their most typical forms in the hard cheeses.

The hard cheeses show two types of texture. A cut cheese may appear smooth, free from holes or with a few angular cracks or seams, or it may show round holes or "eyes." In the smooth textured forms every effort is made to prevent gassy fermentations, usually by controlling the fermentation of the curd in the making process. When "eyes" are present, the end sought has been a development of a particular form of gassy fermentation which gives this appearance and brings about the characteristic ripening texture and flavor.

The hard cheeses have been developed in groups of national varieties. The best known of these groups are those which may be represented by English Cheddar, American Factory Cheddar, Danish, the Edam of Holland, Swiss and Parmesan with many related varieties in Italy and neighboring countries of southern Europe.

181. The Danish group.—The Danish cheeses are related in appearance and flavor to the English group represented by Cheddar. The demand for butter in Europe has been so great that the Danish cheese-makers have developed skim and part skim varieties largely to the exclusion of the whole milk form. Skillful handling of their process has resulted in a product which has had a very large and appreciative market in England and Germany.

182. The Dutch group.—Edam and Gouda are the two forms of cheese made in Holland and most widely known among other peoples. Both reach America in considerable quantities; both are shipped in large amounts to tropical countries. Although attempts have been made to manufacture them in America, no commercial production of these cheeses has been successful. Although whole milk grades of these cheeses are known, they are to a large measure part skim in manufacture. The presence of one or both of these forms in every large market in America makes the general facts of their production of general interest. Parts of a report on experimental work in the making of Edam and Gouda are, therefore, given here.

183. Edam cheese[84] is a sweet-curd type, made from partially skimmed-milk. It comes to the market in the form of round red balls, each weighing from 3½ to 4 pounds when cured. It is largely manufactured in northern Holland and derives its name from a town famous as a market for this kind of cheese.[85] Milk from which one-fourth to one-third of the fat has been removed is used. Too great pains cannot be taken in regard to the condition of the milk. It should be fresh, free from every trace of taint; in brief, it should be in as perfect condition as possible.

184. Method of manufacture.—The following paragraphs give the steps in the manufacture of Edam cheese:

Treatment of milk before adding rennet.—The temperature of the milk should be brought up to a point not below 85° F. nor much above 88° F. When the desired temperature has become constant, the coloring matter should be added. Cheese color is used at the rate of 1½ to 2 ounces for 1000 pounds of milk. The coloring matter should, of course, be added to the milk and thoroughly incorporated by stirring before the rennet is added.

Addition of rennet to milk.—The rennet should not be added until the milk has reached the desired temperature (85° to 88° F.) and this temperature has become constant. When the temperature reaches the desired point and remains there stationary, the rennet extract is added. Rennet extract may be used, 4½ to 5½ ounces being taken for 1000 pounds of milk, or enough to coagulate the milk in the desired time, at the actual temperature used. The milk should be completely coagulated, ready for cutting, in about twelve to eighteen minutes from the time the rennet is added. The same precaution observed in making Cheddar cheese should be followed in making Edam cheese with reference to care in adding the rennet, such as careful, accurate measurement, dilution with pure water before addition to milk.

Cutting the curd for Edam.—When the curd breaks clean across the finger, it

[84] These paragraphs were taken from N. Y. Exp. Sta. Bul. 56, Experiments in the manufacture of cheese; Part I. The manufacture of Edam cheese, 1893. See also, Haecker, T. L., Experiments in the manufacture of cheese, Minn. Exp. Sta. Bul. 35, 1894.

[85] Boekhout, F. W. J., and J. J. O. de Vries, Cracking of Edam, Verslag. Landbouwk. Onderzoek. Rykslandboupoefstat. (Netherlands), 20 (1917), pages 71-78, fig. 1.

Boekhout, F. W. F., and J. J. O. de Vries, Sur le défaut "Knijpers" dans le fromage d'Edam, Rev. Gen. Lait, 9 (1913), no. 18, pages 420-427.

should be cut; it is cut a very little softer than in the Cheddar process as ordinarily practiced. As stated, this stage of hardness in the curd which fits it for cutting should come in twelve to eighteen minutes after the rennet is added. First, a vertical knife is used and the curd is cut lengthwise, after which it is allowed to stand until the slices of curd begin to show the separation of whey. Then the vertical knife is used in cutting crosswise, after which the horizontal knife is at once used. Any curd adhering to the bottom and sides of the vat is carefully removed by the hand, after which the curd-knife is again passed through the mass of curd lengthwise and crosswise, continuing the cutting until the curd has been cut as uniformly as possible into very small pieces.

Treatment of Edam curd after cutting. — When the cutting is completed, one commences at once to heat the curd up to the temperature of 93° to 96° F. The heating is done as quickly as possible. While the heating is in progress, the curd is kept constantly agitated to prevent settling and consequent overheating. As soon as the curd shows signs of hardening, which the experience of the worker will enable him to determine, the whey is drawn off until the upper surface of the curd appears, when one should commence to fill the press molds.

Filling molds, pressing and dressing Edam. — The molds, which are described later in detail, are well soaked in warm water previous to use, in order to prevent too sudden chilling of curd and consequent checking of separation of whey. As soon as whey is drawn off, as indicated above, one begins to fill the pressing molds (Fig. 27). The filling should be done as rapidly as possible to prevent too great cooling of curd. When the curd has been put into the molds, its temperature should not be below 88° F. Unless care is taken to keep the curd covered, the portion that is last put into the molds may become too much cooled. In making Edam cheese on a small scale, it is a good plan to squeeze the moisture out with the hands as much as possible and then break it up again before putting in the molds, when the curd should be pressed into the mold firmly by the hands. The molds should be filled as nearly alike as possible. The cheese should weigh from 5 to 5¼ pounds each when ready for the press. When the filling of molds is completed, they are put under continual pressure of 20 to 25 pounds for about twenty-five or thirty minutes. While the cheese is being pressed, some sweet whey is heated to a temperature of 125° or 130° F., and this whey should not be allowed to go below 120° F. at any time while it is being used. When the cheeses are taken from their molds, each is put into the warm whey for two minutes, then removed and dressed. For dressing Edam cheese, the ordinary cheese bandage cloth is used. This is cut into strips, which should be long enough to reach entirely around the cheese and overlap an inch or so, and which should be wide enough to cover all but a small portion of the ends of the cheese when put in place. Before putting on the bandage, all rough projections should be carefully pared from the cheese. In putting on, the cheese is held in one hand and the bandage is wrapped carefully around the cheese, so that the whole is covered, except a small portion on the upper and lower surface of the cheese. These bare spots are covered by small pieces of bandage cloth of a size sufficient to fill the bare surface. The bandage is kept wet with the warm sweet whey, thus facilitating the process of dressing. After each cheese is dressed, it should be replaced in the dressing mold, care being taken that the bandage remains in place and leaves no portion of the surface of the cheese uncovered and in direct contact with the mold. The cheese is then put under continual pressure of 60 to 120 pounds and kept for six to twelve hours.

Fig. 27.—Edam cheese mold.

185. Salting and curing Edam.—There are two methods which may be employed in salting,—dry and wet. In dry-salting, when the cheese is finally taken from the press, it is removed from the press mold, its bandage is removed completely, and the cheese placed in another mold, quite similar, known as the salting mold. Each cheese is placed in a salting mold with a coating of fine salt completely surrounding it. The cheese is salted in this way once each day for five or six days. Each day the cheese should be turned when it is replaced in the mold, so that it will not be rounded on one end more than the other.

In the method of wet-salting, the cheese is placed in a tank of salt brine, made by dissolving common salt in water in the proportion of about 1 pound of salt to 2½ quarts of water. Each cheese is turned once a day and should be left in the brine seven or eight days. When the cheese is taken from the salting mold or salt bath, it is placed in warm water and given a vigorous, thorough brushing in order to remove all slimy or greasy substances that may have accumulated on the outer surface. When the surface is well cleansed, the cheese is carefully wiped dry with a linen towel and placed upon a shelf in the curing-room. In being put on the shelves, the cheeses should be placed in contact so as to support one another, until they have flattened out at both ends so much that they can stand upright alone. Then they are moved far enough apart to allow a little air space between them. Another method of securing the flattened ends is to support each cheese on opposite sides by wedge-shaped pieces of wood. After being placed on the shelves in the curing-room, they are turned once a day and rubbed with the bare hand during the first month, twice a week during the second month and once a week after that. When any slimy substance appears on the surface of the cheese, it should be washed off at once with warm water or sweet whey. The special conditions of the curing-room will be noticed in detail below. When the cheeses are about two months old, they can be prepared for market in the following manner:

They are first made smooth on the surface by being turned in a lathe or in some other manner, after which the surface is colored. For coloring, some carmine is dissolved in alcohol or ammonia to secure the proper shade, and in this color-bath the cheeses are placed for about one minute, when they are removed and allowed to drain, and as soon as they are dry the outside of each cheese is rubbed with boiled linseed oil, in order to prevent checking. They are then wrapped in tin-foil, which is done very much like the bandaging. Care must be taken to put on the tin-foil so that it presents a smooth, neat appearance. The cheeses are finally packed in boxes, containing twelve cheeses in each box, arranged in two layers of six each with a separate partition for each cheese.

186. Equipment for making Edam cheese.—Careful attention must be given to the moisture and temperature of the curing-room. This room should be well ventilated, quite moist and its temperature kept between 50° and 65° F. These are conditions not easy to secure in any ordinary room. Some form of cellar is best adapted for these conditions. The amount of moisture can be determined by an instrument known as a hygrometer. In a curing-room suited for Edam cheese, the moisture should be between 85 and 95 per cent, or a little short of saturation. When the temperature is between 50° and 65° F., the moisture is between 85 and 95 per cent if the wet-bulb thermometer is from 1 to 2° F. (or ½ to 1° C.) below the dry-bulb thermometer. Cheese will check or crack and be spoiled for market, if the degree of moisture is not kept high enough.

Aside from the molds, press and salting vat, the same apparatus that is used in making Cheddar can be used for Edam cheese. The pressing mold is turned preferably from white wood or, in any case, from wood that will not taint. Each mold consists of two parts; the lower constitutes the main part of the mold, the upper portion is simply a cover. The lower portion or body of the mold has several holes in the bottom, from which the whey flows when the cheese is pressed. Care must be taken to prevent these holes being stopped up by curd. This part of the mold is about six inches deep and six inches in diameter across the top. The salting mold has no cover and the bottom is provided with only one hole for the out-flow of whey; in other respects it is much like the pressing mold.

187. Qualities and yield of Edam cheese.—The flavor of a perfect Edam cheese is difficult to describe. It is mild, clean, and pleasantly saline. In imperfect Edams, the flavor is more or less sour and offensive. In body, a perfect Edam cheese is solid, rather dry and mealy or crumbly. In texture, it should be close and free from pores. In the experiments here reported the amount of fat in 100 pounds of the partially skimmed-milk varied from 2.45 to 3.20 pounds and averaged 2.77 pounds. Of this amount, from 0.30 to 0.51 pound of fat was lost in the whey, with an average of 0.39 pound. The yield of cheese from 100 pounds of milk varied from 9.60 to 11.82 pounds and averaged 10.56 pounds.

188. Gouda cheese.[86]—This Dutch variety is a sweet-curd cheese made from

[86] Paragraphs taken from N. Y. Exp. Sta. Bul. 56, Experiments in the manufacture of cheese; Part II. The manufacture of Gouda cheese, 1893. See also, Hayward, H., Method of making Gouda cheese, Pa. Exp. Sta. Rept. 1890, pages 79-81, and Haecker, T. L., Experiments in the manufacture of cheese, Minn. Exp. Sta. Bul. 35, 1894, and Monrad, J. H., in N.

whole milk. In shape, the Gouda cheese is somewhat like a Cheddar with the sharp edges rounded off and sloping toward the outer circumference at the middle from the end faces. They usually weigh 10 or 12 pounds, though they vary in weight from 8 to 16 pounds. They are largely manufactured in southern Holland, and derive their name from the town in which they were first made. Fresh sweet milk that has been produced and cared for in the best possible manner should be used.

189. Method of manufacture. — The processes of manufacturing Gouda cheese are as follows:

Treatment of milk before adding rennet. — The temperature of the milk should be brought up to a point not below 88° F. nor much above 90° F. When the desired temperature has been reached and has become constant, the coloring matter is added. One ounce of cheese color for about 1200 pounds of milk may be used. The coloring matter should be thoroughly incorporated by stirring before the rennet is added.

Addition of rennet to milk. — The rennet should not be added until the milk has reached the desired temperature (88 to 90° F.) and this temperature has become constant. The milk should be completely coagulated, ready for cutting, in fifteen or twenty minutes. The same precautions should be used in adding rennet as those previously mentioned in connection with the manufacture of Edam cheese.

Cutting the curd. — The curd should be cut when it is of about the hardness generally observed for cutting in the Cheddar process. The cutting is done as in the Cheddar process except that the curd is cut a little finer in the Gouda cheese. Curd should be about the size of peas or wheat kernels when ready for press and as uniform in size as possible.

Treatment of curd after cutting. — After the cutting is completed, heating and stirring is begun at once. The heating and constant stirring is continued until the curd reaches a temperature of 104° F., which should require from thirty to forty minutes. When the curd becomes rubber-like in feeling, the whey should be run off. The whey should be entirely sweet when it is removed.

Pressing and dressing Gouda. — After the whey is off, the curd is put in molds at once without salting (Fig. 28). Pains should be taken in this process to keep the temperature of the curd as near 100° F. as possible. Each cheese is placed under continuous pressure amounting to ten or twenty times its own weight and kept for about half an hour. The first bandage is put on in very much the same manner as in Edam cheese making. The cheese is then put in press again for about one hour. The first bandage is then taken off and a second one like the first put on with great care, taking pains to make the bandage smooth, capping the ends as before. The cheese is then put in press again and left twelve hours or more.

Y. Produce Rev. 25 (1907), no. 8, page 336, where a home process of making this cheese is given.

Fig. 28.—Gouda cheese mold.

Salting and curing. —When Gouda cheese is taken from the press, the bandage is removed and it is placed for twenty-four hours in a curing-room like that used for Edam cheese, as previously described. Each cheese is then rubbed all over with dry salt until the salt begins to dissolve, and this same treatment is continued twice a day for ten days. At the end of that time, each cheese is carefully and thoroughly washed in warm water and dried with a clean linen towel. The cheeses are then placed on the shelves of the curing-room, turned once a day and rubbed. The temperature and moisture are controlled as described in the curing process of Edam cheese. If the outer surfaces of the cheese become slimy at any time, they are carefully washed in warm water and dried with clean towels. Under these conditions, cheese ripens in two or three months.

190. Equipment for Gouda cheese.—The molds, press and curing-room are the only equipment needed in the making of Gouda cheese that differ from that employed in making Cheddar cheese. The mold used for Gouda cheese consists of two portions, which are shown separately in Fig. 28. These molds are made of heavy pressed tin. The inside diameter at the middle is about 10 inches, that of the ends about 6½ inches. The height of the mold is about 5½ inches, and this represents the thickness of the cheese, but by pushing the upper down into the lower portion, the thickness can be decreased as desired.

191. Composition and yield of Gouda.—In work with milk averaging 4.2 per cent of fat there were lost in the whey from 0.29 to 0.43 per cent with an average of 0.35 per cent of fat. The loss of fat appears to be not much greater than the average loss met with in cheese factories in making Cheddar cheese. From 100 pounds of milk, there were made from 11.60 to 13.35 pounds of green cheese, with an average of 12.50 pounds. The percentage of water in the experimental cheese varied from 41.25 to 45.43 per cent and averaged 43.50 per cent.

CHAPTER XII

CHEDDAR CHEESE-MAKING

The lot-card; The milk; Ripening the milk; Setting or coagulating; Cutting; Heating or "cooking" the curd; Removing the whey; Hot-iron test; Firmness of the curd; Gathering the curd together; Matting or cheddaring; Milling the curd; Salting; Hooping the curd; Pressing the curd; Dressing the cheese; Handling over-ripe and gassy milk; Qualities of Cheddar cheese.

Cheddar is the best known cheese throughout the United States and the one most commonly made in factories. The Cheddar process was brought to America by English immigrants. Similar to Cheddar cheese are Pineapple, English Dairy, Sage cheese, skimmed-milk and California Jack cheese made in this country, and Derbyshire, Leicestershire, Wensleydale and Cheshire made in England. The Cheddar cheese process as employed in the factories to-day has been modified and improved since it was first introduced into this country by the early immigrants.

The following description[87] includes only the practices as found in the factories to-day if whole milk is used. Skimmed-milk Cheddar cheese is discussed later.

Fig. 29.—Delivering milk to the cheese factory.

[87] The authors acknowledge here the helpful suggestions and criticisms of G. C. Dutton, New York State Cheese Instructor.

192. The lot-card.—The Cheddar process involves several hours of manipulation and includes many details which should be closely and accurately observed and recorded. The necessity of carrying observations of several different factors at the same time makes a scheme of recording data essential to convenient work. For this purpose, a lot-card for Cheddar cheese is introduced here and the pages given to particular factors are indicated in the space intended for the recording of observations. The manufacture of Cheddar cheese is a complicated process, because several factors must be given attention at the same time. A careful record of the observations of each step in the successive handling of each lot of milk puts the operator in possession of a permanent record of his experience. This record has several uses. It may help to convince patrons of the importance of eliminating faults in the milk; it furnishes the cheese-maker a cumulative record of his experiences in handling milk with special qualities, such as high or low fat-content, over-acidity or taints. Since Cheddar ripening covers a period of weeks and months, no operator can remember particular lots of milk sufficiently well to be able to use his experience on the interpretation of the qualities found in the ripened product.

193. The milk.—It is the usual practice to deliver the milk to the cheese factory each morning (Fig. 29). The night's milk is cooled and kept clean and cold until delivered at the factory. It is advisable not to mix the cold night's milk and the warm morning's milk, but to deliver them in separate cans to the cheese factory at the same time. The milk is weighed, sample for fat test taken and then run into the vat (Fig. 30). The receiving or taking in of the milk is one of the most important parts of the cheese factory work. It is practically as important as the actual manufacturing of the cheese.

21 CHEESE. This card must remain with lot.............. from the milk room until the finished product is ready to leave the building, then it should be handed to instructor.

MAKING Day and Date.. Vat...................

Milk Used		Milk
....	....	Appearance of Milk ....
....	....	Odor..
....	....	Taste...
Total pounds		Weather conditions........................

...................% fat   ....lbs. fat

	Starter
............% solids not fat ....lbs. s. n. f.	Kind used ....
	Flavor..
	Acidity...
............% casein ....lbs. casein.	Amount used .... % used........

Time of	Minutes	% Acid	Temperature
adding starter....	....	*In Milk*	of milk when received
			when starter added .....
adding rennet	....	when received...................	when rennet added ....
		before adding starter...............	when whey removed....
coagulation	....	after adding starter............	at pressing..................
		when rennet added..................	**Rennet Test**
cutting	....		when milk received....
		In Whey	after adding starter.....
turn'g on steam..	....	after curd is cut................	when rennet added.....
		at dipping..........................	**Hot Iron Test**
turn'g off steam	....	at packing..........................	at dipping..................
dipping	....	at milling...........................	at packing..................
		at salting...........................	at milling....................
packing	....		at salting....................
milling	....	**Condition of Curd**	
salting	....	when cut	
hooping	....	when packed	
		when milled	
pressing...............	....	when salted	
		when pressed	
dressing...............	....		

	Amount per 1000 lbs. milk......	Color	Rennet	Salt
Total time from setting to pressing }	Total Amount............			

....................% fat in whey   ....lbs. fat estimated so lost.
....................% of total milk fat lost in whey

If comments are added on reverse side, put cross here ....

Work and Observations by........................

Assisted by...

YIELD Day and Date... Time.....................

Weight of cheese when removed from press to curing room,.............lbs.   Serial No............

............lbs. milk for one lb. cheese.   Kind of cheese made ....lbs. cheese per 100 lbs. milk

............lbs. cheese for one lb. fat in milk.   No. of cheese made.   ....lbs. cheese for one lb. total solid

If comments are added on reverse side put cross here............

Work and observations by...

Arranged by W. W. Hall.

Fig. 30.—Receiving, sampling, weighing and running the milk into the cheese vat.

Any milk high in acid or with a bad flavor should be avoided. It is often bad policy to reject the milk, for a neighboring factory will accept it and the factory not only loses the milk but also the patron. Factories should have an agreement to prevent this. The acidity can be determined by the acid test, but the detection of flavors must be made by the cheese-maker himself with the aid of smell and taste. Many of the bad flavors in the cheese can be traced to the poor quality of the milk. One of the worst qualities in milk and cheese is the presence of gas-producing organisms.[88] Any milk which shows gassy fermentation should be rejected, for it is difficult to make cheese from this and at best there will be a large loss during the manufacturing process. The cheese may have a bad flavor and develop "pinholes" and in extreme cases may puff up like a ball. The person receiving the milk should talk to the farmers or dairy-men about the proper care of the utensils and milk. He must see that the cans are kept clean. One very bad practice is to deliver milk and take home whey in the same cans. The cans, as they are brought back from the cheese factory full of whey, are often left in the barn or near a hog-pen until the whey is fed. Unless such cans are emptied immediately on returning to the farm and then rinsed out with cold water, thoroughly washed and scalded, bad flavors may develop in the cheese. It is thought that this causes "fruity" or sweet flavor, which resembles that of fruits such as raspberries, strawberries or pineapples.

[88] Russell, H. L., Cheese as affected by gas-producing bacteria, Wis. Exp. Sta. Rept. 1895, pages 139-146.

Marshall, C. E., Gassy curd and cheese, Mich. Exp. Sta. Bul. 183, 1900.

194. Ripening the milk.—A slight development of acidity is required: (*a*) to obtain the formation of a firm curd; and (*b*) to establish immediate dominance of a desirable type of lactic organism which will produce the large amount of acid required later in the cheddaring process. The development of this acidification before the addition of rennet is known as the ripening of the milk. The extent of ripening advised by different schools of makers has varied from an acidity of 0.20 of 1 per cent or even slightly higher percentage titrated as lactic acid, to about 0.17 of 1 per cent as now preferred by some of the most successful groups of workers. The ripeness of the milk can also be determined by the use of the rennet test.

The milk may be ripened by allowing the lactic organisms already present in the milk to develop naturally. This requires considerable time and while the lactic acid-forming bacteria are developing, other and undesirable fermentations may be taking place, so that the good results which should follow the uninterrupted development of the lactic acid-forming organisms are lost. Starter is commonly used to produce the desired ripening of the milk. (For the preparation of starter see Chapter IV.)

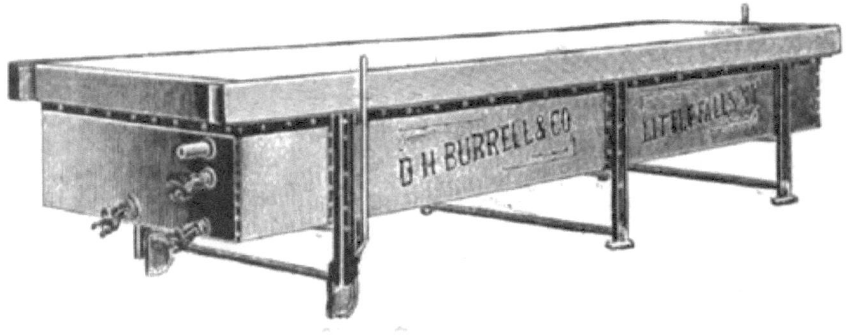

Fig. 31.—Steel cheese vat.

Some makers put the starter into the empty vat (Fig. 31) and add the milk as it is received; others add it to the total volume of cold milk and then begin to heat it. Whenever the starter is used, it should be strained to remove lumps. These lumps might cause a mottled color in the cheese. The best practice calls for an acidity or a rennet test of the mixed milk after it has been brought to the setting temperature in the vat. With milk tested at this stage and the volume of milk in the vat known, the cheese-maker is able to calculate closely the amount of starter needed. When the quantity of starter to use is in doubt, the amount added should be under rather than over the estimate, since the need of more can be determined by making frequent rennet and acid tests in a very few minutes without damage to the cheese. If too much starter has been used, acid or sour cheese is usually obtained, with loss in market quality.

An over-development of acidity at any stage of the manufacturing process affects the flavor, body and texture, color and finish of the cheese. The product is known as a sour cheese, and can usually be identified by its sour taste and smell.

A sour cheese while curing will seldom develop a normal Cheddar flavor and the texture will be hard and harsh and very brittle. The body will not be smooth but harsh and grainy. The over-development of acid will show by fading or bleaching the color. A sour cheese usually leaks whey for a few days after being placed on the curing-room shelves.

Ripening the milk is one of the most important parts of cheese-making. Proper ripening places the acid fermentations under the control of the cheese-maker so that he may know what results will follow his labors. The operator can control the acidity while ripening the milk, but after the rennet is added all control of the acidity is lost. From that time, the moisture must be regulated in proportion to the acidity.

Before setting, the milk should be ripened to such a point as to leave at least two and one-half hours from the time that the rennet extract is added until the acid development has reached the stage at which it is necessary to remove the whey. By the acid test the milk may vary from 0.16 to 0.18 of 1 per cent, but no definite statement can be given for the rennet test. This can be determined only by comparison from day to day. For operation of rennet test see Chapter V. During this period of two and one-half hours, the curd is formed, then cut, and the temperature is raised from 84° or 86° F. (the temperature at which the rennet extract is added) to about 98° to 100° F. The curd must be kept agitated so that the particles will not mat together; this is necessary to obtain sufficient contraction of the particles of curd with the proper reduction of water-content. If the milk becomes too ripe (too sour) before the rennet is added, there will not be sufficient time for these steps to take place naturally. In such cases special means are required to firm the curd. These result in a loss of both quality and quantity of cheese. On the other hand, if the milk is not ripened, but the rennet extract added, regardless of the acid development, one of the important natural forces for expelling the moisture is lost. The time required for the particles of curd to contract is much prolonged, the expulsion of whey is usually inadequate and the curd remains in a soft or wet condition. Using too much starter is almost equally bad, for although it hastens the making process, it produces a sour or acid cheese.

195. Setting or coagulating.—The milk for Cheddar cheese-making is heated to 86° to 88° F. or occasionally a slightly lower temperature. This temperature is found by experiment to give the texture of curd most favorable for the desired results. Although some cheese-makers work as low as 84° F., the texture of such curd is too soft and coagulates too slowly. The very slight change of 2° F. produces curd which coagulates more quickly and is tougher and firmer.

If the cheeses are to be colored, the color should be added after all the starter. It should be thoroughly and evenly mixed with the milk to insure an even color in the cheese. If the color is added before the starter, there are likely to be white specks in the cheese, on account of the coagulated casein in the starter. The amount of color to use depends on the tint desired in the cheese. It varies from ⅓ to ½ ounce to 1000 pounds of milk for a light straw color to 1½ to 2 ounces for 1000 pounds of milk for a deep red color.

Enough rennet should be used to produce a curd firm enough to cut in twenty-five to thirty-five minutes. The necessary amount will vary with the strength of the rennet extract itself, with the acidity, the temperature, the nature of the lot of milk, and with the individual aims of the maker in which he adjusts the other factors to his preferences as to rapidity of rennet action. With the usual commercial extract, the needed amount ranges from 2.5 to 4 ounces for 1000 pounds of milk. As for all varieties of cheese, the rennet extract should be diluted in cold water at about one part rennet to forty parts water and thoroughly stirred into the milk. (See Chapter V.)

196. Cutting.—The object of cutting is to obtain an even expulsion of the moisture from the curd. The curd is cut as soon as it becomes firm enough. To determine this, various tests may be used. Some operators test it by pressing it away from the side of the vat, considering it ready to cut when it separates cleanly from the metal. The test most commonly used is to insert the index finger obliquely into the curd, then to start to split the curd with the thumb and finally to raise the finger gently; if ready to cut, the curd will split cleanly over the finger and clear whey will separate to fill the opened crack. Another arbitrary but more or less satisfactory rule is that the time from adding the rennet until cutting should be two and one-half times that from the addition of rennet until the first sign of coagulation is observed.

The condition of the curd itself is the best guide to show when it is ready to cut. The condition of the curd is constantly changing, so that in a large vat, if the cutting is not begun until the curd is in the best condition, by the time the last of the curd is cut it will be too hard or firm. It is better to begin while the curd is a trifle too soft so that the cutting will be taking place while the curd is at the proper stage. At best the last of the curd may become too hard. If too hard, it will break ahead of the knife instead of cut. Breaking causes more fat loss than cutting because there is more surface exposed and hence more fat globules. The softer the curd when cut, the quicker and easier the moisture can be expelled.

If the curd is cut when soft, care must be exercised not to stir it too hard immediately after cutting. Soft curd breaks very easily. When the curd is cut soft and then stirred vigorously, there is a larger loss of fat than when the curd becomes hard before it is cut.

Two knives are used to cut the curd. (See Fig. 11.) These knives may have either wire or blades for cutting. The space between the wires or blades varies from 5/16 to ½ inch. Knives used should have blades or wires close enough together to cut the pieces as small as desired, without a second cutting. When the curd has to be cut a second time it usually results in pieces of uneven sizes, because the pieces already cut cannot be evenly split in two.

One set of knives has horizontal and the other perpendicular blades or wires. The curd is cut the long way of the vat with the horizontal knife and lengthwise and crosswise with the perpendicular knife so that the result is small cubes or oblongs of curd. Some cheese-makers prefer to use one knife first and some the other, but the result should be a curd cut into pieces of uniform size. The smaller the particles of curd or cubes are cut, the quicker the curd will firm up or cook. If not cut uniformly, the changes taking place later in the curd particles will not be uniform,—the small pieces will be hard and dry while the large ones will be soft and mushy.

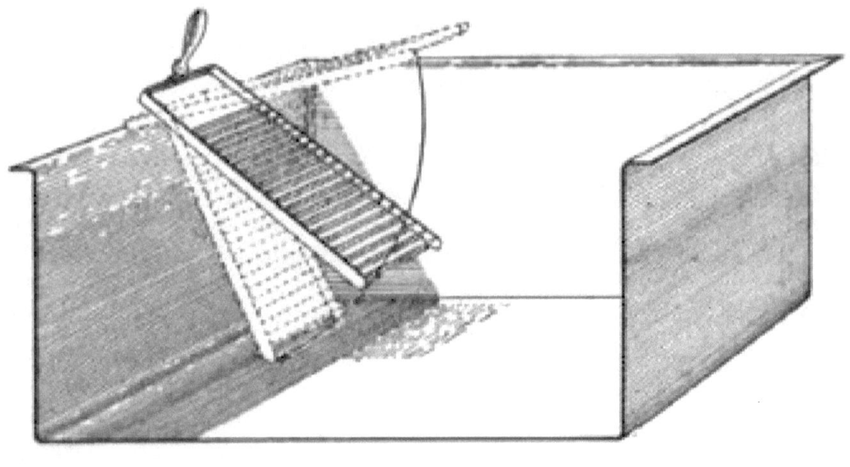

Fig. 32.—The proper way to put the knife into the curd.

Care should be taken to let the knife cut its way into the curd (Fig. 32). If the knife is pushed into the curd, it will break it and cause a large loss of fat. The same is true when taking the knives out of the curd. The loss of fat due to cutting is very similar to the loss of sawdust when sawing a board. It may be considered a necessary evil. The loss due to cutting is about 0.3 of 1 per cent of fat in the whey and the loss of casein about 0.1 of 1 per cent in the whey.

197. Heating or "cooking" the curd.—After the curd is cut, the pieces (cubes) rapidly settle to the bottom of the vat and tend to mat together. To prevent this, the curd must be kept stirred. When stirring first begins, the curd is soft and very readily broken. Some cheese-makers prefer to stir by hand for the first few minutes after cutting, while the curd is soft. The importance of careful handling can hardly be over-emphasized. No matter how well the curd has been cut, if the stirring is performed in a careless manner in the early stages, it will be broken into uneven sized pieces and a considerable loss of fat will result. A wooden hay rake or a McPherson curd agitator (Figs. 33, 34) may be used to stir the curd. Mechanical curd agitators are used in some cheese factories. There are several makes. (See Fig. 35.) These agitators save much hand labor, although some stirring by hand must be done in connection with them. The mechanical agitators do not stir the curd in the corners of the vat; this must be done with the hand rake. It is the usual practice to stir the curd immediately after cutting for five to ten minutes before the mechanical agitators are used. This is necessary to give the curd a slight chance to firm as the mechanical agitators tend to break it up. After cutting, a thin film forms on each piece of curd. This film holds the curd particles, especially the fat. Breaking the films on the cubes causes loss of fat. If lumps form at the early stage, by matting of the curd particles, violent stirring is required to separate them. When such lumps are broken up, new cleavage lines are formed with loss of fat, because the original films surrounding the soft curd fuse so firmly that the curd cubes do not separate but actually break. New surfaces are thus formed with consequent fat loss. Rapid shrinkage with expulsion of whey takes place during the first few minutes of gentle agitation. Before any heat is applied to the vat, sufficient whey should have separated or formed to float each piece of curd separately. This will require ten to fifteen minutes from the time of cutting.

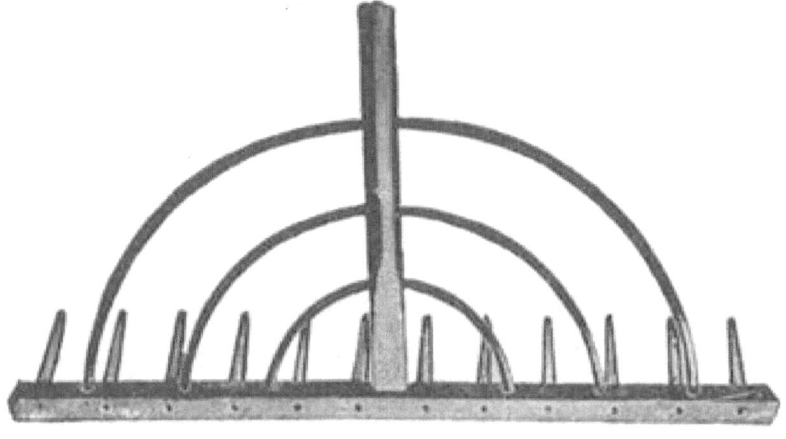

Fig. 33.—Acme curd rake.

Fig. 34.—McPherson curd agitator.

Fig. 35.—Two types of mechanical curd agitators.

Thus far the first of three distinct factors which expel the moisture from the curd has been considered: (1) the action of the rennet; (2) the development of the lactic acid; and (3) the application of heat. These forces must have time to act naturally. If heat is applied too soon after the curd is cut or if the temperature is raised too rapidly, it causes a thick film to form on the pieces of curd which interferes with the escape of the whey. The outside of the curd becomes firm but the inside remains very soft. A curd which is cooked on the outside only feels firm when stirred by hand in the whey, but when a handful is squeezed the soft centers are noticed. To firm such curd masses requires violent stirring, which will break the thick tough film. This allows the moisture to escape and also increases the fat loss. The rapidity of heating should depend on the condition of the curd and the amount of acid developed. The heat should keep pace with these. When ready to raise the temperature, the least amount of steam possible should be allowed to pass through the valve. This should raise the temperature very gradually. If heat is applied too quickly at first, it will cause the curd to lump. A safe rule is to raise the temperature one degree in the first five minutes after the steam has been turned on. The heating should progress slowly until the whole mass of curd in the vat has reached a temperature of 90° to 92° F. The usual temperature to which the curd is heated or cooked is 98° F. to 100° F. The lower the temperature that can be used and properly firm the curd, the better will be the body of the cheese. If the curd is heated too high, it will become hard, which causes a dry hard "corky" cheese. After this temperature has been reached, there is not such a tendency for the curd particles to stick together nor are they so easily broken in stirring. It should require, under normal conditions, not less than thirty to forty-five minutes, from the time the steam is turned on, to raise temperature of the curd from the setting temperature to that necessary to "firm" the curd. If a shorter time is allowed to raise the temperature, the curd will not have opportunity to contract naturally.

The temperature required to expel the moisture properly varies with the percentage of fat in the milk. If rich in fat (4.5 to 5.5 per cent) milk requires a temperature of 98° to 104° F. to firm the curd, while the same result can be accomplished with milk testing 3.0 to 3.5 per cent fat at a temperature of 94° to 96° F. A higher temperature is needed in winter than in summer because the milk is usually richer in fat. In a water-jacketed vat, allowance must always be made for the rise in temperature due to the water surrounding it. The water may be removed if there is danger of the temperature going too high. However, it is better to gauge the heat so that the water may be left, as this helps to hold the curd at an even temperature, especially in cold weather. In a steam-heated vat there is not so much danger of the temperature running up.

The stirring must be kept up after the steam has been turned off until the curd has reached such a stage of contraction that it will not readily pack or mat in the bottom of the vat. After the curd reaches this stage it may be allowed to settle to the bottom and stirred only occasionally until it is time to remove the whey. If the cheese room is not warm and there is danger of the curd cooling, a cover should be placed on the vat. The curd should not be allowed to settle for more than fifteen minutes without stirring to keep each piece separate. This is necessary to obtain uniform contraction of all curd masses.

198. Removing the whey.—To permit the normal changes in the curd to take place naturally, two and one-half hours from the time the rennet extract is added is ordinarily required before the whey is drawn. The time of removing the whey is determined by two factors: one, the acid development, and the other, the firmness of the curd. For the best results, it is better to have the firmness of the curd a trifle ahead of the acid development. When the proper acid development has been reached, the whey must be removed, regardless of the firmness of the curd. If the curd has not become firm enough by natural forces, when the acid development has reached the proper stage to remove the whey, it must be firmed by other means. If it is not firm enough, either by natural or artificial means, when the whey is removed, a sour cheese is the result. The acid development should not be allowed to go beyond 0.16 to 0.19 of 1 per cent acidity in the whey by the acid test or 1/16 to 1/8 of an inch of acid on the hot-iron test, before the whey is removed.

199. Hot-iron test.[89]—This test is employed to determine the amount of acid in the curd. A piece of iron, such as an iron pipe two feet long, is heated in the fire to proper temperature. If the iron is too hot it will burn the curd, and if not hot enough the curd will not stick to the iron. When hot, it is taken from the fire and wiped clean with a cloth. A handful of curd is taken from the vat and squeezed dry, either in the hand or in a cloth. This curd is carefully pressed against the hot iron and drawn away. If the iron is at the right temperature and the curd has sufficient acid development, the curd will stick to the iron and when pulled away will form fine threads. The length of these threads determines the amount of acid in

[89] S. M. Babcock, Hot iron test of cheese curd, Wis. Exp. Sta. Rept. 1895, pages 133-134.

the curd. The acid is usually spoken of in terms of the length of threads, as ⅛ inch of acid, ½ inch of acid and the like. The curd must have a slight development of acid before it will stick to the iron. This test takes advantage of the peculiar properties[90] of curd which are produced by the action of the acid on the casein.

200. Firmness of the curd.—The cheese-maker must be able to judge the firmness of the curd by physical examination. The particles of curd should have shrunken to about one-half their original size and should be of uniform consistency throughout; they should not have any soft centers. The curd should be firm and springy. When a double handful is pressed and suddenly released, the curd particles should spring apart. The curd should have a "shotty" feeling when in the whey. If the curd has attained the proper firmness, and the acid has not reached the correct stage to remove the whey, it may be left in the whey until sufficient acid development has been attained. This is liable to cause the curd to become too firm and to result in a hard dry cheese. If there is no evidence of the presence of undesirable organisms, such as bad odors, or gas holes in the curd, it is better to remove the whey and develop the acid when the curd is in the "pack." The pack refers to the first piling of the curd.

Fig. 36.—Whey siphon with strainer.

[90] Van Slyke, L. L., and E. B. Hart, A study of some of the salts formed by casein and paracasein with acids, their relation to American Cheddar cheese, N. Y. (Geneva) Exp. Sta. Bul. 214, 1902.

The whey may be removed either by means of a faucet or gate in the vat or by a siphon (Fig. 36). With either form of removal a whey-strainer (Fig. 37) should be used to prevent loss of curd particles. It requires considerable time for the whey to escape from a large vat. After the curd has been heated to the proper temperature, it is well to remove a portion of the whey. In doing this the surface of the whey should not be drawn down quite to the top of the curd. When ready, the remaining whey can be quickly removed.

If it is decided that the curd is not firm enough, when the whey is drawn down to the surface of the curd and the acid has developed sufficiently, the curd should be firmed up in the whey by stirring it vigorously by hand before the remainder of the whey is removed. This is commonly called "hand stirring." This difficulty results either from the use of too much starter or from holding the milk until too much acid development has taken place before adding the rennet. Hand stirring accomplishes what natural forces would accomplish if given sufficient time. If the curd does not firm naturally in the whey, there is a large loss of fat and other solids, because the pieces of curd will have to be broken up to allow the water to escape from the soft centers of these masses. This loss can usually be reduced by firming the curd in the whey or adding water rather than by stirring without either water or whey. If the curd is not properly firmed, it carries extra whey into the cheese. With the increase in whey, the amount of milk-sugar carried into the cheese increases. This extra milk-sugar attacked by bacteria produces an excess of lactic acid, which results in "sour" cheeses. This explains why the curd is placed beyond the danger of over-development of acid by removing so large a portion of the whey. If the curd is properly firmed in the whey and the whey is removed before too much acid has developed, it is impossible to make a sour cheese.

201. Gathering the curd together.—Before the last of the whey has been removed, the curd should be pushed back from the faucet into the upper two-thirds of the vat and spread in an even layer. This layer should be six to eight inches thick. The curd can be pushed back with the rake or a board which will fit crosswise in the vat, in which are many holes. As soon as the whey has been removed so that there is not enough to wash the curd into the lower part of the vat, the vat should be tilted and a ditch eight to ten inches wide cut in the curd through the center. The curd from the ditch should be removed to either side and spread evenly. As soon as all the whey has been removed, the pieces of curd scattered about in the vat should be gathered up and placed with the remainder.

In some factories, instead of matting the curd in the vat, a curd sink is used. This is a wooden receptacle about the size of the vat but not so deep, with a slatted false bottom. It is fitted with castors so that it can be easily moved about. A cloth is placed in the sink and the curd and whey are dipped upon the cloth. The whey escapes very rapidly through the cloth. The curd sink is an advantage in those cases in which it is desirable to remove the whey from the curd quickly, such as high acid curds which have to be hand stirred to firm the curd. The disadvantage lies in the work required to keep the sink and the large cloth clean.

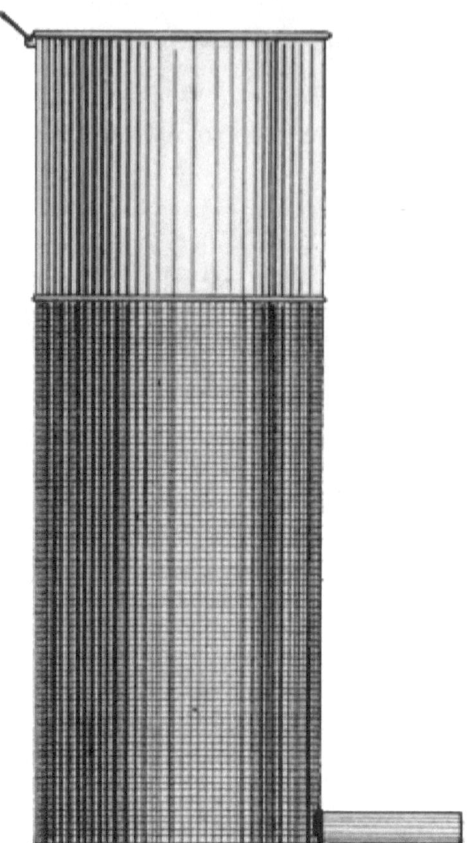

Fig. 37.—Whey strainer with spout to fit into the gate in the vat.

202. Matting or cheddaring is the distinctive feature of the Cheddar process. It is the piling and matting of the curd. Whether the curd is matted in the vat or in the curd sink, the process is practically the same. The object of cheddaring is three-fold: (1) to control the incorporation of moisture; (2) to control undesirable ferments, if present in the curd; (3) to develop the texture desired in the cheeses.

After the curd in the vat has become matted so that the particles stick together, the masses on either side of the central channel are cut crosswise into strips with a cheese knife (Fig. 38). The width of the strip depends on the water-content of the curd at this stage. The more water, the smaller should be the pieces of curd. This allows the whey to drain away much more rapidly. As soon as the strips of curd are cut, they should be turned over or stood on edge. A drain should be left along the middle line of the vat and on each side. This permits the whey to run away freely. If, on the other hand, the outlet is dammed up, the curd may become "whey-soaked." This produces a soft mushy cheese which sometimes is "acidy" or sour. After the curd is turned each time, all crumbs of curd broken off should be brushed underneath the masses of curd so that they will mat with it. They should never be placed on top of the curd because they will not unite but will become dry and hard. If the crumbs are not kept brushed up, they become dry and will cause an open textured granular cheese and possibly lumps in the cheese. After the pieces of curd have been turned several times, and the whey has fairly completely drained away, they may be piled first two deep, then three deep and so on, the depth of the piling being gauged by the softness or amount of water in the curd and the temperature. The higher the curd is piled, the more water it will retain (assimilate), so that the amount of moisture in the curd is regulated by the size of the pieces into which it is cut and the rapidity and depth to which it is piled.

Fig. 38.—A cheese knife.

The curd should not be left too long from the time it is turned until it is turned again. This period is usually about ten to fifteen minutes. The moister the curd, the more often it should be turned. In turning, care should be taken to keep the ends at the same temperature as the remainder. This can be done by piling them inside, thereby keeping them warm. There is a tendency for the ends of the pieces of curd to remain granular and so cause an open-textured cheese.

During the cheddaring process, the temperature should be reduced uniformly and gradually. If there is danger of the curd becoming too cold, the vat should be covered and a pail of hot water may be placed inside, if it is deemed necessary. The temperature of the curd should not be allowed to go below 85° to 90° F. If kept too warm, the curd will become soft and plastic, and if too cold, it will not mat together.

While the curd is being turned and piled, its physical properties are changing. The acid develops. When the cheddaring process is completed, the curd should be elastic, smooth and fibrous. The curd should have the close meaty texture desired in the cheese. If this step in the process is neglected, defects may appear later in the body, texture and flavor of the cheese. Attempts to pile the curd too fast result in a soft, mushy, open-textured product. Such cheese has mechanical holes, in which moisture collects, and so is likely to cause rot while curing.

If gas is detected either before or during the cheddaring process, the curd should be piled until the gas holes are no longer round but flat. If the gas holes are not flattened or obliterated during this process, the cheeses will be very liable to puff on the shelves in the curing-room. The curd should be handled until the gas holes flatten out evenly, although this may require considerable time. At best, gassy curd will never produce the highest grade of cheese.

Cheddaring or piling the curd is not thoroughly understood by most cheese-makers. Because the moisture contains the milk-sugar, there is danger of having so much moisture present in the cheese that it will become sour from the action of the lactic acid-forming bacteria on the milk-sugar. A cheese may be sweet when made and later become sour because it contains too much moisture or milk-sugar. This is known as "shelf souring." For the proper cheddaring of a curd, it is necessary that it be properly firmed in the whey. If the moisture is not evenly incorporated, the cheese will have a mottled color. The pieces that have the more moisture will be lighter colored. If the proper amount of moisture is not incorporated, the cheese will be dry and hard, and if too much, soft and pasty.

203. Milling the curd.—The large pieces formed by the cheddaring process must be cut into small ones before the curd can be easily put into the hoop. This is called "milling." Properly milled curd can be salted evenly, cools more quickly and uniformly and can be distributed evenly in the hoops.

The proper time to "mill" the curd is determined by its physical condition. Some curds will cheddar much more rapidly than others, hence no definite length of time can be given. Curd, when ready to mill, should have a fibrous texture somewhat like the white meat of a chicken breast. The pieces of curd should split very easily. When cut, the curd should show a close, solid, smooth interior. The amount of lactic acid developed may vary within rather wide limits. The hot iron may show strings ½ to 1 inch long. The acidity (by titration of the freshly separating whey) may be 0.45 to 0.65 of 1 per cent. If the curd has been properly made, that is, firmed up in the whey with the proper acidity so far, acid development during the cheddaring process will take care of itself. The physical condition remains the principal means of determining the time when the curd should be milled.

Fig. 39.—Gosselin curd-mill.

Fig. 40.—Barnard curd-mill..

Fig. 41.—Junker curd-mill...

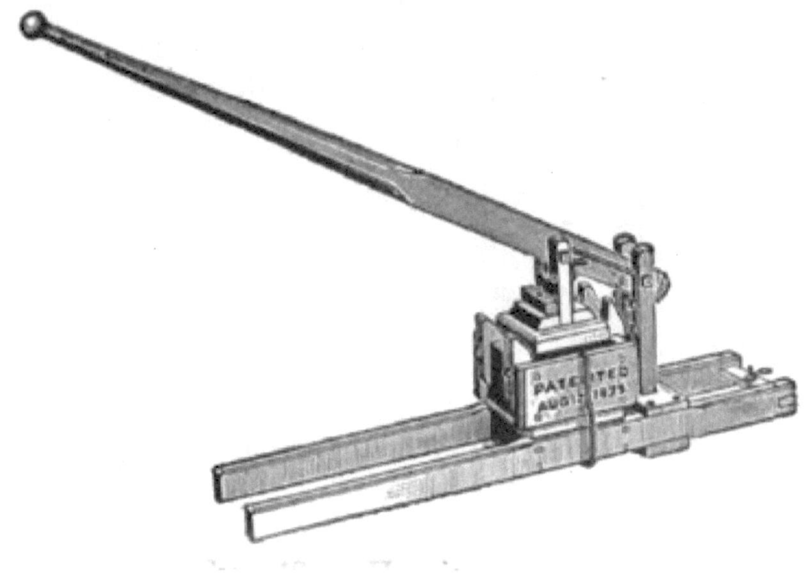

Fig. 42.—Harris curd-mill...

There are many kinds and styles of curd-mills on the market. Gosselin, Barnard, Pohl, Junker, Victor, Harris are well-known kinds (Figs. 39-42). Some are hand, others power mills. Some of these tear the curd into pieces of unequal size, others cut it into uniform pieces. A mill that will do the work with the least possible pressure on the curd and which will cut it into small uniform-sized pieces is most desirable. The ideal mill should release the least fat and leave the curd in the best condition to receive the salt. It is impossible to run curd through any mill without exposing some fat on the freshly cut surfaces, and if the curd is put under pressure, more fat will be pressed out and lost. Cutting in the mill, like cutting the curd after coagulation by rennet, may be called a necessary evil. There is an unavoidable mechanical loss which may be greater or less according to the mill used. If the curd has been properly handled so that the water in it has become thoroughly assimilated (properly incorporated), this loss will be reduced to the minimum. If the curd contains free moisture and many of the particles have soft interiors, a stream of white whey will run down the vat as the curd masses are cut. Some samples of such white whey will test as high as 15 per cent fat. This not only causes a loss in yield but in quality of cheese, according to the amount of fat lost. White whey is an indication of loss of fat. If the proper amount of moisture is present and is so thoroughly incorporated in the curd that it can be separated only by evaporation, the ideal condition has been reached. While milling, the cut curd should be stirred as fast as milled to prevent matting again and to allow odors to escape. This stirring is usually performed with a curd fork (Fig. 43). At the same time the temperature will be lowered. The milled curd should be spread evenly over the upper three-quarters of the bottom of the vat. The flavor of the curd that has been made from tainted milk can be very much improved by stirring at this time so that air can enter.

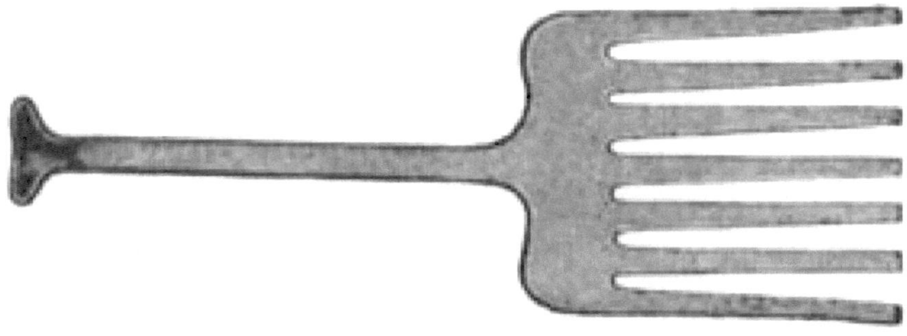

Fig. 43.—A curd fork.

A gassy curd, which has been held until the holes have become flattened, should be stirred very frequently during this stage to allow the gas to escape, thereby improving the flavor.

204. Salting.—Salt is added to Cheddar curd for several purposes: (1) for its taste; (2) to aid in the removal of the whey and to harden and shrink the curd; (3) to influence the fermentation by slowing down acidification, checking the growth of unfavorable organisms and delaying ripening. The salt should be pure. It should be coarse-grained, because the large grains dissolve more slowly and permit its absorption to a much larger extent than the fine-grained salt. Salt that dissolves slowly is, therefore, to be sought for this purpose.

The following factors must be considered in determining the amount of salt to be used: (1) the amount of curd from the milk; (2) the percentage of water in the curd; (3) the acidity of the curd; (4) the particular market form of cheese desired. The custom of determining the quantity of salt by the weight of milk is an inaccurate practice. The amount of salt should be based on the amount of curd. If the amount of fat in the milk is known, a fairly accurate estimate of the amount of curd can be made. It would be more accurate to weigh the curd before salting, but this is not practicable or necessary to insure a good quality of cheese. The amount of salt varies from 1½ to 2½ pounds of salt to the curd from each 1000 pounds of milk.

The salt should not be added directly after milling because, at that time, it would cause a large loss of fat. After milling there should be time before salting for the freshly cut surfaces to dry or "heal over." When first milled the curd has a dry harsh feeling; when ready to salt it will feel soft and mellow and some moisture can usually be squeezed out easily. Fifteen to twenty minutes from the time of milling are required before the curd is ready for the salt. When ready, the curd should be spread evenly over the bottom of the vat. The salt should be carefully weighed, and then applied, evenly, over the surface of the curd, in two or three applications. The curd should be thoroughly stirred after each application of salt. While the salt is being dissolved and absorbed, the curd should be stirred occasionally to prevent lumps from forming.

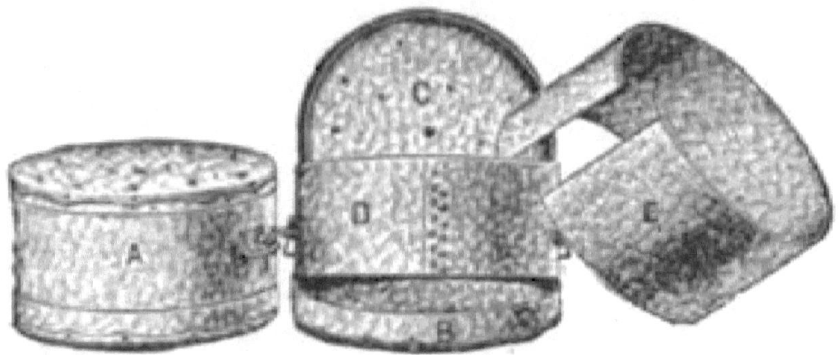

Fig. 44.—Wilson press hoop. A, complete hoop; B, bottom cover with wide flange; C, top cover with narrow flange; D, closed body; E, bandager.

205. Hooping the curd.—When the salt has become dissolved and the curd as soft and mellow as before the salt was added, it is ready to be put into the hoop. Various sized hoops may be used, depending on the desired size of the cheese. Two types are the Wilson and the Fraser (Figs. 44, 45). With either type, a dampened press cloth should be cut just to fit the bottom of the hoop. A starched circle may or may not be used; if used, it should be placed on top of the press cloth. The bandage now commonly employed is the seamless one which comes in the form of a tube of various sizes for different sized hoops. The lengths of bandage cut for each hoop or cheese depend on the height of the cheese plus about one and one-half inches' lap on each end. The bandage, after being cut the desired length, is placed on the part of the hoop made to hold it, so that it is suspended about the side of the hoop and laps about one and one-half inches on the bottom. The bandage should be free from ravelings and placed squarely in the hoop.

Fig. 45.—Fraser press hoop. A, complete hoop; B, bandager; C, follower; D, fibrous press ring.

The hoop is now ready to fill with curd. Enough hoops should be prepared to hold all the day's curd as fast as it is ready. In order to have all the cheeses as nearly as possible of the same size, it is advisable to weigh the curd into the hoops. The curd may be measured into the hoops, but this is not so accurate. The curd may be dipped with a flat-sided curd pail or a curd scoop into the hoops (Fig. 46).

Fig. 46.—Curd scoop and pail.

206. Pressing the curd.—The natural changes sought in the curd require a period of at least five hours between the time of setting (addition of the rennet) and the pressing of the curd. Less time than this involves loss in yield and quality of the cheese. In other words, the time requirement for these changes cannot be ignored. The object of pressing is not primarily to remove whey but to produce the physical conditions essential to ripening the cheese in a mass and put it in convenient form for handling. The whey should have been removed during the cooking and cheddaring. When ready for the press, the temperature of the curd should be about 80° to 85° F.; it should be brought down to this point during the milling, salting and hooping processes. If the curd is put to press too warm or too cold, the following results may be expected:

Too high temperature during pressing produces several faults, as:

(1) Favors the development of undesirable ferments.

(2) Causes excessive loss of fat.

(3) Gives the curd pieces a greasy surface so that they will not readily pass into a compact cheese. If a cheese is greasy, the bandages will not stick.

(4) Favors the formation of mechanical holes in the cheese.

(5) Causes "seamy" color in the cheese by the collection of fat between pieces of curd.

Too low temperature has its difficulties, such as:

(1) The pieces of curd will not fuse together.

(2) The rind does not form properly.

(3) It appears to cause mottled cheese.

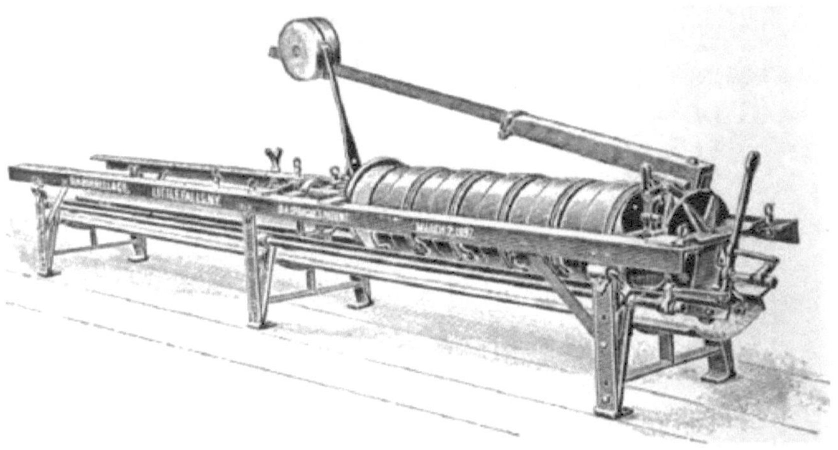

Fig. 47.—Continuous pressure gang cheese-press.

Fig. 48.—Filling the hoops and pressing the curd.

The commonly used gang press may or may not have an arrangement to cause continuous pressure to be applied to the cheese (Figs. 47, 48). When fresh cheeses are first placed in the press, the pressure should be applied very gradually. The curd, after being cut through the mill, will have many exposed fat globules. A heavy pressure at first will force out the whey set free by the extracting power of the salt. The whey will carry away the exposed fat globules, and therefore reduce the yield. As soon as white whey starts from the hoops, the increased application of the pressure should be stopped until the whey regains the appearance of clear brine. More pressure can then be gradually applied until full pressure is reached.

The cheeses should remain under heavy pressure for one-half to one hour, when they should be removed from the press and dressed.

207. Dressing the cheese.—When ready to dress the cheese, the press is opened and the hoops turned down. The hoops are opened so that the bandages can be lapped over the top of the cheeses about 1½ inches. Before turning a bandage down, it should be carefully pulled up to remove any wrinkles from the sides of the cheese, but not hard enough to pull it free from the bottom. After it is pulled up, the bandage should be lapped over the top about 1½ inches, and if not even should be trimmed with a sharp knife. It should then be sopped down with warm water. Plenty of warm water to wet the bandage and cloths helps to form a good rind. If starched circles are used, one should be placed on the top of the cheese and sopped down with warm water. If not, the press cloth should be wrung out of warm water and put on smoothly, so there will be no wrinkles. The hoop is then put together and placed back in the press under heavy pressure for twelve to eighteen hours. The pressure should be sufficient to cause the curd particles to unite so that the surface of the cheese will be smooth. The next day the cheeses are taken from the hoops and placed in the curing-room. If they do not come out of the hoop easily, they may be loosened by cutting between the sides of the cheese and the hoop with a knife. A special thin-bladed knife for this purpose is called a speed knife (Fig. 49). Care should be taken not to cut the bandage when trying to loosen the cheese. If starched circles are used, the press cloths are removed from the cheese, when they are put in the curing-room. If neither starched circles nor press cloth are left on the cheese in the curing-room, the rind will crack on account of drying out on the exposed surface. This allows mold and insects to enter the cheese. The flavor, body and texture and color of the cheese are all dependent on the skill of the cheese-maker and the quality of the milk from which it is made. The finish is dependent entirely on the skill and carefulness of the maker. An operator should see that the cheese press is straight so that there will be no crocked cheese and that the bandage and press cloths are properly put on, because the finish or appearance of the cheese is an index of his ability.

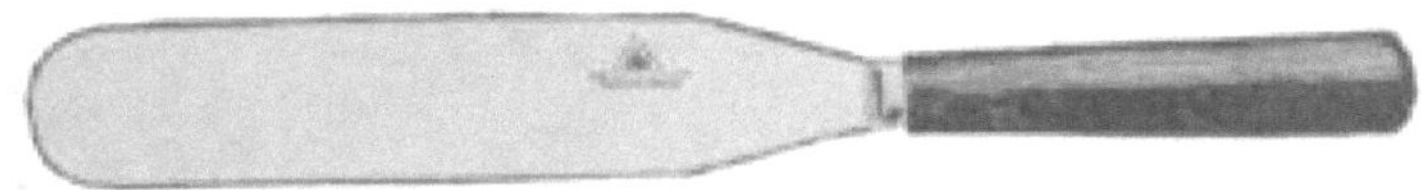

Fig. 49.—Speed knife.

208. Handling over-ripe and gassy milk.—Because it is sometimes necessary to make over-ripe[91] or gassy milk[92] into cheese, special directions or precautions

[91] Decker, J. W., Cheesemaking from sour milk, Wis. Exp. Sta. Rept. 1898, pages 42-44.

[92] Russell, H. L., Cheese as affected by gas producing bacteria, Wis. Exp. Sta. Rept. 1895, pages 139-146.

Marshall, C. E., Gassy curd and cheese, Mich. Exp. Sta. Bul. 183, 1900.

are necessary. The best way is to reject this milk. When it is necessary to make it into cheese, the losses are much more than with normal milk. It is a question of making as good a cheese as possible, and the subject of losses is ignored.

(1) *Over-ripe milk.*—The fact that the milk is over-ripe shows that there is already too much acid present. Every effort must be made to get the curd as firm as possible in the whey with the acid development as low as possible or before the acid has had time to develop any more than can be helped. Although the milk is over-ripe, it is a good plan to add about ¼ of 1 per cent of starter just before the rennet. This starter will not begin to work until the curd is being cheddared and it will help the flavor, especially if any bad fermentation should be present.

The rennet is added at 80° F., as this lower temperature tends to check the acid development. More rennet is used, commonly from 4 to 4½ ounces to 1000 pounds of milk. This gives a quicker coagulation. The curd is cut soft, as this tends to expel the moisture more quickly. The heat is turned on sooner after cutting. The time to turn it on and the length of time to heat are determined by the amount of acid. A curd should not be heated in less than fifteen minutes. If the curd has enough acid and has not begun to firm up much, the whey should be drawn down to the surface of the curd, water the temperature of the whey and curd put into the vat, and the curd firmed up in this water. The water washes the acid out of the curd and because of the lack of milk-sugar checks the acid development.

If the milk is not so ripe and the curd nearly firm enough, the whey may be drawn off and the curd firmed up by hard stirring in the vat or sink. The curd should not be pushed back enough to be very deep or thick when ready to cheddar.

The curd should be cut into very small pieces to cheddar. The smaller the pieces, the faster the whey drains away. Sometimes it is necessary to cut the curd into pieces six inches square. The pieces should not be piled but should be turned often and stood on edge to let the whey drain away and sometimes pressed with the hands to force the whey out. It is often all one man can do to keep the curd turned.

Fig. 50.—At the left is a regular shaped, close, solid textured cheese; at the right one puffed up with gas.

Moore, V. A., and A. R. Ward, Causes of tainted cheese curds, N. Y. (Cornell) Exp. Sta. Bul. 158, 1899.

The curd is not cheddared very long but is milled early so that the whey can escape. If it is thought that the cheese will be sour, the curd should be washed in cold water to remove the acid and milk-sugar. A little more salt is sometimes used. A product made from over-ripe milk, no matter how skillful the cheese-maker, will show traces of a sour cheese.

(2) *Gassy milk.*—If a cheese-maker knows that there is "gassy" fermentation, he should add more starter and develop more acid when ripening the milk to try to overcome this. There are different kinds of gassy fermentation. Some produce acid and some do not. Some will not show until the cheeses have been on the curing-room shelves several days. Others will cause the curd to float in the whey. Usually the gas shows as pin-holes while the curd is being cheddared.

Fig. 51.—This shows the same cheeses as in Fig. 50, cut open to show the solid and gassy texture.

The gas causes tiny round holes in the cheese, resulting in the cheese swelling or puffing out of shape and sometimes breaking open (Figs. 50, 51). The only time to overcome the gas is during the cheddaring process. The curd is piled and rep-iled until the holes flatten out. This shows that the gas-producing organisms have weakened and will not cause any more holes. Because the curd has to be piled so many times and so long, the pieces become very thin. The curd is ready to mill when most of the holes have flattened. After milling, the curd should be stirred and aired for some time before salting to allow the bad odor to escape.

Because of the high acid development, it often happens that the cheese will not be gassy but will be sour. At best a cheese made from milk having gassy fermentation will have a bad flavor. The quality of the cheese can be no better than that of the milk from which it is made, plus the skill of the cheese-maker.

209. Qualities of Cheddar cheese.—The cheese should be neat, clean and attractive. If unclean, and the bandage not put on the cheese properly, it shows that the manufacturer is not particular to keep the curing-room shelves tidy nor careful and painstaking in dressing. The cheese should not be lopsided or bulged. When cut, it should have a uniformly colored interior. The principal color defects are too high, or too light color, mottled or seamy. The texture should be solid and close. A common defect is mechanical holes or openings and another is gas pockets. The body can be tested by rubbing the cheese between the thumb and fingers. It should be smooth and waxy and free from lumps. It should rub down like cold butter. The common defects are graininess and lumpiness. Graininess may be caused by too much acid or too much moisture in the cheese. Lumpiness is due to uneven curing. If too much moisture is present, the body will be soft and mushy; if not enough moisture, the body will be hard and dry.

The cheese should have a pleasant, clean, mild aroma and the characteristic flavor which is usually somewhat similar to that of nuts and so is spoken of as a nutty flavor.

CHAPTER XIII

COMPOSITION AND YIELD OF CHEDDAR CHEESE

Composition of milk, whey and cheese; Relations of fat to casein in normal milk; Influence of fat in milk on yield of cheese; Fat loss in cheese-making; Effect of bacterial-content of milk on yield of cheese; Factors affecting the moisture-content of Cheddar; Variations of the Cheddar process; Cheddar-type cheese from pasteurized milk; Club cheese; The stirred-curd or granular process; California Jack cheese; The washed-curd process; English dairy cheese; Pineapple cheese; Leyden; Cheddar cheese with pimientos; Sage cheese; Skimmed-milk cheese; Full skimmed-milk Cheddar cheese; Half skimmed-milk Cheddar cheese; Yield and qualities of skimmed-milk Cheddar cheese.

So many factors affect the composition and yield of Cheddar cheese that no positive or exact statement can be made unless other facts are definitely known. The following factors affect both the composition and yield:

1. The chemical composition of the milk.
2. Amount of moisture incorporated into the cheese.
3. The amount of solids lost in cheese-making.
4. The skill of the cheese-maker.
5. The bacterial-content of the milk.

210. Composition of milk, whey and cheese.—The following Tables[93] VI, VII, VIII, which are the average of forty-eight factories for the season of 1893, show the minimum, maximum and average composition:

TABLE VI

AVERAGE COMPOSITION OF THE MILK

	MINIMUM	MAXIMUM	AVERAGE
Water	86.28	88.30	87.28
Total solids	11.70	13.72	12.72
Fat	3.30	4.40	3.77
Casein	2.20	2.85	2.48
Albumin	0.52	0.81	0.69

[93] Van Slyke, L. L., Investigations relating to the manufacture of cheese, N. Y. (Geneva) Exp. Sta. Bul. 68, 1894.

	MINIMUM	MAXIMUM	AVERAGE
Sugar and ash, etc.	5.63	5.89	5.78

TABLE VII
AVERAGE COMPOSITION OF THE WHEY

	MINIMUM	MAXIMUM	AVERAGE
Water	92.75	93.28	93.00
Total solids	6.72	7.25	7.00
Fat	0.24	0.51	0.38
Casein, albumin	0.66	0.90	0.86
Sugar and ash, etc.	5.63	5.86	5.76

TABLE VIII
AVERAGE COMPOSITION OF THE GREEN CHEESE

	MINIMUM	MAXIMUM	AVERAGE
Water	33.16	43.80	37.33
Total solids	66.84	56.11	62.67
Fat	30.00	35.89	33.41
Casein	20.80	25.48	23.39
Sugar and ash, etc.	4.86	7.02	5.89

Table VI shows the minimum, maximum and average composition of the milk and Table VIII the composition of the cheese made from that milk. The average composition of the cheese in Table VIII shows that it contains 37.33 per cent of water. The tendency to-day seems to be for a softer cheese so that the average would probably be higher. Table VIII also shows the wide variation in the composition of the cheese. The moisture and total solids both vary about 10 per cent. In order to judge the variation in composition, one must know the composition of the milk and the moisture-content of the cheese and then only a very inaccurate estimate of the composition of the cheese can be formed.

211. Relation of fat to casein in normal milk.—In order to understand the relation of the composition of the milk to yield of cheese, one must be familiar with the relation of the fat to the casein in normal milk. The following table[94] shows the relation of fat to casein in normal milk:

---

[94] Van Slyke, L. L., Investigations relating to the manufacture of cheese, N. Y. (Geneva) Exp. Sta. Bul. 62, 1893.

TABLE IX

SUMMARY SHOWING THE RELATION OF FAT TO CASEIN IN NORMAL MILK

GROUP	PER CENT OF FAT IN MILK	NUMBER OF SAMPLES	AVERAGE PER CENT OF FAT IN EACH GROUP	AVERAGE PER CENT OF CASEIN IN EACH GROUP	AVERAGE POUNDS OF CASEIN FOR EACH POUND OF FAT IN MILK
I	3.0-3.5	22	3.35	2.20	0.66
II	3.5-4.0	112	3.72	2.46	0.66
III	4.0-4.5	78	4.15	2.70	0.65
IV	4.5-5.0	16	4.74	3.05	0.64
V	5.0-5.25	7	5.13	3.12	0.61

Table IX shows that the pounds of casein for each pound of fat are not constant but that the casein does not increase in proportion to the fat above 4.0 per cent of fat in the milk.

212. Influence of fat in milk on yield of cheese.—The following table shows the influence which fat in the milk has on the yield of cheese:[95]

TABLE X

SUMMARY SHOWING RELATION OF FAT IN MILK TO YIELD OF CHEESE

GROUP	SVERAGE PER CENT OF FAT IN MILK	POUNDS OF GREEN CHEESE MADE FROM 100 LB. OF MILK	POUNDS OF GREEN CHEESE MADE FOR 1 LB. OF FAT IN MILK
I	3.35	9.14	2.73
II	3.72	10.04	2.73
III	4.15	11.34	2.70
IV	4.74	12.85	2.71
V	5.13	13.62	2.66

Table X shows that as the fat in the milk increases, the pounds of cheese made from 100 pounds of that milk increases; but the amount of cheese made for each pound of fat in the milk does not increase. This is due to the fact pointed out in Table IX, namely, that as the fat increases in the milk the casein does not increase in the rich milk in proportion to the fat. From Tables IX and X this conclusion may be drawn: that as the percentage of fat increases in the milk the more cheese can be made from 100 pounds of that milk, but after the increase in fat gets above 4 per cent the amount of cheese that can be made for each pound of fat in the milk is decreased because the casein does not increase in proportion to the fat. No exact statement of yield can be made without first stating the moisture-content of the

[95] Van Slyke, L. L., Investigations relating to the manufacture of cheese, N. Y. (Geneva) Exp. Sta. Bul. 62, 1893.

cheese. The losses also must be considered.

Van Slyke[96] in the following Table XI shows the effect of the fat-content of normal milk on the yield of cheese.

The moisture-content of all the cheeses is reduced to a uniform basis of 37 per cent. (See cut showing yield of cheese, Fig. 52.)

Fig. 52.—The figures represent the relative yield of cheese containing different percentages of fat, but all have a uniform content of 37 per cent water.

TABLE XI

TABLE SHOWING THE EFFECT OF THE FAT-CONTENT OF NORMAL MILK ON THE YIELD OF CHEESE

Per Cent of Fat in the Milk	Per Cent of Casein in the Milk	Amount of Cheese Made from 100 Lb. 100 Lb. of Milk	Pounds of Amount of Cheese Made for Each Pound of Fat in the Milk
3.00	2.10	8.30	2.77
3.25	2.20	8.88	2.73
3.50	2.30	9.45	2.70
3.75	2.40	10.03	2.67
4.00	2.50	10.60	2.65
4.25	2.60	11.17	2.63
4.50	2.70	11.74	2.61
4.75	2.80	12.31	2.59
5.00	2.90	12.90	2.58

213. Fat loss in cheese-making.—The amount of solids lost in the whey also affects the yield. The following table gives the amount of fat lost in whey with

[96] Van Slyke, L. L., Methods of paying for milk at cheese factories, N. Y. (Geneva) Exp. Sta. Bul. 308, 1908.

normal milk containing different percentages of fat:

TABLE XII

SUMMARY SHOWING AMOUNT OF FAT IN MILK LOST IN
CHEESE-MAKING

Group	Pounds of Fat in 100 Lb. of Milk	Pounds of Fat Lost in Whey for 100 Lb. of Milk	Per Cent of Fat in Milk Lost in Whey
I	3 to 3.5	0.32	9.55
II	3.5 to 4	0.33	8.33
III	4 to 4.5	0.32	7.70
IV	4.5 to 5	0.28	5.90
V	5 to 5.25	0.31	6.00

Table XII shows that the percentage of fat in the whey is approximately the same for milk high or low in fat. But the milk low in fat loses a higher percentage of the total milk-fat in each 100 pounds of whey.

214. Effect of bacterial-content of milk on yield of cheese.—The bacterial-content[97] of the milk influences the yield by affecting both the moisture-content and the losses. If the milk is sour or has bad fermentation, the losses will be increased because the curd cannot be carefully handled, and the moisture cannot be incorporated to the extent that it can in clean milk, without injury to the quality. The proper-cooling of the milk in one instance increased the yield 0.3 pound of cheese for each 100 pounds of milk. The more moisture that can be incorporated into the cheese up to the legal limit, the greater the yield.

215. Factors affecting the moisture-content of Cheddar.—The amount of moisture that can be incorporated in a curd depends on several factors.[98] The following increase the moisture-content control of the cheese:

1. Cutting the curd coarse.
2. High setting temperature.
3. Low acid in the curd at time of removing whey.
4. Not stirring the curd with the hand as the last of the whey is removed.

---

[97] Farm Bur. Exchange, St. Lawrence Co., N. Y., Vol. 1, no. 9, 1915. Cooling milk before delivery at the cheese factory.

[98] Sammis, J. L., et al., Factors controlling the moisture content of cheese curds, Wis. Exp. Sta. Research Bul. 7, 1910.

Ont. Agr. College and Exp. Farm Rept. 1909, pages 111-124, Cheese making experiments.

Ont. Agr. College and Exp. Farm Rept. 1910, pages 111-128, Cheese making experiments.

Fisk, W. W., A study of some factors influencing the yield and the moisture content of Cheddar cheese, Cornell Exp. Sta. Bul. 334, pages 515-537, 1913.

    5. Slow pressure.

    6. High piling of the curd in the cheddaring process.

    7. Small amount of salt.

    8. Holding the curd at low temperature after the whey is removed.

    9. Large amount of rennet.

    10. Cutting the curd hard.

The following factors decrease the moisture-content of the cheese:

    1. Fine cutting.

    2. Low setting temperature.

    3. High acid in the curd at time of removing the whey.

    4. Stirring the curd with the hand as the last of the whey is removed.

    5. Fast pressure.

    6. Low piling of the curd in the cheddaring process.

    7. Large amount of salt.

    8. Holding the curd at high temperature after the whey is removed.

    9. Small amount of rennet.

    10. Cutting the curd soft.

From this discussion, it is evident that the yield of cheese from 100 pounds of milk increases with higher percentages of fat and casein in the milk, with reduced losses of solids during manufacture, with the absence of undesirable fermentations, and with the incorporation of large amounts of water.

216. Variations of the Cheddar process.—The Cheddar process, as already described, is widely employed in cheese factories. Many varieties are found, however, and varietal names are used for such products. A whole series of these forms are either locally or widely made in England and taught in the English dairy schools. Some of these varieties resemble the factory Cheddar product fairly closely; others are clearly different products. A typical series of the variations as developed in America will be considered.

In the commercial trade Cheddar cheese is usually designated by some name which indicates its size. The size of the cheese is determined by that of the hoops. The hoops vary both in diameter and height. The table on the following page shows the usual sizes of the hoops and the weight and name applied to the cheese.

217. Cheddar-type cheese from pasteurized milk.—Sammis and Bruhn[99] have described a variation of the Cheddar process to overcome the difficulties of making cheese from pasteurized milk. Such milk curdles in very unsatisfactory manner unless some chemical is added to compensate for the salts lost and to offset the other changes resulting from heat. For this purpose, they found the use of hydrochloric acid satisfactory.

---

[99] Sammis, J. L., and A. T. Bruhn, The manufacture of cheese of the Cheddar type from pasteurized milk, U. S. Dept. Agr. Bur. An. Ind. Bul. 165, pages 1-95, 1913.

TABLE XIII

SIZE OF CHEESE HOOPS, WEIGHT, AND TERM APPLIED TO CHEESE

DIAMETER OF HOOP	HEIGHT OF CHEESE	WEIGHT OF CHEESE POUNDS	TERM APPLIED TO CHEESE
6-7 in.	7-8 in.	9-11	Young America
Tapers 5-7 in.	10-14 in.	10-16	Long Horn
12-14 in.	3½-4½ in.	18-24	Daisy or Picnic
14-15½ in.	4-6 in.	30-40	Twin (two in same box)
14-16 in.	4-7 in.	35-40	Flat
13½-15 in.	10-12 in.	40-50	Cheddar
14-16 in.	12-15 in.	75-90	Export

"The acidulation of milk with hydrochloric acid after pasteurization is accomplished without difficulty or danger of curdling by running a small stream of the acid, of normal concentration, into the cooled milk as it flows from the continuous pasteurizer into the cheese vat. One pound of normal-strength acid is sufficient to raise 100 pounds of milk from 0.16 percent to 0.25 percent acidity (calculated as per cent of lactic acid). The amount of acid needed each day to bring the milk up to 0.25 per cent acidity is read from a table or calculated from the weight of the milk and its acidity, determined by the use of Manns's acid test (titration with tenth-normal sodium hydrate and phenolphthalein). The preparation of standard-strength acid in carboy lots for this work and the acidulation of milk present no great difficulty to any one who is able to handle Manns's acid test correctly.

"After the milk is pasteurized and acidulated three-fourths per cent of first-class starter is added and the vat is heated to 85°. It is set with rennet, using 2 ounces of rennet per thousand pounds of milk, so that the milk begins to curdle in 7 minutes and is cut with three-eighth inch knives in 25 minutes. All portions of the work after adding rennet are carried out in an unvarying routine manner, according to a fixed-time schedule every day. As soon as the rennet has been added the cheese maker is able to calculate the exact time of day when each of the succeeding operations should be performed, and the work of making the cheese is thus simplified and systematized. It is possible that the routine process here described may be varied somewhat with advantage at different factories."

This cheese usually lacks characteristic Cheddar flavor or contains it in very mild form. It therefore satisfies only those who seek very mild flavored products. Efforts are now being made to find a flavor producing substance or organism which will bring the flavor of this product more nearly to that of typical Cheddar.

218. Club cheese is known by a variety of trade names. It is made from Cheddar cheese, so that it is especially liked by persons who care for strong Cheddar flavor. It has a soft texture so that it spreads easily, and is therefore much used for sandwiches. Well-ripened or old Cheddar cheese is ground in a food chopper. The older the Cheddar, the stronger will be the flavor of the club cheese. Cheese of good flavor should be used. In order to do away with all lumps in the texture, it is sometimes necessary to run the mixed cheese through the food chopper a second time. While all lumps must be worked out, care should be taken not to work the cheese so much that it will become salvy and sticky.

Usually a little pepper is added, to give the cheese a biting taste. Some manufacturers add a great variety of substances, but these are not necessary and destroy the flavor of the cheese.

Club cheese may be wrapped in tin-foil or put up in air-tight glass jars. The latter practice, while more expensive, has the advantage of making the cheese keep longer; but for local trade tin-foil is just as satisfactory as glass. In filling the glass, care must be taken not to leave any air spaces between the cheese and the glass, as this is likely to permit the cheese to mold. A glass jar can be filled and air spaces prevented by first smearing a very thin layer of cheese over the glass.

219. The stirred-curd or granular process.—The original practice as brought from England and followed in the farm dairies before the development of the factory system is now known variously as the "stirred-curd" or "granular curd" process. With the introduction of the cheese factory, as known to-day, this system was replaced by the Cheddar cheese. The old farm process is still used on some farms and in a few factories. As the name indicates, the curd for such cheeses is kept stirred so that it remains in granular condition instead of being allowed to mat as in the Cheddar process.

The early steps of the two processes are identical. They diverge at the point at which in the factory Cheddar process the whey is drawn and the curd is allowed to mat. In some factories the curd and part of the whey are dipped into a curd sink. This allows the whey to escape more easily and quickly. In the stirred-curd process, the pieces of curd are kept separated by stirring and not allowed to mat. The whey is drawn off and the stirring continued by hand. After stirring fifteen to twenty minutes, the curd becomes so dry as not to mat easily. As soon as the curd has reached this stage, the salt is evenly and thoroughly mixed with it. More salt is added than in the Cheddar process because the curd is more moist than Cheddar curd at the time of salting. The whey freely separating carries away much of the salt. The quantity of salt to use depends on the amount of whey draining from the curd. After salting, the curd is allowed to cool, with occasional stirring to prevent the formation of lumps. The advantage of the stirred-curd practice lies in the shorter time required for making cheese and in the greater yield due to increased water-content. It has several disadvantages, among them being: (1) lack of control of undesirable fermentation; if gas organisms are present, the cheeses more frequently huff than with the Cheddar system; (2) there is more fat lost while stirring the curd, hence quality and yield suffer; (3) the water is not so thoroughly incorporated, which more frequently results in mottled cheeses; (4) the body is commonly soft and "weak," shows mechanical holes, and cures too rapidly. These faults are closely correlated with the presence of higher percentages of water than in cheeses made by the Cheddar process. In other words, the stirred-curd process usually produces a cheese with higher water-content, hence more subject to the development of unfavorable fermentation than the Cheddar cheeses.

220. California Jack cheese[100] is very similar to the stirred-curd or granular process. This cheese was originally made in Monterey County on the coast of California, about twenty-five years ago, in small quantities, but after it was found to sell well other counties started to manufacture it. As Monterey was the first county to make this product, it was named "Monterey" cheese. In order to distinguish the cheese made in other counties from this, it was suggested that it be given a name and, consequently, it was called "Jack" cheese. This has been accepted as its true name. The cheese is made mostly by Portuguese and Italian-Swiss, although some of the best of the variety is now manufactured near Modesto, California.

This cheese is adapted for manufacture on small dairy farms, where there is inexpensive and scanty equipment. The smaller sizes of cheese are made and ripened quickly. It has become widely used in California.

The cheese is made every morning, from evening's and morning's milk. The former is put into the cheese vat at night, and morning's milk is added as milking is going on. When the milk is all in the vat, it is immediately warmed to 86° to 88° F. and rennet extract is added (when milk has 0.2 to 0.21 of 1 per cent acidity) at the rate of 6 to 8 ounces to 1000 pounds of milk. No coloring matter is used. It is ready for the curd-knife in thirty to thirty-five minutes, its readiness being determined the same as in making Cheddar cheese. The curd is first cut lengthwise of the vat with the horizontal curd-knife and allowed to stand until the whey rises over and partly covers the curd, when it is cut again with the vertical curd-knife crosswise of the vat. It is then hand-stirred, gently at first, and the stirring is finished with the rake.

Either a steam-heating or self-heating vat is used (the steam-heating vat is preferred) and temperature increased about one degree in five minutes. The curd is heated to 98° F. in winter, and to 105° F. to 110° F. in summer. After temperature is up, it is stirred occasionally with a rake until the whey is drawn at 0.14 to 0.15 of 1 per cent acidity.

The curd is hand-stirred as soon as the whey is nearly drained off, and raked to each side of the vat to drain more thoroughly, when it is quickly stirred again to keep it from lumping or matting. Salt is now added at the rate of 1½ pounds to 100 pounds of curd, and stirred in thoroughly several times. During the salting process, cold water is allowed to run under the vat, the hot water having been run off previously.

Curd is put into cloths at a temperature of 80° to 85° F. No cheese hoops are used. Two sets of press cloths are necessary; one set is ready to use while the other is still on the cheese in the press. These press cloths are about one yard square. The press cloths are all laid out evenly one on top of the other, as many as there are cheeses. They are then taken together and spread out over the top of a large, open tin milk-pail, and pushed down in the center to the bottom of the pail, with the edges hanging over the top. A common one-gallon lard pail is used to measure the curd into the press cloths. A lard pail full will make a cheese weighing six and one-half pounds, which is the popular size. After a pailful has been put into the

---

[100] New York Prod. Review, Vol. 34, no. 2, page 66.

press cloth, the four corners are caught up with the left hand, while with the right hand the curd is formed round and the press cloth straightened and the other corners in turn taken up. The press cloth is now taken up tight over the curd with the left hand, while the cheese is given a rolling motion on the table with the right hand, pressing at the same time to expel some of the whey. This twists the press cloth tight over the curd, where it is tied with a stout string. After fixing them all (as many as there are cheeses) in this way, they are ready for the press.

The cheeses are pressed between two wooden planks, 12 inches wide, 1½ inches thick, by whatever length is required for the number of cheeses to be pressed. One plank is nailed on supports at a convenient height from the floor on a little slant for the whey to drain off better. The cheeses in the press cloths are placed at the proper distance apart so they do not touch. Then the other plank is put squarely over the top of the cheese and levers about four feet long at an interval of five feet are placed over this plank, from a cleat in the wall, on the other end of which is placed a heavy weight of about 100 pounds, which acts as an automatic pressure. The cheeses are left in the press until the next morning, when they are taken out and put on the shelves in the curing-room. The cheeses have no bandage or covering, and do not seem to crock, and they form a very good rind.

The cheese is a sweet variety, weighs six and one-half pounds cured and cures in about three weeks ready to ship, and sells at 16 to 25 cents a pound wholesale. Most of the work seems to lie in forming and rolling the curd in press cloths before pressing. Trouble is experienced by the makers, especially in warm climates in summer, in not having the milk at a uniform acidity when rennet is added. Great improvements could be made in this cheese by using an acidimeter, paraffining and curing the cheese in an even temperature, not much over 60° F.

Old and hard Jack cheese is also employed for grating and cooking, while the fresh is used for the table.

221. The washed-curd process has been developed in recent years largely in the state of New York. In this method, a regular Cheddar curd is made up to the time of milling. This curd is washed or soaked in cold water during or directly after milling. The theoretical object of this washing is to carry away bad flavors and to reduce over-development of acidity by washing away all traces of whey. However, cheese-makers soon found that it increased the yield and this led some to carry it to extremes.

After the curd has been milled, it is covered with cold water. The temperature of this water ranges from 50° F. to 70° F. The curd is stirred in this water for various lengths of time according to the judgment of the cheese-maker. This time varies from five minutes to one hour. Sometimes the vat is partly filled with water and the curd milled directly into the water. This process has certain advantages and disadvantages.

The advantages are: if too much acid has developed in the curd, this washing will reduce it so that the cheese will not be sour. Sometimes when bad flavors are present in the curd, washing will tend to overcome or remove them. Its disadvantages are: the larger yield due to excessive soaking tempts the makers to soak curd beyond the time needed to relieve the initially sour condition. Curd soaked in this way produces cheeses containing percentages of water so high as to lower their quality. This increases the yield sometimes as much as 3 to 5 per cent. Such a cheese is very soft in texture and does not cure like a Cheddar cheese which has not been washed. Part of the lactic acid, milk-sugar[101] and the inorganic salts are removed by this washing. A washed-curd cheese will sometimes rot, due to the activity of the putrefactive bacteria, and to the lack of the restraining effect of the lactic acid-forming bacteria. Some washed-curd cheeses are so soft that they will not retain their normal shape.

A washed-curd cheese is never sour because the milk-sugar and lactic acid have been removed by washing.

222. English dairy cheese.—In some localities cheeses are still made on the farms. These are mostly produced after the stirred-curd process, hence are soft-bodied and open-textured. They usually weigh ten to twelve pounds and are three to four inches thick and twelve inches in diameter.

223. Pineapple cheese.—This variety derives its name from the fact that the cheeses are made in about the size and shape of a pineapple. The curd is made after the Cheddar process from either whole milk or partly skimmed milk. It is pressed in molds shaped like a pineapple. The cheeses are then hung in nets to give the checked appearance on the surface. They are rubbed with linseed oil to prevent the surface cracking, and finally are shellacked.

224. Leyden.—Among specialties, a cheese called Leyden originating in Holland is made in Michigan and New York. This is a part skim cheese heavily spiced with caraway seed. The ripe cheese is colored red as it goes to market.

225. Cheddar cheese with pimientos.—Recently some Cheddar cheeses have been made with pimientos added. This gives a mixture of characteristic Cheddar and pimiento flavors, which seems to be desired by some persons. An ordinary Cheddar curd is made and the pimientos added just before salting. The pimientos are ground rather coarsely and then added to the curd together with the liquid which was with the pimientos in the can. The pimiento should be thoroughly and evenly mixed with the curd to insure a uniform distribution and mottled color in the cheese. The salt is then applied. The remainder of the process is the same as for ordinary Cheddar cheese.

226. Sage cheese is a product flavored from the leaves of the ordinary garden sage. It is made by two methods: one, in which the sage leaves are used, and the other, in which a part of the curd is colored to imitate that given by the sage leaves, and sage oil or tea is used to give the flavor.

In the leaf method, a regular Cheddar cheese curd is made up to the time of salting. Just before the salt is added, sage leaves are mixed with the curd. The

---

[101] Babcock, S. M., et al., Cheese ripening as influenced by sugar, Wis. Exp. Sta. Rept. 1901, pages 162-167.

E. G. Hastings, et al., Studies on the factors concerned in the ripening of Cheddar cheese, Wis. Exp. Sta. Research Bul. 25.

leaves should be dried and freed from stems and other coarse particles and the leaves themselves broken up rather finely. The leaves are then added at the rate of 3 ounces for every 1000 pounds of milk. Care must be exercised to see that the leaves are evenly mixed through the curd or an evenly mottled cheese will not result. The salt is then added. This sequence seems to increase the absorption of the flavor by the curd.

If these cheeses are consumed as soon as well cured, no fault can be found. On the other hand, if they are held for any length of time, yellow areas form about each piece of sage leaf; the leaves decay rapidly and spoil the cheese. This method gives a very true flavored sage cheese, the only objection being that it cannot be held in storage for any length of time without a marked deterioration.

In the other method of making sage cheese, either a vat with a movable partition or a large and a small vat must be used. In many cases the receiving can is used as the small vat. After the milk is properly ripened and ready to set, one-sixth to one-seventh of the milk is put into the small vat. To this small vat, green coloring matter is added. Juice from the leaves of corn, clover, or spinach was formerly used as coloring. Consequently the manufacture of sage cheese by this method was limited to the seasons of the year when these leaves could be obtained. Now, however, the dairy supply houses have a harmless green color paste which is much cheaper and can be secured at any season of the year. The amount of color paste to use will vary from 30 to 35 c.c. for every 1000 pounds of total milk. This should be added to the small vat of milk. It gives a green milk and later a green curd.

Both vats are worked along together, until the time for removing the whey. Then the partition in the vat is removed or the small vat is mixed with the large one. The green curd should then be evenly mixed with the white one or an even green mottled cheese will not result. The curds should not be mixed until they are well firmed or the white curd will take on a greenish cast and spoil the appearance of the cheese.

After the whey is removed, the curd is allowed to mat as in ordinary Cheddar but care must be exercised to pile the curd so that it cannot spread or "draw" out. If it does draw out, the small green spots will be stretched out and large blotches or patches of green will be the result. The cheese-maker must watch the curd closely or he may not secure the much desired small green mottles. When the curd is well matted, it is milled as in Cheddar. Just before the salt is added, the sage extract is applied to the curd.

The sage extract can be obtained from dairy supply houses, or a sage tea can be made by steeping the sage leaves. In many cases the commercial extract gives the cheese a strong disagreeable flavor, but not a true sage flavor. The sage tea gives a flavor more like that of the leaves themselves. Too much of the extract or the leaves will give a very rank flavor. The sage extract can best be put on the curd by means of a sprayer or atomizer with which it can be evenly sprayed over the entire surface. The extract should be applied two or three times and the curd well stirred after each application. The amount of the extract to use depends altogether on its strength; an ounce of the extract or three ounces of sage tea to 1000 pounds of milk is about the correct amount. After the extract has been added, the salt is used at the same rate as with a normal Cheddar curd and the sage curd is carried along the same as a Cheddar.

This extract method gives a sage cheese mottled with small green spots which somewhat resemble the green of sage leaves. A cheese made in this way can be held for a long time, as nothing has been added which can decay. The only objection to this method is that the sage extract may not give a true sage flavor. Therefore, the maker must try to obtain the best extract possible or make his own from the sage leaves.

227. Skimmed-milk Cheddar cheese.[102]—The process of making skimmed-milk cheese after the Cheddar process is varied with the amount of fat left in the milk. Before attempting to make skimmed-milk Cheddar, one should become familiar with the process for whole-milk Cheddar. Skimmed-milk cheeses are usually highly colored.

When part skimmed-milk cheese is manufactured, there is often difficulty in getting the milk in the vat to test the desired percentage of fat. Some cheese-makers skim all the milk and then put in the desired amount of cream. This practice seems wasteful, not only because of the cost of separation, but because the fat will not mix easily with the milk but will tend to float on the surface. If the fat floats, there will be a large loss. After a very few trials an operator can tell about how much of the whole milk must be skimmed in order to have the mixed skimmed-milk and whole milk test the desired percentage of fat. The necessary percentage of fat in the mixed milk to produce cheese of a certain grade can be determined by testing the cheese by the Babcock test. (See Chapter XIX.)

228. Full skimmed-milk Cheddar cheese.—In the summer there is not much demand for full skimmed-milk cheese, but it is made in large quantity in winter. The method of manufacture is as follows:

Skimmed-milk as it comes from the separator is at a temperature of about 88° to 90° F.; it is ripened and set at this temperature. It is ripened rather highly on the acid test, from 0.18 to 0.20 of 1 per cent, and to correspond on the rennet test which will not be many spaces. In about twenty-five to thirty minutes it is coagulated ready for cutting. The curd of skimmed-milk cheese is cut a little softer than is that of whole-milk cheese. Milk is usually set at 88° to 90° F. The curd is not ordinarily cooked above this temperature. If the milk was 84° to 86° F. when set, then the curd should be raised to 88° to 90° F. The curd firms in the whey very rapidly. When firm enough, it should have a slight development of acid. On the acid test it should show 0.17 to 0.19 per cent, and on the hot iron ⅛ to ¼ of an inch. The milk should be ripe enough or starter enough should have been used, so that the acid will continue to develop in the "pack" very rapidly. During the cheddaring process the curd is piled more rapidly and in higher piles than is customary with whole-milk cheese. This is necessary to incorporate or assimilate a large percentage of water or whey in the cheese. Therefore the process of skimmed-milk Cheddar cheese is much shorter. More acid is developed with the skimmed-milk than

---

[102] Fisk, W. W., Skim-milk Cheddar cheese, N. Y. (Cornell) Exp. Sta. Ex. Bul. 18, 1917.

with the whole-milk cheese because it seems necessary to develop proper texture. If the acid is not developed sufficiently, the cheese will be very rubbery and cure very slowly, in which case bad fermentation and flavor may and often do develop. The curd is turned, piled or cheddared in the vat until it begins to become meaty and fibrous. If there is danger of too much acid, the curd may be rinsed off with water. It is then milled and salted at the rate of 1 or 1¼ pounds of salt to the curd from each 1000 pounds of milk. The remainder of the process is the same as that for making whole-milk cheese.

229. Half skimmed-milk Cheddar cheese.—No definite directions can be given for the manufacture of part skimmed-milk cheese, because the process varies with the amount of fat left in the milk. As the fat is decreased, the process becomes more like that for making full skimmed-milk cheese; as the fat is increased, the process becomes more like that for whole-milk cheese. However, the process of making half skimmed-milk cheese is about midway between the two. The milk is ripened more than it would be for whole-milk cheese, usually until it tests from 0.15 to 0.17 of 1 per cent acid. The curd is coagulated and cut the same as for the other skimmed-milk cheeses. It is cooked to a temperature just sufficient to firm the curd, usually from 94° to 96° F. The lower the temperature at which the curd can be cooked and yet become firm, the better is the texture of the cheese. When the curd has firmed enough, or when sufficient acid development, from 0.15 to 0.17 of 1 per cent, has taken place, the whey is removed. The curd is then turned, piled or cheddared. A skimmed-milk curd may be piled much more rapidly than a whole-milk curd without danger of injuring it. When the curd becomes meaty or fibrous, it is milled. It should be salted at the rate of 1¼ to 2 pounds of salt to the curd from each 1000 pounds of milk. The remainder of the process is the same as that for making whole-milk cheese.

The cheese-maker should observe the following points when making skimmed-milk cheese: (1) Have clean-flavored sweet milk; (2) use clean-flavored commercial starter; (3) ripen the milk sufficiently, but not too much; (4) firm the curd at as low a temperature as possible; (5) have the curd properly firmed when the whey is drawn; (6) cheddar the curd faster than the curd from whole milk; (7) make the cheeses all the same size; (8) keep the cheese neat and clean in the curing-room.

230. Yield and qualities of skimmed-milk Cheddar cheese.—The results of skimming different percentages of whole milk containing varying percentages of fat are given in the following table. As the percentage of fat in the milk decreases, the yield of cheese also decreases, according to the table. As the percentage of fat decreases in the milk, the percentage of moisture in the cheese increases, showing that moisture is substituted for fat. The yield of cheese from 100 pounds of milk is also given in this table. This yield varies with the amount of moisture incorporated into the cheese, the amount of solids not fat in the milk, and the solids lost in the whey.

In some creameries and cheese factories, the milk is skimmed and the cream made into butter and the skimmed-milk into cheese by the Cheddar process. In making cheese without the milk-fat, it is difficult to standardize a method that will produce the flavor and body of the whole-milk Cheddar cheese. A skimmed-milk cheese lacks the softness and mellowness of texture of the whole-milk product. It is very likely to be tough, dry or leathery. It is attempted to remedy this defect by incorporating more moisture into the skimmed-milk cheese. The added moisture tends to replace the fat in giving a soft mellow body. It requires skill on the part of the cheese-maker to incorporate moisture to take the place of the fat in giving the cheese mellowness and smoothness of body.

TABLE XIV

TABLE SHOWING THE COMPOSITION AND YIELD OF SKIMMED-MILK CHEDDAR CHEESE						
PERCENTAGE OF FAT IN THE MILK	PERCENTAGE OF THE MILK SKIMMED	PERCENTAGE OF FAT IN THE MILK IN THE VAT AFTER SKIMMING	NUMBER OF POUNDS OF CHEESE FROM 100 POUNDS OF MILK	COMPOSITION OF THE CHEESE		
				PERCENTAGE OF TOTAL SOLIDS	PERCENTAGE OF FAT	PERCENTAGE OF WATER
4.7	50	2.4	9.92	54.74	22.00	45.25
4.7	60	2.0	9.74	52.46	17.50	47.54
4.7	70	1.5	9.26	49.87	13.50	50.13
4.7	80	1.0	8.42	48.26	10.00	51.74
4.0	50	2.0	9.70	53.29	21.00	46.71
4.0	60	1.6	9.50	50.89	17.00	49.11
4.0	70	1.2	9.30	48.06	13.50	51.94
4.0	80	0.9	9.20	45.24	10.50	54.76
3.5	50	1.8	8.54	54.20	19.50	45.80
3.5	60	1.5	8.10	51.10	16.50	48.90
3.5	70	1.1	7.44	52.62	13.00	47.38
3.5	80	0.9	7.00	49.64	9.54	50.36
3.4	50	1.9	8.24[103]	54.50	20.00	45.50
3.4	60	1.5	7.82	52.05	16.50	47.95
3.4	70	1.4 1.2	7.80 7.28	49.04 50.76	14.00 14.00	50.96 49.24
3.4	80	0.9	7.24	47.41	10.50	52.59

The grades of skimmed-milk cheese vary between rather wide limits—from those made entirely of skimmed-milk to those made of milk from which only a small amount of fat has been removed and which are almost like whole-milk cheese. Because of the gradations of skimmed-milk cheese, it is difficult to make anything but general statements and to base comparisons with whole-milk cheese.

---

[103] Curd was spilled but practically all recovered.

CHAPTER XIV

CHEDDAR CHEESE RIPENING

Fat; Milk-sugar; The salts; Gases; Casein or proteins; Causes of ripening changes; Action of the rennet extract; The action of the bacteria; Conditions affecting the rate of cheese ripening; The length of time; The temperature of the curing-room; Moisture-content of the cheese; The size of the cheese; The amount of salt used; The amount of rennet extract; The influence of acid; Care of the cheese in the curing-room; Evaporation of moisture from the cheese during ripening; Paraffining; Shipping;. Defects in Cheddar cheese: Defects in flavor; Feedy flavors; Acid flavors; Sweet or fruity flavors; Defects in body and texture; Loose or open texture; Dry body; Gassy textured cheese; Acidy, pasty or soft body and texture; Defects in color; Defects in finish;. Cheddar cheese judging: Securing the sample; How to determine quality; Causes of variations in score; The score-card.

Freshly made Cheddar cheese is hard, tough and elastic and lacks characteristic cheese flavor. In this condition it is called "green," unripe or not cured. Before the cheese is ready to be eaten, it passes through a complex series of changes which are collectively known as ripening. In the ripening process the texture becomes soft and mellow and the characteristic cheese flavors develop. Cheese ripening must be considered from two view-points, first, the changes taking place inside the cheese and secondly the outside conditions necessary for ripening. Some of the chemical changes during ripening are known, while others are not understood. The different agents causing ripening, and the constituents of the milk, will be discussed.

231. Fat.—Numerous investigations have been made to ascertain what chemical changes the fat undergoes in the ripening process. Suzuki,[104] in studying the fat, found no enzyme capable of producing lactic acid or volatile fatty acids. However, these acids were found in increasing amounts during the ripening process and after the lactose had disappeared. Acetic and propionic acids reached a maximum at three months and then decreased, while butyric and caproic acids continually increased during the experimental period covered. Formic acid was detected in the whole-milk cheese only at the five and one-half month stage. In the

---

[104] Suzuki, S. K., et al., Production of fatty acids and esters in Cheddar cheese, Wis. Exp. Sta. Research Bul. 11.

judgment of the experimenter the principal source of acetic and propionic acids was probably lactates. Traces of these acids may have had their origin in protein decomposition or further fermentation of glycerine. The principal sources indicated for butyric and caproic acids were fats and proteins.

The distillate from the experimental cheese was designated "flavor solution" and contained alcohols and esters, giving a close resemblance to the cheese aroma. The "flavor solution" from the mild whole-milk cheese contained esters made up largely of ethyl alcohol and acetic acid, while from the more pungent skimmed-milk cheese the esters were largely compounds of ethyl alcohol and caproic and butyric acids. The alcohol may have come from the lactose fermentation. It appears to be an important factor in flavor production. The agencies operative in the production of volatile acids and syntheses of esters are as yet undefined.

232. Milk-sugar. — The milk-sugar (lactose) is changed into lactic acid by the lactic acid-forming organisms, within the first few days after the cheese is made. This acid is combined with the other constituents as fast as it is formed. After a few days, the milk-sugar will have entirely disappeared from the cheese.[105] The relation between the milk-sugar and lactic acid is very close. It is necessary that milk-sugar be present in order later to have the lactic acid develop.

233. The salts. — Just what changes the salts[106] undergo or how they combine with the other compounds is not definitely known. It is supposed that the calcium salts first combine with the phosphates and later, as the lactic acid is formed, they combine with the lactic acid, forming a calcium lactate.

234. Gases. — In the process of cheese ripening, gases are formed, the commonest being carbon dioxide.[107] Exactly how this gas is formed is not known. It may be due to the formation of lactic acid from the milk-sugar or to the living organisms in the cheese.

235. Casein or proteins. — Complex ripening changes in the cheese take place in the casein compounds or proteins. Because of the complex chemical nature of the proteins and the various agents acting on them, it is difficult to follow these

[105] Babcock, S. M., et al., Cheese ripening as influenced by sugar, Wis. Exp. Sta. Rept. 1901, pages 162-167.

[106] Bosworth, A. W., and M. J. Prucha, Fermentation of citric acid in milk, N. Y. (Geneva) Exp. Sta. Tech. Bul. 14, 1910.

Van Slyke, L. L., and A. W. Bosworth, Condition of casein and salts in milk, N. Y. (Geneva) Exp. Sta. Tech. Bul. 39, 1914.

Van Slyke, L. L., and E. B. Hart, A study of some of the salts formed by casein and paracasein with acids; their relation to American Cheddar cheese, N. Y. (Geneva) Exp. Sta. Bul. 214, 1902.

Van Slyke, L. L., and E. B. Hart, Some of the relations of casein and paracasein to bases and acids and their application to Cheddar cheese, N. Y. (Geneva) Exp. Sta. Bul. 261, 1905.

Van Slyke, L. L., and O. B. Winter, Cheese ripening investigations, N. Y. (Geneva) Exp. Sta. Tech. Bul. 33, 1914.

[107] Van Slyke, L. L., and E. B. Hart, The relation of carbon dioxide to proteolysis in the ripening of Cheddar cheese, N. Y. (Geneva) Exp. Sta. Bul. 231, 1903.

changes. This has led to different opinions regarding the ripening process. The various compounds thought to be formed from the casein or proteins are as follows:[108]

Paracasein (formed by the action of the rennet on the casein). Insoluble in brine and warm 5 per cent salt brine.

Protein. Soluble in warm 5 per cent salt brine.

Protein. Insoluble in warm salt brine or water.

Paranuclein. A protein soluble in water and precipitable by dilute hydrochloric acid.

Caseoses and proteoses. Protein derivations soluble in water and not coagulated by heat.

Peptones. Protein derivations simpler than the proteoses, soluble in water and not coagulated by heat.

Amido acids. Protein derivations soluble in water, least complex except ammonia.

Ammonia. The simplest protein derivations.

From the discussion of the constituents in the milk and cheese, it is evident that practically all the principal ripening changes are concerned with those taking place in the proteins.

236. Causes of ripening changes.—Authorities disagree as to the exact agents which cause the ripening changes. Some think they are due to the action of the enzymes in the rennet and those secreted in the milk. Others hold that these changes are due entirely to bacterial action. A combination of the two seems probable. The action of the rennet extract renders the casein insoluble and in the ripening process the proteins become soluble, the degree depending on the length of time the cheese is ripened. The amount of water-soluble proteins and protein derivatives is used as a measure of the extent of cheese ripening, considered from a chemical standpoint.

237. Action of the rennet extract.—Some authorities hold that rennet extract contains two enzymes, rennin and pepsin, while others think it is a single peptic ferment. These enzymes produce effects[109] closely related to, if not identical with, those of pepsin in the following particulars: neither the rennet enzyme nor pepsin causes much, if any, proteolytic change except in the presence of acid; the quantitative results of proteolysis furnished by the rennet enzyme and pepsin agree closely, when working on the same material under comparable conditions; the classes of soluble nitrogen compounds formed by the two enzymes are the same, both

[108] Van Slyke, L. L., and E. B. Hart, Some of the compounds present in American Cheddar cheese, N. Y. (Geneva) Exp. Sta. Bul. 219, 1902.

[109] Van Slyke, L. L., et al., Action of rennin or casein, N. Y. (Geneva) Exp. Sta. Tech. Bul. 31, 1913.

Van Slyke, L. L., et al., Cheese ripening investigations; rennet enzyme as a factor in cheese ripening, N. Y. (Geneva) Exp. Sta. Bul. 233, 1903.

quantitatively and qualitatively; neither enzyme forms any considerable amount of amido compounds and neither produces any ammonia; the soluble nitrogen compounds formed by both enzymes are confined to the group of compounds known as paranuclein, caseoses and peptones.

Rennet exerts a digestive effect on the casein[110] which is intensified by the development of acid in the curd. The soluble nitrogenous products formed in Cheddar cheese by the rennet enzymes are the albumoses and the higher peptones. Experiments show that no flavor develops until the amido acids and ammonia are formed. When the rennet enzymes were the only digesting ferments in the cheese, there was no trace of cheese flavor. This is probably due to the fact that the rennet enzyme changed the casein into caseoses and peptones but did not form amido acids and ammonia. Some authorities[111] think that the enzyme galactase carries the ripening of the protein from this stage. The question arises whether these intermediate compounds must be found before other agents can form the amido acids and ammonia.

TABLE XV[112]

SHOWING THE EFFECT OF DIFFERENT AMOUNTS OF RENEET EXTRACTS ON THE RATE OF FORMATION OF SOLUBLE NITROGEN COMPOUNDS IN CHEESE RIPENING				
QUANTITY OF RENNET ADDED PER 100 LB. OF MILK	PER CENT OF WATER SOLUBLE NITROGEN COMPOUNDS IN THE CHEESE			
	Initial	32 days	80 days	270 days
2 oz	0.14	0.47	0.68	1.30
2 oz	0.14	0.47	0.68	1.30
4 oz	0.16	0.75	1.13	1.74
8 oz	0.16	0.90	1.50	1.97
16 oz	0.14	1.26	1.70	2.04

The above table shows that the more rennet extract used the faster the cheese cures, measured by the amount of water-soluble nitrogen compounds formed in the cheese.

238. The action of the bacteria.—Authorities[113] disagree as to the groups of bacteria found in Cheddar cheese. This may be due to lack of proper classification. Some of the groups are: *Bacterium lactis acidi, B. coli communis, B. lactis aerogenes, B.*

[110] Bosworth, A. W., Studies relating to the chemistry of milk and casein, N. Y. (Geneva) Exp. Sta. Tech. Bul. 37, 1914.

[111] Wis. Exp. Sta. Rept. 1898, Distribution of galactase in milk from different sources, pages 87-97.

Wis. Exp. Sta. Rept. 1903, pages 195-197, 201-205, 222-223, Action of proteolytic ferments on milk.

[112] Wis. Exp. Sta. Rept. 1900, pages 102-122.

[113] Harding, H. A., and M. J. Prucha, The bacterial flora of Cheddar cheese, N. Y. (Geneva) Exp. Sta. Tech. Bul. 8.

casei, Streptococci, *B*.[114] *Bulgaricum* and Micrococci. Authorities agree that the *B. lactis acidi* group is the most prominent. This group makes up 90 per cent or more of the total bacteria flora of the cheese in the early stages of ripening. In the course of a few weeks, however, this group is largely replaced by the *B. casei* group.[115]

TABLE XVI

Showing the Number of Bacteria to a Gram in Cheddar Cheese as Determined by Lactose-Agar Plate Cultures				
Time of Plating	Cheese Number			
	580.	581.	582.	583.
Milk	8,000,000	500,000	700,000	500,000
Curd at salting time	160,000,000	326,000,000	912,000,000	839,000,000
12 hours	332,000,000	1,048,000,000	623,000,000	965,000,000
1 day	586,000,000	736,000,000	709,000,000	569,000,000
2 days	235,000,000	405,000,000	848,000,000	580,000,000
4 days	235,000,000	405,000,000	848,000,000	580,000,000
6 days	165,000,000	184,000,000	853,000,000	184,000,000
14 days	51,000,000	211,000,000	369,000,000	401,000,000
21 days	284,000,000	290,000,000	348,000,000	319,000,000
28 days	285,000,000	453,000,000	314,000,000	144,000,000
35 days	104,000,000	261,000,000	326,000,000	504,000,000
49 days	132,000,000	228,000,000	436,000,000	661,000,000
70 days	128,000,000	291,000,000	193,000,000	168,000,000
98 days	114,000,000	212,000,000	45,000,000	55,000,000

FROM WIS. BUL. 150.

The large number of bacteria in the cheese is very striking. The number as given in the accompanying table is not that actually in the cheese, as it is very difficult to obtain the sample in suitable condition for plating.[116]

The principal action of the lactic acid-forming bacteria in the cheese ripening is the changing of the milk-sugar or lactose into lactic acid and the formation of small amounts of other substances, such as acetic, succinic and formic acids, alcohol, aldehydes and esters and some gases, carbon dioxide and hydrogen. While the amount of these substances other than lactic acid is small, it is thought that the

[114] Bacterium, Bacillus and Lactobacillus are preferred by different authors as generic placing of the Bulgarian sour milk species.

[115] Hastings, E. G., Alice C. Evans and E. B. Hart, The bacteriology of Cheddar cheese, Wis. Exp. Sta. Bul. 150, pages 1-52, 1912.

[116] Harding, H. A., The rôle of the lactic acid bacteria in the manufacture and in the early stages of ripening of Cheddar cheese, N. Y. (Geneva) Exp. Sta. Bul. 237, 1903.

effect of these on the cheese may be important. Heinemann shows[117] that lactic acid exists in two optical modifications, the levorotatory and dextrorotary acids. In cheese they are usually found in the inactive or racemic form, the levorotatory and dextrorotary acids being present in equal amounts. What importance the question of optical activity of the lactic acid may assume is not definitely known. Just as some groups of bacteria have a specific effect on the lactose, producing only one modification of lactic acid, so bacteria attacking lactic acid may exercise a selective action and use only one or the other optically active modification. In other words, the early flora of cheese-ripening bacteria may determine the later flora by the production of a form of lactic acid attacked by one group of bacteria and not by another, and the effect on the flavor will differ accordingly. The amount of lactic acid in the cheese increases for a time, then decreases.

The errors in determining lactic acid are considerable. It seems that the tendency is toward an increase of lactic acid in the cheese long after the lactose has disappeared. Two explanations are offered: one, that in the lactic acid fermentation an intermediate compound or compounds are formed which exist for some time, the conversion into lactic acid being complete at about three months; the other is that lactic acid is formed as a product of paracasein proteolysis.

The lactic acid formed in cheese ripening does not exist in a free state but reacts with the calcium salts in the cheese and forms calcium lactates. It is thought that there is sufficient of these salts to neutralize all the acid formed, and therefore the acid does not enter into combination with the paracasein salts. It has been found that lactates are the principal source of acetic and propionic acids. These are supposed to have some effect on the flavor of the cheese.

The effect of lactic acid as a determinant of bacterial and enzymic changes is very important. Early in the ripening process, lactic acid suppresses the growth of undesirable micro-organisms. It also furnishes the acid medium necessary for the best action of both the coagulating and peptic enzymes.

The importance of the lactic acid bacteria in cheese ripening has been summed up by Hastings[118] as follows: "The functions of this group of bacteria in Cheddar cheese are through their by-product lactic acid as follows: (*a*) To favor the curdling of milk by rennet. (*b*) The bacteria of the milk are held in great part in the curd. Through the acid they influence the shrinkage of the curd and expulsion of the whey, (*c*) The acid so changes the nature of the curd as to cause 'matting,' or 'cheddaring' of the curd, (*d*) The acid activates the pepsin of the rennet extract, (*e*) The acid prevents the growth of putrefactive bacteria in the cheese. (*f*) It has been shown that *Bacterium lactis acidi* is able to form acid in the absence of the living cell. (*g*) The development of *Bacterium lactis acidi* is followed by the growth of another group of acid-forming bacteria, the *Bacillus Bulgaricus* group. They reach numbers comparable with those of the first group, reaching their maximum number within the first month of ripening. Since they develop after the fermentation of

[117] Heinemann, P. G., The kinds of lactic acid produced by lactic acid bacteria, Jour. Biol. Chem., Vol. 2, pages 603-608.

[118] Hastings, E. G., et al., The bacteriology of Cheddar cheese, U. S. Dept. Agr. Bur. An. Ind. Bul. 150, 1912.

the milk-sugar, they must have some other source of carbon and of energy than milk-sugar." It is also probable that other groups constantly present contribute to the changes.

From the preceding discussion it is evident that each of the ripening agents has its important part to play in the ripening process and a normal ripening of the cheese is a composite result of these various agencies.

239. Conditions affecting the rate of cheese ripening.—The rate at which these agents cause ripening of the cheese depends on several factors.[119] Most of these factors are within the control of man. They are as follows: the length of time; temperature of the curing-room; moisture-content of the cheese; size of the cheese; the quantity of salt used; the amount of rennet; the influence of acid.

240. The length of time.—The water-soluble nitrogen compounds increase as the cheese ages, other conditions being uniform. The rate of increase is not uniform; it is much more rapid in the early than in the succeeding stages of ripening.

241. The temperature of the curing-room.—Very few cheese factories have made any provision for regulating the temperature of the curing-room. Without such provision the temperature follows closely that of the outside air. In some cases the curing-room is located over the boiler-room and hence becomes very hot. In the cheese warehouses, provision has been made to control the temperature very closely. Experiments show that the soluble nitrogen compounds increase, on the average, closely in proportion to an increase of temperature, when the other conditions are uniform.

The temperature of the curing-room has a material effect on the quality of the cheese. Cheese made from the same day's milk, and part cured at 40° F., part at 50° F., part at 60° F. show considerable differences, the greatest seeming to be in the flavor and texture. Those kept at the low temperature cure more slowly and develop a milder flavor, those at the higher temperature cure faster and develop undesirable flavors. At the higher temperature the undesirable organisms seem to be more active. Some very skillful makers and judges of cheese have always contended that if Cheddar is properly made, firmed to the body and texture of a high-class cheese, ripening at 55 to 60° F. gives a higher quality. Such a cheese must be low in moisture, perhaps 3 to 5 per cent lower than one cured successfully by the cold process.

The following tables[120] XVII, XVIII show the effect of different temperatures of curing cheese on the total score and on the points of the flavor, body and texture:

---

[119] Van Slyke, L. L., and E. B. Hart, Conditions affecting chemical changes in cheese ripening, N. Y. (Geneva) Exp. Sta. Bul. 236, 1903.

[120] Van Slyke, L. L., et al., Cheese ripening at low temperatures, N. Y. (Geneva) Exp. Sta. Bul. 234, 1903.

TABLE XVII

TABLE SHOWING THE RELATION OF TEMPERATURE OF
CURING TO TOTAL SCORES

TIME OF PLATING	CHEESE NUMBER
40°	95.7
50°	94,2
60°	91.7

TABLE XVIII

TABLE SHOWING THE RELATION OF TEMPERATURE OF CURING
TO SCORE OF BODY AND TEXTURE, AND FLAVOR

TEMPERATURE OF CURING	40° F.	50° F.	60° F.
Body and texture	23.4	32.0	22.2
Flavor	47.4	46.4	44.8

Of the three temperatures of curing, the lowest gave a higher total score and a higher score for flavor, body and texture.

The curing temperature should not go low enough to freeze the cheese, as this lowers the quality. The cheese will cure very slowly and have a mealy texture.

242. Moisture-content of the cheese.—Other conditions being equal, there is a larger amount of water-soluble nitrogen compounds in cheese containing more moisture than in that containing less moisture. Therefore, a high moisture-content of the cheese causes it to cure faster. The presence of moisture also serves to dilute the fermentation products which otherwise would accumulate and thus check the action of the ripening agents.

243. The size of the cheese.—Cheeses of large size usually cure faster than smaller ones, under the same conditions. This is due to the fact that the large cheeses lose their moisture less rapidly by evaporation and therefore after the early period of ripening have a higher water-content.

244. The amount of salt.—The relation of salt to the rate of ripening is more or less directly associated with the moisture-content of the cheese, since an increase in the amount of salt decreases the moisture. Thus, cheese containing more salt forms water-soluble nitrogen compounds more slowly than that containing less salt. The salt also has a direct effect in retarding one or more of the ripening agents.

245. The amount of rennet extract.—The use of increased amounts of rennet extract in cheese-making, other conditions being uniform, results in the production of increased quantities of soluble nitrogen compounds in a given period of time, especially such compounds as paranuclein, caseoses and peptones.

246. The influence of acid.—It is necessary that acid be present but the exact relation of varying quantities of acid to the chemical changes of the ripening process is not fully known. If too much acid is present, it imparts a sour taste to the cheese. It also causes the texture of the cheese to be mealy or sandy instead of smooth and waxy.

Conditions that may increase the rate of ripening:

1. Increase of temperature.
2. Larger amounts of rennet.
3. More moisture in the cheese.
4. Less salt.
5. Large size of the cheese.
6. Moderate amount of acid.

Conditions that may retard ripening:

1. Decrease of temperature.
2. Smaller amounts of rennet.
3. Less moisture in the cheese.
4. More salt.
5. Small size of the cheese.
6. No acid or an excess of acid.

247. Care of the cheese in the curing-room. — The cheeses need daily attention while in the curing-room (Fig. 53). They should be turned every day to prevent sticking and molding to the shelf and to secure an even evaporation of moisture. If not turned, the moisture will not evaporate evenly from all surfaces and will result in an uneven distribution in the cheese, which causes uneven curing, and usually gives the product an uneven color.

The surface of the cheese should be watched to see that the cloths stick. If they do not, the surface will crack, due to the evaporation of the moisture. If the cloths are loosened, they should be removed and the surface of the cheese greased with butter. The grease will tend to prevent the rind from cracking. If the surface of the cheese is not smooth, due to wrinkles in the bandage, or if it cracks, due to the lack of cloths, it furnishes the opportunity for insects to lay their eggs and the larvæ to develop within the cheese. Molds also lodge and grow in such cracks.

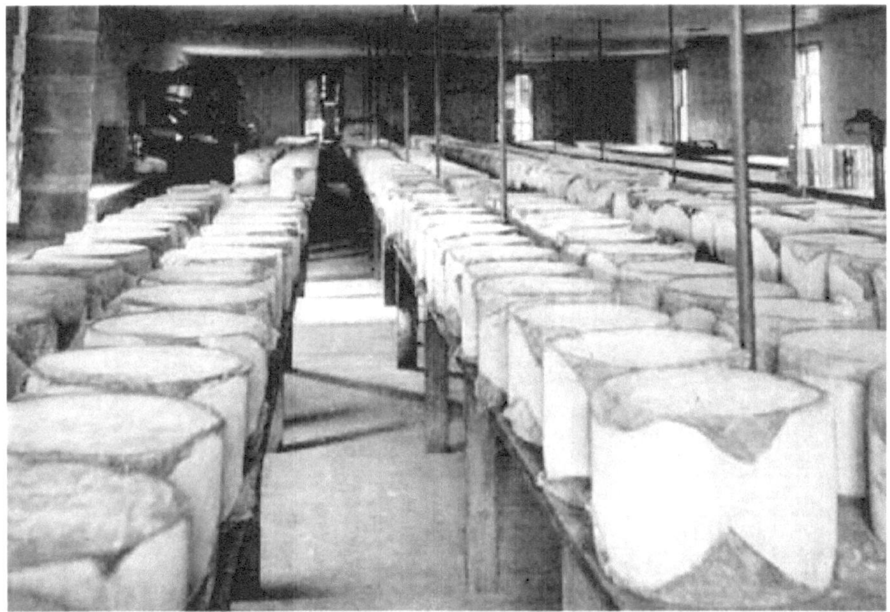

Fig. 53.—Cheddar cheese curing-room.

The cheese should be kept clean while in the curing-room. This means that the hands of the person handling the cheese must be clean. The shelves should be washed with good cleaning solution and scalded with hot water whenever they become greasy or moldy.

Some means should be provided for regulating the temperature and humidity of the curing-room. In most factories this is accomplished by opening the doors and windows at night to admit the cool air and closing them in the morning to keep out the hot air. Care should be taken to keep the doors and windows closely secured. The windows should have shades to keep out the sun. If the room becomes too dry, the floor may be dampened with cold water.

The length of time in the curing-room depends on how often shipment is made to some central warehouse or to the market. This usually varies from two to six weeks.

When the surface of the cheese becomes dry and the rind is well formed, the cheese may be paraffined. It usually requires four to six days after cheeses are taken from the hoop before they are ready for this process. The object of paraffining is to prevent the escape of moisture and to keep the cheese from molding.

248. Evaporation of moisture from the cheese during ripening.—The losses due to evaporation while the cheeses are curing are a considerable item. The rate of evaporation depends on the temperature and humidity of the curing-room, the size of the cheese, the moisture-content and protection to the surface.

Table XIX[121] shows the effect of size of cheese and temperature of the curing-room, on losses while curing. This table shows that the evaporation of moisture is more as the size of the cheese decreases and the temperature is increased. This is probably due to the fact that the smaller cheese has more surface to a pound than a large cheese. The evaporation increases with temperature, probably because of lowered relative humidity. The humidity can be tested with an hygrometer.

TABLE XIX

SHOWING THE VARIATION OF LOSSES IN WEIGHT OF CHEDDAR CHEESE WHILE CURING, DUE TO SIZE OF CHEESE AND TEMPERATURE OF CURING-ROOM			
WEIGHT OF CHEESE IN POUNDS	WEIGHT LOST PER 100 POUNDS OF CHEESE IN 20 WEEKS AT		
	40° F.	50° F.	60° F.
70	2.5	2.4	4.2
45	2.7	3.7	5.1
35	3.9	5.9	8.5
12½	4.6	8.1	12.0

The higher the moisture-content of the cheese, usually the more rapid is the evaporation. This is due to several causes: there is more moisture to evaporate; the moisture is not so well incorporated; a moist cheese does not form so good a rind.

249.Paraffining[122] consists of dipping the cheese in melted paraffin at a temperature of about 220° F. for six seconds. Fig. 54 shows an apparatus for paraffining. This leaves a very thin coat of paraffin on the cheese; at a lower temperature, a thicker coat would be left. The thicker coating is more liable to crack and peel off. If the cheese is not perfectly dry before it is treated, the paraffin will blister and crack off.

Before a cheese is paraffined, the press cloth is removed and also the starched circles, if loose. After a cheese has been paraffined, if the coating is not broken, the loss due to evaporation is greatly reduced. The amount of paraffin to coat a 35-pound cheese will depend on the temperature of the paraffin and the length of time the cheese is immersed. Usually at 220° F. it requires about 0.15 of a pound for each 35-pound cheese. After the cheeses have been paraffined, they may be left on the curing-room shelves or boxed ready to ship.

[121] Van Slyke, L. L., et al., Cheese ripening at low temperatures, N. Y. (Geneva) Exp. Sta. Bul. 234, 1903.

[122] Doane, C. F., Methods and results of paraffining cheese, U. S. Dept. Agr. Bur. An. Ind. Circ. 181, pages 1-16, 1911.

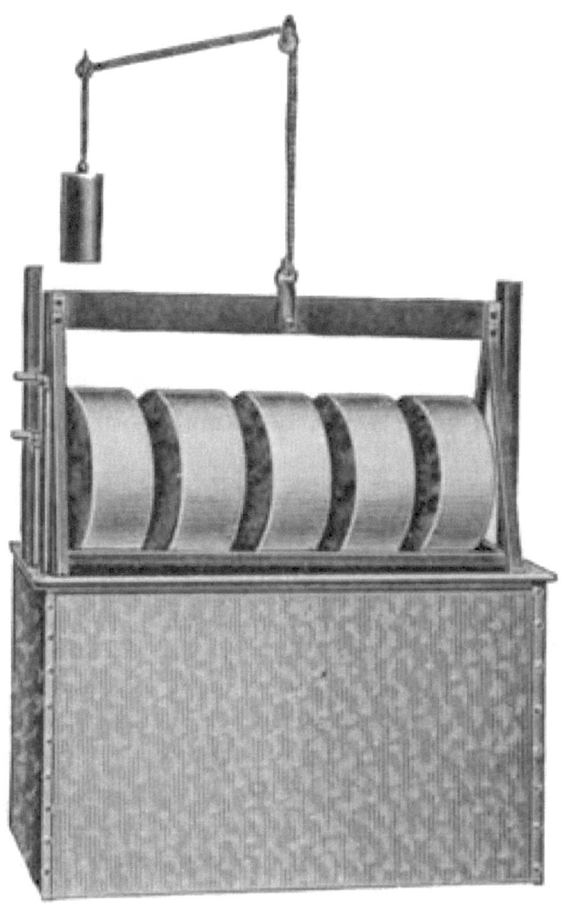

Fig. 54.—A paraffiner for cheese.

250. Shipping.—When ready to ship, each cheese should be carefully and accurately weighed and boxed. Usually these cheeses are boxed after being paraffined. If press cloths are left on the cheese in the curing-room, they should be removed just before weighing. These cloths should not be left in a pile in the factory after being removed as they have been known to heat and sometimes cause fires. They should be washed clean and dried ready for use again. If starched circles are used, they should be left on the cheese. A scale board should be placed on each end of the cheese to prevent its sticking to the box and also to keep the box from wearing the surface of the cheese.

The box should be a trifle larger in diameter than the cheese so that the latter can be easily placed in it. The sides of the box should be the same height as the cheese.

The weight of each cheese should be neatly and accurately marked on each box. Care should be exercised to keep the boxes clean.

DEFECTS IN CHEDDAR CHEESE

A great number of defects may occur in Cheddar cheese. Certain of these are due to known causes and proper remedies are definable, while neither cause nor remedy has been found for other defects. Some of the common defects and their causes and remedies are discussed under different headings of the score-card as: defects in flavor, their causes and remedies; defects in body and texture, their causes and remedies; defects in color, their causes and remedies; defects in finish and their causes and remedies.

251. Defects in flavor.—Any flavor differing from the characteristic Cheddar cheese is a defect. Certain of these defective flavors can be recognized and causes and remedies given for them, while others may be distinguished as such but no cause or remedy can be given.

252. Feedy flavors.—Flavors may be characteristic of certain feeding stuffs. Feeding strong-flavored foods, such as turnips, cabbage, decayed silage, certain weeds and sometimes rank green feed, give their peculiar flavors to both milk and cheese. Freshly drawn milk usually absorbs these odors from the air in barns filled with such foods. Certain of these materials may be fed just after milking in moderate amounts without affecting the milk drawn at the next milking. Others should not be used. Milk should not be exposed to strong volatile odors. Some of the objectionable odors may be removed by airing the curd for a longer time after milling before the salt is applied.

253. Acid flavors.—A cheese with an acid flavor has a pronounced sour smell and taste. This is caused by the over-development of acid which may be due to any of the following causes: (*a*) receiving milk at the factory which is sour or has too high development of acid; (*b*) using too much starter; (*c*) ripening the milk too much before adding rennet; (*d*) not firming the curd sufficiently in the whey before removing the latter; (*e*) developing too much acid in the whey before it is removed; (*f*) retaining too much moisture in the curd.

The trouble can be reduced or eliminated by one or more of the following precautions: (*a*) receiving only clean, sweet milk at the cheese factory; (*b*) maintaining the proper relation between the moisture and acidity; (*c*) adding the rennet at the proper acidity; (*d*) using less starter; (*e*) adding the rennet extract so that there will be sufficient time to firm the curd before the acid has developed to such a stage that it will be necessary to draw the whey; (*f*) producing the proper final water-content in the newly made cheese.

254. Sweet or fruity flavors.—These are the sweet flavors characteristic of strawberry, raspberry and the like. Such flavors are very objectionable and usually increase with the age of the cheese. They appear to be caused by: (*a*) carrying both milk and whey in the same cans without properly cleaning them; (*b*) exposing milk near hog-pens where whey is fed; (*c*) dirty whey tanks at the cheese factory; (*d*) micro-organisms which get into the milk through any unclean conditions.

These troubles can be controlled: (*a*) if milk and whey must be carried in the same cans, the cans should be emptied immediately on arrival at the farm and thoroughly washed and scalded; (*b*) the whey vat at the factory should be kept clean and sweet; (*c*) the starter must have the proper clean flavor.

Other defects may be classed as "off flavors," "dirty flavors," "bitter flavors" and the like. These are undoubtedly due to unsanitary conditions whereby undesirable organisms get into the milk, even though the particular organism is often not determined. The flavors may be improved by the use of a clean-flavored commercial starter and by airing the curd after milling before salting. The best remedy is to remove the source of the difficulty.

255. Defects in body and texture.—The body and texture should be close. A sample rubbed between the thumb and fingers should be smooth and waxy. Any condition which causes a body and texture other than this is to be avoided.

256. Loose or open texture.—A cheese with this defect is full of irregularly shaped holes and usually soft or weak-bodied. This is serious if the cheese is to be held for some time. Moisture and fat are likely to collect in these holes and cause the cheese to deteriorate, thereby shortening its commercial life.

Several causes may bring about this condition: (*a*) insufficient cheddaring; (*b*) pressing at too high a temperature; (*c*) inadequate pressing; (*d*) development of too little acid.

The corresponding remedies are: (*a*) cheddar the curd until the holes are closed and the curd is solid; (*b*) cool the curd to 80° F. before putting to press; (*c*) press the curd longer, possibly twenty-four to twenty-six hours; (*d*) develop a little higher acid in the whey before removing the curd.

257. Dry body.—A cheese with this defect is usually firm, hard and dry, sometimes rubbery or corky. This may result from lack of moisture, fat or both, and may be due to the following causes: (*a*) making the cheese from partly skimmed-milk; (*b*) heating the curd in the whey for too long a time; (*c*) heating the curd too high; (*d*) stirring the curd too much in the whey or as the last of the whey is removed; (*e*) using too much salt; (*f*) developing of too much acid in the whey; (*g*) curing the cheese in too hot or too dry a curing-room; (*h*) not piling the curd high or fast enough in the cheddaring process.

The cause should be located and the corresponding remedy found, as follows: (*a*) make cheese only from whole milk; (*b*) draw the whey sooner; (*c*) firm the curd at as low temperature as possible in the whey; (*d*) stir the curd in the whey only enough to keep the curd particles separated but do not hand-stir it; (*e*) use less salt; (*f*) develop less acid in the whey; (*g*) cure the cheese in a cool moist curing-room; (*h*) pile the curd sooner and higher during the cheddaring process.

The number of causes which may singly or in combination produce dry cheese demands experience and technical skill that calls for the development of a high degree of judgment.

258. Gassy textured cheese.—Gassy cheese has large numbers of very small round or slightly flattened holes. When round these are called "pin-holes," and when slightly flattened "fish eye" openings. These are due to the formation of gas by the micro-organisms in the cheese. When a cheese is gassy, it usually puffs up from gas pressure as in the rising of bread. If enough gas is formed, it will cause the cheese to break or crack open. Instead of being flat on the ends, such a cheese becomes so nearly spherical as to roll from the shelf at times.

The gas-producing organisms enter because of unclean conditions somewhere in the handling of the milk and the making of the cheese. Some of the common sources of gas organisms are: (*a*) unclean milkers; (*b*) dirty cows; (*c*) aërating the milk in impure air, especially air from hog-pens where the whey is fed; (*d*) allowing the cows to wade in stagnant water or in mud or in filthy barnyards and then not thoroughly cleaning the cows before milking; (*e*) exposing the milk to the dust from hay and feed; (*f*) dirty whey tanks; (*g*) drawing milk and whey in the same cans without afterward thoroughly washing them; (*h*) unclean utensils in the factory; (*i*) using gassy starter; (*j*) ripening cheese at high temperatures.

Some of these causes are within the control of the cheese-maker after the making process is begun. Many of them are avoided only by eternal vigilance. Among the recommendations for meeting gassy curd are the following: use only milk produced under clean sanitary conditions; use a clean commercial starter.

If gas is suspected in the milk, a larger percentage of commercial starter should be used. More acid must be developed before the whey is removed. If the gas shows while cheddaring, the curd should be piled and repiled until the holes flatten out before milling.

The curd should be kept warm during the piling or cheddaring process. This may be accomplished by covering the vat and setting a pail or two of hot water in it. After milling, the curd should be stirred and aired for a considerable length of time before salting. This will aërate the curd and allow it to cool. The cheese should then be placed in a cool curing-room. (See handling of gassy milk.)

259. Acidy, pasty or soft body and texture.—A cheese with acidy body may be either hard and dry or soft and moist. It has a mealy or sandy feeling when rubbed between the fingers. The causes and remedies are the same as for cheeses with acid flavors. When rubbed between the fingers, it is pasty and sticks to the fingers. It is caused by the cheese containing too much water. (See control of moisture.)

260. Defects in color.—Any color which is not uniform is a defect. The proper color depends on the market requirement. Some markets prefer a white and others a yellow cheese; however, if the color is uniform, it is not defective.

Mottled color is a spotted or variegated marking of the cheese. Several causes may give the same general effect: (*a*) uneven distribution of moisture, the curd having extra moisture being lighter in color; (*b*) neglecting to strain the starter; (*c*) adding the starter after the cheese color has been added; (*d*) mixing the curd from different vats.

Remedies for this mottled color are: (*a*) to maintain a uniform assimilation of moisture (see discussion of moisture); (*b*) to strain the starter to break up the lumps before adding to the milk; (*c*) to add all of the starter before adding the cheese color; (*d*) not to mix curds from different vats.

Seamy color. —In "seamy" colored cheese, the outline of each piece of curd may be seen. There is usually a line where the surfaces of the curd come together. It may be caused by the pieces of curd becoming greasy or so cold that they will not cement. This may be remedied by having the curd at a temperature of 80° to 85° F. when put to press. If it is greasy, this may be removed by washing the curd in cold water.

Acid color. —This is a bleached or faded color and is caused by the development of too much acid. (See acid flavor for causes and remedies, page 266.)

261. Defects in finish. —Defects of this class differ from those previously mentioned in being entirely within the control of the cheese-maker. All are due to carelessness or lack of skill in manipulation. Anything which detracts from the neat, clean, workmanlike appearance of the cheese is a defect that may interfere with the sale of an article intrinsically good. Some of the common defects are: (*a*) unclean surfaces or dirty cheese; (*b*) cracked rinds; (*c*) moldy surfaces; (*d*) uneven sizes; (*e*) cracked cheese; (*f*) wrinkled bandages; (*g*) uneven edges.

CHEDDAR CHEESE JUDGING

Judging of cheese is the comparison of the qualities of one product with those of another. To make this easier it is customary to reduce the qualities of the cheese to a numerical basis. This is accomplished by the use of a score-card, which recognizes certain qualities and gives to each a numerical value. Each of these score-cards gives a perfect cheese a numerical score of 100. Two score-cards are used to judge cheese, one for export and the other for home-trade product. The latter is more commonly used.

Export Score-card		Home-trade Score-card	
Flavor	45	Flavor	50
Body and texture	30	Body and texture	25
Color	15	Color	15
Finish	10	Finish	10
	— —		— —
Total	100	Total	100

The same qualities are recognized in each score-card, but different numerical values are given them.

262. Securing the sample. —The sample of cheese to be examined is best obtained by means of a cheese-trier (Fig. 55). This is a piece of steel about five or six inches long fitted with a suitable handle. It is semicircular in shape, about ½ to ¾ of an inch in diameter. The edges and end are sharpened to aid in cutting. This is inserted into the cheese and turned around and then drawn out. It removes a long cylinder of cheese, commonly called a "plug." This plug should be drawn from the top rather than from the side of the cheese, because when the bandage is cut it often splits, due to the pressure against it and so exposes the cheese.

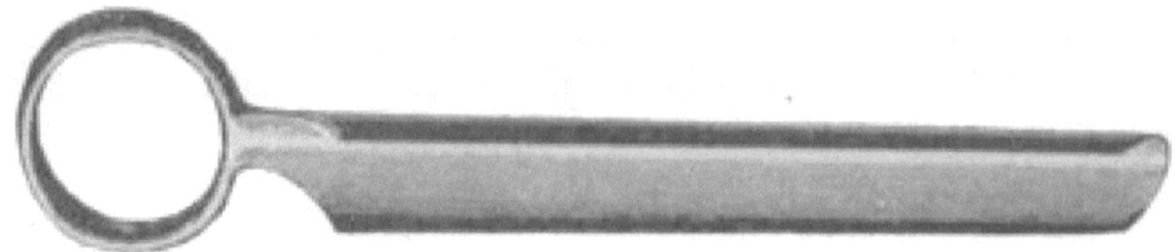

Fig. 55.—A cheese-trier.

263. How to determine quality.—As soon as the plug has been removed, it should be passed quickly under the nose to detect any volatile odors which are liable to leave the cheese quickly. Next, the compactness of the plug should be noticed and the color carefully examined. Then the outer end of the plug should be broken off and placed back in the cheese in the hole made by the trier. It should be about an inch long and pushed in so that the surface of the cheese is smooth. This prevents mold and insects entering the cheese. Usually the cheese will mold after a short time where the plug has been removed. The remainder of the plug should be saved for determining the flavor and the body and texture.

The flavor can be determined by the first odor obtained from the cheese on the trier and by mixing or crushing a piece of the plug between the thumb and fore-finger and then noting the odor. Mixing and thoroughly warming causes the odor to be much more pronounced. The cheese should seldom be tasted to determine the flavor, for when many are to be judged, they all taste alike after the first five or six. This is probably due to the cheese adhering to the teeth, tongue and other parts of the mouth, making it difficult to cleanse the mouth sufficiently. The body and texture can be determined by the appearance and the feeling of the cheese when rubbed between the thumb and fingers. The body and texture are distinct, yet they are more or less interchanged. The body refers to the cheese as a whole and the texture to the arrangement of the parts of the whole. The openness of texture or the holes can be noted when the plug is first removed. The firmness of body and smoothness of texture can be determined when the cheese is rubbed between the thumb and fingers. The color can be judged when the plug is first removed. The finish or appearance may be noted either before or after the other qualities by carefully examining the cheese.

Cheddar cheese should have a neat, clean, attractive appearance; when cut it should show a close, solid, uniformly colored interior. It should have a clear, pleasant, mild aroma and a nutty flavor. It should possess a mellow, silky, meaty texture and when rubbed between the thumb and fore-finger should be smooth and free from hard particles.

CHEESE SCORE-CARD

Sample.. *Date*..

	SCORE		REMARKS
Flavor...........	50	....	
Body and Texture....	25	....	
Color...........	15	....	
Finish...........	10	....	
Total...........	100	....	

Recommendations..

....

....

....

....

....

....

....

Name of Judge..

SUGGESTIVE TERMS

FLAVOR
Desirable

Clean   Pleasant Aroma   Nutty Flavor

Undesirable

Due to Farm Conditions

Weedy Feedy Cowy Old Milk Bitter

Due to Factory Conditions

Too much acid   Too little acid

Due to either Farm or Factory Conditions

Yeasty   Fruity   Fishy   Rancid
Sour   Bitter   Sweet   Tainted

BODY AND TEXTURE
Desirable

Smooth   Waxy   Silky   Close

Undesirable

Pasty Greasy Curdy Mealy Lumpy
Corky   Loose   Gassy   Yeasty
Acidy   Sweet   Watery   Too dry

COLOR
Desirable

Uniform

Undesirable

Streaked   Mottled   Acid cut
White specks   Wavy   Too high
Seamy   Rust spots   Too light

FINISH
Desirable

Clean surfaces Neat bandage Attractive

Undesirable

Wrinkled bandage   Greasy
Unclean surfaces   No end caps
Cracked rinds   Uneven edges
Undesirable size

264. Causes of variations in score.—It is very seldom, if ever, that a cheese is given a perfect score, for it usually has one or more defects which may be hardly noticeable or very pronounced. The seriousness of the defect is determined by the individual tastes of the judges and the market requirements. It is customary for the judge to pick out several samples and score them in order to fix the standard and if there are several judges this serves to unify their standard. Ordinarily judges will vary because of their individual tastes, unless they begin with a uniform standard.

Certain markets require cheese with given qualities which on other markets would be considered defects. For example, the Boston market requires a very soft, pasty cheese which other markets would consider undesirable.

The cheese is constantly undergoing changes due to the ripening agents so that it may not always be scored the same. For example, a cheese may have little or no flavor and after several weeks a very considerable flavor may have developed. This is probably due to the action of the ripening agents, and therefore the second time it would be scored differently.

265. The score-card.—When judging several samples of cheese, the type of score-card on the opposite page is used for each one.

This gives the date of judging and the sample number, the judge's name and reasons for cutting the score and recommendations to avoid these troubles.

CHAPTER XV

THE SWISS AND ITALIAN GROUPS

Swiss cheese: The Swiss factory; The milk; Rennet extract; Starter; The
making process; Curing Swiss; Block Swiss; Shipment; Qualities
of Swiss cheese; Composition and yield; The Italian group: Parmesan; Regianito.

Certain varieties of hard cheese of foreign origin are now made to some extent
in this country. If not manufactured in sufficient quantities to supply the demand,
the remainder is imported. These hard cheeses are now considered.

SWISS CHEESE

Swiss cheese, variously known as Gruyère, Emmenthal, Schweitzer and Swiss,
had its origin in the Alpine cantons of Switzerland. From this region its manufacture has been carried by Swiss dairy-men and emigrant farmers into widely separate lands. The Swiss colonies settled in the United States in the Mohawk Valley
and in Cattaraugus County, New York; in Wayne, Stark, Summit, Columbiana and
Tuscarawas counties of Ohio, and in Green and Dodge counties in Wisconsin. Of
all these, the Wisconsin colonies have become the most extensive. Similar colonies
have developed the making of this type of cheese in Sweden and Finland.

266. The Swiss factory.—Swiss cheese cannot be made in a vat like other types
for reasons that will be explained later. In place of the vat is used a kettle, generally
of copper, and it may or may not be jacketed for steam or for hot water (Fig. 56).
These kettles vary in capacity from 600 to 3000 pounds of milk. The cheese-maker
takes the best care possible of his kettle, for an unclean utensil is one of the easiest
sources of contamination of the milk. When the kettle is not jacketed, and it is only
in recent years that this has been done, it is suspended in a fireplace by means of
a crane arrangement.

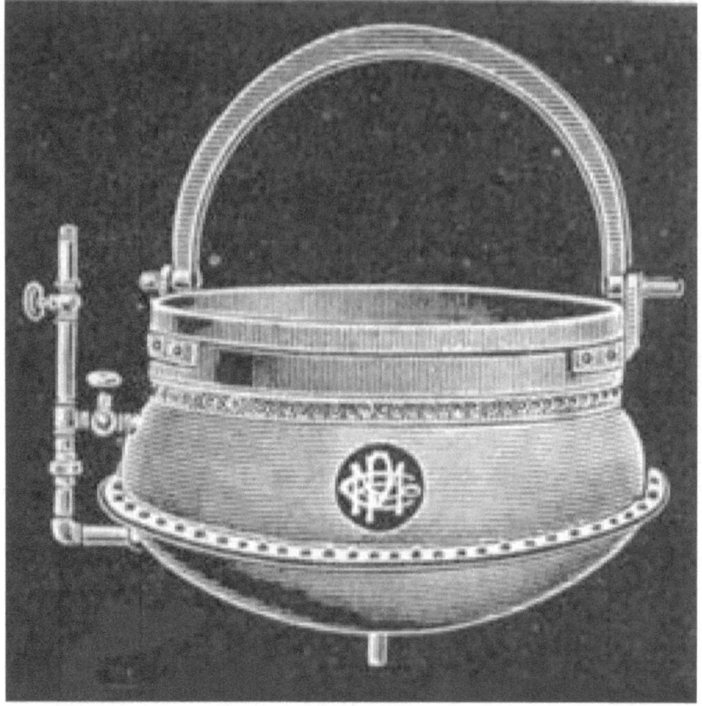

Fig. 56.—Swiss-cheese kettle.

This fireplace uses wood, and is built of brick or stone, so that the kettle rests on the edge and is provided with a door which swings upon another crane, and can be closed while the fire is going. When the kettle is swung on a crane, it is possible to swing it under the weigh-stand for filling. This requires a lid to swing down over the fire, and keep the room free from smoke. The chimney generally has a rather high stack to secure a good draft. This kettle is fastened to the crane by a large iron band passing around the neck, to which a bail or handle is attached. The kettle may be raised or lowered by means of a simple screw on this beam. The crane consists of a heavy beam working in sockets in the floor and a beam or cross brace, which has another and shorter beam braced to it, to take the weight of the kettle.

The weigh-stand, and its efficient location, is a matter of extreme importance. It is elevated a little above the remainder of the floor to allow gravity to do the work. The next most important equipment is the press and draining table. The table is made of wood or stone, and has a slight slope to allow the whey to drain off. The press is generally a jack screw which, braced against a beam, will exert an enormous pressure on the table below.

Swiss cheeses are made in two styles, the "round" or drum and the "block" or rectangular forms, each of which has its advantages. For the round style, which is most commonly made, the forms for hooping are of metal or of elm wood, and consist of strips of a given width, generally six inches, but of an undetermined length. These strips are then made into a circle and held by a cord, which is easily lengthened or shortened, thus varying the diameter of the hoop.

Besides these hoops, cheese boards or followers are needed. These are heavy circular boards, of a size to fit that of the cheese generally made, and are banded with iron around the edge and cross-braced on the bottom for rigidity. The small tools of the factory consist of knives to cut the curd, and of a "Swiss harp" or other similar tool to stir the curd. Many clean bandages are also needed, and a kettle brake.

267. The milk.—Swiss cheese requires clean sweet milk. Dirt, high acid and infections with undesirable bacteria involve difficulties of manufacture and frequent losses of cheese. One common practice rejects milk if it shows acidity above 0.15 per cent. To secure milk in this condition, factories are small and located so close to the producing farms as to secure 1000 to 3000 pounds of milk delivered warm from the cow twice a day. The cheese is made twice daily from this fresh milk. If, however, milk is properly cared for, it is possible to mix night's and morning's milk without bad results. In fact, in working experimentally with high grade milk and taking precautions against loss of fat, it has been necessary to skim (separate) part of the milk, thus reducing the ratio of fat to casein. Analysis of good Swiss cheeses shows that the desired texture is more uniformly obtained with milk in which the fat is less than the normal ratio. This assumes that the manufacturing loss is kept down so that the fat removed offsets the extra loss from curd-breaking.

268. Rennet extract.—Most Swiss cheese-makers prefer to make their own rennet extract from the stomach. This results in a product which is not uniform in strength and so requires good judgment to secure the desired coagulation in the allotted time. Some cheese-makers roll fifteen to twenty well salted calves' stomachs together and dry them. From this they cut off a definite amount each day to be soaked for twenty-four hours in two to five quarts of whey at 86° F. Four quarts of this solution added to 2000 pounds of milk at 90° F. should produce a curd ready for cutting in twenty to thirty minutes.

269. Starter.—Makers do not agree as to the use of "starters" for Swiss cheese. Those opposed to such use say that a starter will give the cheese a decided Cheddar flavor, while those in favor of it state that it will control undesirable fermentations, and that, with the use of a starter, it is possible to make Swiss cheese throughout the year, and have uniform success.

Doane,[123] working with *Bacillus Bulgaricus* as a starter, found that these starters did not always overcome the undesirable fermentations. If a cheese-maker is having difficulty to develop the holes or "eyes," this may be overcome by making a starter[124] as follows from good cheese and whey or milk: Select a cheese which has the desirable "eyes" or holes and a good flavor. Grind up some of this and add

[123] Doane, C. F., and E. E. Eldredge, The use of Bacillus Bulgaricus in starters for making Swiss or Emmenthal cheese, Dept. of Agr. Bur. An. Ind. Bul. 148, 1915.

[124] N. Y. Produce Rev. and Am. Creamery, Vol. 37, no. 25, page 1112, Starter for Swiss cheese.

about ¼ of a pound to one gallon of milk or whey. Hold this for twenty-four hours at a warm temperature (85° to 90° F.). Strain it into the vat of milk just before the rennet is added.

270. The making process. — The milk is delivered twice a day without cooling. It usually reaches the factory at a temperature of 92° to 96° F. It is strained into the kettle, and starter and rennet added at the same temperature as received. (For method of adding rennet, see Chapter V.) Enough rennet should be used to give a coagulation ready for cutting in twenty to thirty minutes. The firmness of the curd is tested by inserting the index finger in an oblique position, then raising it slightly and with the thumb of the same hand starting the curd to break or crack. When the curd is coagulated ready for cutting, it will give a clear break over the finger.

It is important to keep the temperature uniform while coagulation is in process, and this is best accomplished by the use of a little pan arrangement which fits into the top of the kettle. When this is full of water at 100° F., the temperature of the air above the milk will be about 90° F. When the curd is ready for cutting, a scoop may be used and the top layer carefully turned under to equalize the temperature more closely.

Cutting the curd. — In some cheese factories, knives resembling Cheddar cheese knives are employed to cut the curd. In other factories, a "Swiss harp" is used to break the curd. The curd is usually cut or broken into pieces about the size of kernels of corn. The practice of "breaking" curd instead of cutting it with sharp curd-knives produces excessive loss at times. Experimental study has shown that the loss of fat may be kept as low as 0.3 per cent if modern curd-knives are substituted for the breaking tool formerly used. Study of Swiss cheeses of all grades supports the opinion that the removal of a small part of fat from usual grades of factory milk produces a better quality of product than the use of rich whole milk. This may be accomplished through the escape of fat in the whey on account of breaking the curd and stirring it vigorously, or by skimming a part of the milk which is then curdled, cut and stirred under such conditions as to minimize the loss of fat.

Cooking the curd. — After cutting, the curd is stirred in the whey for about twenty minutes before the steam is turned on and is then heated to 128° to 135° F. While this heating is in progress, constant stirring must be given to avoid matting. This excessive stirring breaks the curd up into pieces about the size of wheat kernels, and accounts for the large fat loss, which is one of the main sources of loss in making Swiss cheese. This stirring is accomplished by a rotary motion, and the use of a brake, which is a piece of wood closely fitting the side of the kettle. This creates an eddy in the current at that point and gives a more uniform distribution of temperature. The process of cooking takes from thirty to forty minutes, and at the end of that time the degree of toughness may be determined by making a roll of curd in the hand, and noticing the break when it is given a quick flip. A short sharp break indicates the desired toughness.

Draining and hooping. — In this process, the cheese-makers' skill is displayed. With the hoop prepared, and the curd at the correct stage of toughness, the operator takes a press cloth, wets it in whey, slips it over a flexible iron ring which can be made to fit the shape of the kettle, gives the contents of the kettle a few swift revolutions, then suddenly reverses the motion, with the result that the contents form into a cone, and the ring and bandage are dexterously slipped under this cone, and drawn up to the surface of the whey with a rope or chain and pulley. This part of the process is the most important, as a cheese must have a smooth firm rind, else it will quickly crack. With too large a batch of milk, the curd can be cut into two pieces and hooped separately. With the mass of curd at the top of the whey, the piece of perforated iron plate just the size of the hoop is slipped under the mass, and attached to the pulley by four chains. Then the top of the mass is carefully leveled off, because while still in the whey, it cannot mat badly and so tend to develop a rind crack. Now the mass is raised clear of the whey, and run along a short track to the drain table, where it is put in the press.

Pressing.—The mass of curd is dropped into the hoop, the edges of the cloth carefully folded under, and the cloth laid on top, then the pressure is applied, gradually at first, but increasing until the final pressure is about fifteen to twenty pounds to a pound of cheese.

During the first few hours the cloths must be changed frequently, and the cheese carefully turned over each time, to secure a more uniform rind. After a time the changes are less frequent, and at the end of twenty-four hours the cheese is taken to the salting-room.

Salting may be done by either the brine or dry method. To prepare a brine bath, add salt to a tank of water until it will float an egg, and add a pailful or more of salt every few days thereafter to keep up the strength. The cheese is then placed in this bath and left for three to five days, depending on the saltiness desired. As the cheese floats with a little of the rind above the surface, it should be turned a few times to insure uniformity of salting. With dry salting, the salt is rubbed on the cheese by hand or with a stiff brush, and any excess carefully wiped off, leaving only a slight sprinkle on the surface to work into the cheese.

271. Curing Swiss.—From the salting-room, the cheese goes to the first one of two curing-rooms, where the unique process of the development of the characteristic eyes takes place.

During the curing period of either round or block Swiss, constant attention must be paid to the cheese. They must be turned every day at first, and then every second or third day toward the end of the curing period. Also, great care must be taken that no mold starts growing, as it will soon work into the cheese, and spoil its flavor. The best way of preventing mold is by washing the cheese, in either clean or slightly salted water, as often as possible. A stiff brush is mostly used for this.

The development of the "eyes" or holes is the difficult part of the whole process. It is not known exactly what causes the development, but it is attributed to micro-organisms or enzymes. The gas in these eyes has been examined and found to be carbon dioxide and free nitrogen. Sometimes hydrogen is found. This comes from the original fermentation of the milk-sugar and remains to contaminate the normal eye. The nitrogen[125] is included from the original air. Propionic acid is formed at the same time as the eyes, and they are said to be the result of a propionic ferment of lactic acid. The interior of the cheese is anaërobic, due to low permeability and high oxygen-absorbing quality. This propionic bacterium cannot, however, account for all the carbon dioxide produced.

After the eyes have started, their further development depends on temperature and humidity of the air, and on the moisture of the cheese, as regulated by the amount of salt used. The first room has a temperature of 70° F. to start the eyes, which is later lowered in the second curing-room to about 60° to check the development. When any local fermentive action starts, it may be checked by rubbing salt on the affected part. The humidity of the room is very important, because a cheese will quickly dry out in a dry room, due to evaporation from the surface. To prevent this, it is well to spray the floor with water, or to have a steam jet in the room.

If the curd has been cooked too long the cheese may be too dry. Such cheeses may be piled two or more deep in the curing-room. It is held by some cheese-makers that this process causes them to absorb more moisture. Probably this is due to the checking of evaporation.

The development of the "eyes" may be watched by trying the following test: Place the middle finger on the cheese and let the first finger slip from it, striking the cheese smartly; a dull sound indicates solidity, while a ring indicates a hole, and an expert maker can tell the size of the holes by the sound. This requires long practice for the operator to become proficient.

After a cheese has remained in the first room for about two weeks and the holes are well started, it is removed to the second curing-room, which is held at a cooler temperature and slightly drier atmosphere. The cheeses are held in this room from three to ten months, depending on market conditions, and capacity of the curing-rooms. In Switzerland, it is customary to hold cheese to secure a well ripened product, while in America most of the cheeses are shipped comparatively green, hence do not bring so high a price.

272. Block Swiss.—In making block Swiss, the same procedure is followed through the cooking stage. Then the curd is pressed in a square form or in one large piece, each form six inches square on the ends and twenty inches long, and later cut into sections. These are then pressed, salted and cured in the same way as round forms. In this type of cheese there is a much smaller cross-section; therefore

[125] Clark, W. M., On the formation of "eyes" in Emmenthal cheese, Jour. Dairy Sci. 1 (1917), no. 2, pages 91-113.

Among important studies of Swiss cheese ripening are the following: Freudenreich, E. v., and Orla Jensen, Ueber die in Emmentalerkäse stattfindende Proprionsäuregärung, Centralb. f. Bakt. etc. 2 Abt. 17, page 529.

Jensen, Orla, Biologische Studien über den Käsereifungsprozess unter spezieller Berucksichtigung der flüchtigen Fettsäuren, Centralb. f. Bakt. etc. 2 Abt. 13 (1904), page 161.

Eldredge, E. E., and L. A. Rogers, The bacteriology of cheese of the Emmenthal type, Centralb. f. Bakt. 2 Abt. 40 (1914), no. ⅛, pages 5-21.

the development of holes is much more easily controlled on account of the ease with which the salt can work into the cheese and control undesirable ferments. As it is easy to control, this variety is made in the fall and winter when the ferments are especially hard to keep in check. However, this cheese has the disadvantage of cutting eye-development short by the rapid entrance of salt.

The curing consists of the developing of the flavor and eyes and the changing in body and texture. Just what causes these changes is not known.

273. Shipment.—When ready for shipment, the drum cheeses of the same general diameter are sorted out and packed four to six in a cask. Care must be taken to put boards between them to prevent sticking. These are called scale-boards, and are made of thin sections of wood fiber. The cheeses are crowded into the cask to make a snug fit, and the head carefully fastened.

274. Qualities of Swiss cheese.—The peculiar Swiss cheese flavor may be characterized as a hazel-nut taste. It is a trifle sweet and very tempting. The "eyes" or holes should be about the size of a cherry with a dull shine to the inner lining. The "eyes" usually contain a small amount of a briny tasting liquid. These eyes should be uniformly distributed. The color should be uniform. The cheese should have a neat, clean, attractive appearance, and the rind should not be cracked or broken.

There are several common defects in Swiss cheese. If the milk is not clean-flavored, the cheese will have the same flavor as the milk. The greatest difficulty is to produce the eyes or holes. A cheese which does not have these is called "blind." A product which has many small pin-holes due to gassy fermentations is called a "niszler"; this means a cheese with a thousand eyes. If gas forms in the cheese and causes cracks, it is called "glaesler." If the cheese contains too much moisture, it will be soft and pasty. Such a cheese does not readily form eyes.

275. Composition and yield.—A large number of analyses of Swiss cheese have been made but there is wide variation. This is due to the fact that the composition and yield are both dependent on the following factors: composition of the milk, losses during manufacture, amount of moisture in the cheese. The losses in Swiss cheese are much larger than with some of the other hard cheeses, such as Cheddar. This is because more fat is lost in the whey, due to breaking instead of cutting the curd and the subsequent hard stirring. The possibility of reducing these excessive losses has already been indicated.

Swiss cheeses of high grade show about the following range of composition:

Water	30-34 per cent
Fat	30-34 per cent
Protein	26-30 per cent
Salt (NaCl)	1-1.4 per cent

The water-content of this type of cheese is low and the protein-content is proportionately high. Both conditions lead to firm textures, long ripening and long keeping periods.

The following score-card is used to judge both block and drum Swiss cheese:

Flavor	35
Appearance on trier holes	30
Texture	20
Salt	10
Style	5
	——
	100

The yield of Swiss cheese varies from 8 to 11 pounds to 100 pounds of milk. The more solids in the milk, the more moisture incorporated in the cheese; the smaller the loss of solids in the manufacturing process, the larger will be the yield from a given amount of milk.

THE ITALIAN GROUP[126]

A group of varieties, best known in America by Parmesan, are made in Italy with related forms in Greece and European Turkey. These forms are very hard, usually uncolored, with small eyes or holes. They are made in large cheeses which ripen very slowly. Cow's milk is regularly used for Parmesan and Grana in northern Italy; other varieties contain goat or sheep milk or various mixtures. Aside from Parmesan, few of the other forms are known outside the place of origin except as they are exported in a small way to satisfy the demand of emigrants from these regions.

276. Parmesan.—One type of Italian cheese, however, the Parmesan, has become very widely known. In general the consuming trade does not discriminate between Parmesan, Grana and closely related forms. Parmesan is made in large cheeses which require one to three years for proper ripening; in texture it is very hard with small eyes or holes formed by very slow fermentation. Such cheeses are ripened in large storehouses in which hundreds and even thousands are brought together and cared for by experts. The surfaces of these cheeses are kept clean and free from insects by rubbing with linseed oil. So hard are these forms that the cheese-trier is not used in testing, but the texture of the surface is tested by pricking with an awl-like tool and the stage of eye-formation and associated ripening is determined by the sound given out when the cheeses are tapped with a hammer.

When ripe, the cheeses of this group are used in cooking principally. The broken cheese is grated and added to macaroni, spaghetti and other cooked cheese dishes. Parmesan is usually made from partly skimmed-milk; the ratio of fat to protein in analysis runs from 1:2 to 3:4 in contrast to the normal relation of about

[126] Gorini, C., Studi sulla fabricatione razionale del fromaggi Grana, Boll. uff. del Ministero Agr. Ind. e Comm. Anno X, serie C, Fasc. 10, pages 1-7, Roma, 1911.

Gorini, C., On the distribution of bacteria in Grana cheese, Centralb. f. Bakt. etc. 2 Abt. 12 (1904), pages 78-81.

Fascetti, G., The technological chemistry of the manufacture of Grana cheese in Reggio, Staz. Sper. Agr. Ital. 47 (1914), no. 8, pages 541-568.

4:3 in whole-milk cheese. In water-content much variation is found, but ripe Parmesan is usually about 30 per cent water. Other members of the group are made with different amounts of skimming, some of them from whole milk. The group in general represents the requirements of cheese for the trade of warmer regions (see Mayo and Elling): (1) a low fat-content so incorporated that the cheese does not become greasy or oily in hot weather; (2) a water-content low enough to prevent rapid spoilage during the necessary exposure of handling under warm conditions.

The equipment for Parmesan manufacture has more resemblance to that of the Swiss factory than the English and American cheeses. The milk is curdled in deep copper kettles (Fig. 57), below which there is commonly a provision for direct heating by fire which is sometimes carried on a truck, and therefore can be withdrawn when heating is sufficient. The steam-jacketed kettle has replaced this earlier form to a large measure.

Fig. 57.—Parmesan cheese kettles.

The general character of the manufacturing process is indicated in the following abstract of one of the methods. Many variations are to be found. The milk for Parmesan is allowed to stand overnight. Some acidity is, therefore, developed in contrast to the absolutely fresh condition of the milk used in Swiss and the acidification developed during the making of Cheddar (Fascetti). It is then skimmed, heated to 72° to 75° F. Rennet is added in amount sufficient to produce firm curd in one hour or slightly less. When the curd is firm, a wood fire is made under the kettle and the curd is broken with a special implement into small particles. After breaking, four grains of powdered sulfur to twenty-two gallons of milk are added. The curd is stirred with a rake. By the time the temperature rises to 77° F., the curd should be in very small pieces. Stirring and heating continue until the temperature reaches 131° F. At this temperature, it stands fifteen minutes, after which it is removed from the fire (or the fire is drawn). Nine-tenths of the whey is then drawn. The cheese-maker then collects the curd into a compact lump under which he slips a cheese cloth. With the aid of an assistant he removes the mass to a perforated vessel for draining. After this the curd goes into large wooden hoops, lined with cloth, which stand upon a slanting draining table until evening. No pressure is used. Before night they are taken to the cellar. The cloths are removed next day. After standing four days, they are salted by covering the upper surface with coarse salt. This is repeated with daily turning for twenty days, then salted on alternate days for another period of twenty days. At the end of the forty days' salting, the cheese is removed from the hoop, scraped, sprinkled with whey and the rind rubbed smooth. A dressing of linseed oil either with or without bone black is applied.

Fig. 58.—A typical cheese-market in France.

The cheeses are kept in special ripening rooms, and rubbed frequently with linseed oil to keep the surfaces free from molds and vermin. Careful grading as to quality of product and consequent response to ripening conditions produce cheeses of many degrees of excellence. Those in which a ripening of three to four years is possible are most highly esteemed.

277. Regianito.—A cheese of the Italian group is now made in Argentina and imported to the United States under the name Regianito.

CHAPTER XVI

MISCELLANEOUS VARIETIES AND BY-PRODUCTS

Caciocavallo; Sap sago; Albumin cheese; Mysost, Norwegian whey
cheese; Whey butter.

As already discussed in Chapter VI, there are a large number of varieties of cheese. Very many are entirely unknown in America. A considerable number of forms are occasionally imported and may be found by visiting the markets and delicatessen stores in the foreign districts of our large cities. Certain forms not widely known are made in America in a few factories or are imported in sufficient quantity to call for brief discussion. Some of these are brought together here.

The importance of the by-products of cheese-making has not been sufficiently recognized, for manufacture on a large scale is only beginning to be appreciated in America. Certain cheese names, such as Mysost, are applied to whey products. In addition, milk-sugar is extensively made and whey-butter has been carefully studied and found to be practicable under some conditions.

278. Caciocavallo originated in Italy, but is now made in certain factories of New York and Ohio. Some factories in Lombardy[127] use whole milk, others use half-skimmed milk. The latter practice is probably the more common. In making this cheese, the milk is coagulated with rennet, cut and firmed in the whey, allowed to settle and the whey drawn. The curd is then piled on the draining table and allowed to mat or fuse into fairly solid masses. After several hours of draining and matting, the curd is cut into strips and placed in a vat of hot water. In the hot water, the blocks of solid curd melt into taffy-like masses which are worked and molded by hand into more or less standard shapes. Indian club or ten-pin forms are most commonly produced. When the proper shape has been gained, each mass is thrown into cold water which solidifies it in that form. Cheese masses heat and cool slowly; several hours of cooling are required to insure a firm cheese. The newly made cheeses are salted in a brine bath, then hung by a string to ripen. Sometimes these cheeses are eaten fresh, again they are ripened several months. They vary in size from one to six pounds. Cornalba gives the composition of Italian Caciocavallo made from whole milk as water 32 to 34 per cent, fat 34 to 36 per cent, protein 28.5 to 29.5 per cent, salt 1.7 to 1.8 per cent; when made from half skimmed-milk, water 28 per cent, fat 27 to 28 per cent, protein 35 to 40 per cent, salt 2.2 per cent. Other analyses vary widely from these figures on account of the

---

[127] Cornalba, G., Caciocavallo in Lombardy, L'Industria del Latte 3, page 105, Abs. in Jahresb. f. Tierchemie 36 (1906), page 250.

differing fat-content of the milk. No standardized practice has been established in America.

Provolono resembles Caciocavallo in method of manufacture and composition, the main difference being in the shape of the cheese. It is more or less round and is held by a coarse net made of small rope. The cheeses are treated while curing the same as Caciocavallo.

279. Sap sago.—This hard green cheese imported from Switzerland is made in cakes, tapering from perhaps two inches in diameter to a rounded top with a height of about two inches. These are made from skimmed-milk curd, partially ripened then mixed with powdered leaves of *Melilotus cœruleus*, a clover-like plant. The mixture is then pressed into the market form and dried until very hard. It is handled without special care since the water-content is so low that fermentations are exceedingly slow. This low-priced cheese may be used in cooking.

280. Albumin cheese.[128]—In the rennet cheeses, the albumin, which constitutes about 0.7 per cent of the milk, passes off in the whey. This albumin is not curdled by rennet. It is, however, coagulated by heating. The presence of acid hastens such coagulation but does not cause it when used alone. When the whey is heated to about 200° F., the albumin rises and may be skimmed off. In this form it is recovered and used. It may be shaped is hoops under pressure, as Ricotte, an Italian form. This cheese is pressed firmly and dried. Such albumin is frequently prepared as a poultry feed.

281. Mysost, Norwegian whey cheese.—The whey contains nearly 5 per cent of milk-sugar which can be recovered by boiling. The Norwegian process which produces Mysost consists in raising the whey to the boiling point, skimming off the albumin as it rises, then concentrating the remainder of the whey. As it reaches sufficient concentration, the albumin is thoroughly stirred back into the mass and the mass finally cooled into forms. Mysost is a brown, hard brittle mass consisting principally of caramelized milk-sugar. Analysis shows such percentage composition as follows: water 10 to 20 per cent, protein 10 to 15 per cent, milk-sugar 30 to 55 per cent. Mysost is found in the larger markets of the United States.

Primost is an albumin cheese somewhat similar to Ricotte and Mysost. It is made by precipitating the albumin by acid and heat. The main difference is in the firmness of the cheese. This is regulated by drying.

282. Whey butter.[129]—The loss of a percentage of fat, rarely less than 0.3 per cent and in some cheeses very much greater, has led to the making of whey butter. For this purpose a separator is introduced and all whey is separated daily. The fat recovered in the form of cream is then ripened and churned. Whey butter is not

[128] Babcock, S. M., Albumin cheese, Wis. Exp. Sta. Rept. 12 (1895), page 134.

[129] Doane, C. F., Whey butter, U. S. Dept. Agr. Bur. An. Ind. Circ. 161, pages 1-7, 1910.

Sammis, J. L., Making whey butter at Cheddar cheese factories, Wis. Exp. Sta. Bul. 246, 1915.

Ellenberrger, H. B., and M. R. Tolstrup, Skimming whey at Vermont cheese factories, Vt. Dept. Agr. Bul. 26, 1916.

rated as equal to butter made from whole milk but a fair market can usually be found for the product. The recovery of 0.25 per cent fat means two and one-half pounds of fat to 1000 pounds of whey. This will make about three pounds of butter.

Whether whey butter shall be made depends on the volume of business, the extra equipment required, the extra help necessary and the market for the product. As a rule, whey butter is economically recoverable only in large factories. It is not considered advisable to attempt to make it unless one has the whey from 10,000 pounds of milk. In some instances, the combination of small cheese factories with one churning plant has proved to be economical. The objection to the making of whey butter is, that it stimulates carelessness on the part of the cheese-maker because he thinks that the fat will be recovered by skimming. He does not realize that the other milk solids are being reduced in the same proportion as the fat, to the great loss in yield of cheese.

CHAPTER XVII

CHEESE FACTORY CONSTRUCTION, EQUIPMENT, ORGANIZATION

Locating the site; The building; Heating plant; Curing-rooms; Light; Ventilation; Boiler-room; whey tanks; Store-room; The floors; Arrangement of machinery and rooms; Arrangements for cleanliness; Equipment and supplies list; Factory organization.

The principal factor in determining the location of a cheese factory is the available supply of milk. This is usually ascertained by making a canvass, and finding out the number of cows whose milk would be brought to the factory. The quantity of milk or the number of cows necessary to insure sufficient milk for the successful operation of the factory, depends on the variety of cheese to be made. When making types of cheese for which very sweet milk is necessary, the milk must be delivered twice a day. This demand limits the area from which the factory can secure its supply. The length of time the cheeses are held in the curing-room and the work necessary to care for them also limits the area which the factory can serve, because a very large amount of milk cannot be handled when the cheese must be given considerable attention in the curing-rooms. Swiss, Limburger and Brick cheese factories usually do not require a large supply of milk; therefore the factories may be built close together. The size of the Cheddar cheese factories varies but it is generally considered unprofitable to make Cheddar cheese unless there are 5000 pounds of milk available daily. Conditions have changed so that at present different kinds of cheese are made from the surplus milk in market milk plants. In such cases a uniform supply is not absolutely necessary. The climate must also be suitable for the industry.

283. Locating the site.—In a farming community, several factory sites are usually available. It is best to consider carefully the desirable features of each before trying to make a definite choice. Many of the present cheese factories were located in hollows because it was easy to secure a supply of water, but no thought or attention was given to the disposal of the sewage. The following points should be considered in choosing a site:

(1) *Drainage.*—A factory should be so located that it has good drainage. Ground that slopes away from the factory makes the disposal of sewage easy. Sewage should not be allowed to run out on the ground and left to decay, thus forming a breeding place for flies, but should run into a cesspool or septic tank.[130] Even in

[130] Farrington, E. H., and G. J. Davis, The disposal of creamery sewage, Wis. Exp. Sta.

a porous soil, a cesspool frequently clogs and gives trouble. The septic tank seems to be the best method to dispose of the sewage unless the factory is so located that connection can be made with a city sewage system.

(2) *Water.*—An abundant supply of pure water is essential to a factory. This may come either from deep wells or springs. The value of a never-failing water supply cannot be overestimated.

(3) *Exposure.*—The factory should be so located that the receiving room is away from the prevailing winds. This prevents dust being blown into the factory. The curing-room should be on the side not exposed to the sun as this will keep it cool. Fig. 59 shows a clean cheese factory of the ordinary type. When it is desirable to cure the cheese in a cellar, it is better to locate the factory on the side of a hill. Then the receiving and manufacturing room may be on the ground level and the curing-room, a cellar, back of the manufacturing room and yet all on the same level. This saves carrying the cheese up and down stairs.

(4) *Accessibility to market* should not be overlooked. Often the quality of the cheese is injured by long hauls. An important item in marketing both milk and cheese is the use of the automobile. By its use the products are not so long in transit, and losses from exposure in delivery are reduced. Both milk and cheese, when exposed to the heat of the sun for any length of time, become warm. This gives undesirable organisms chance to develop.

Fig. 59.—A cheese factory of neat appearance.

284. The building.—Details of construction or estimates of cost will be omitted in the present discussion. A local contractor can do this satisfactorily and also the cost of materials is constantly changing. Only general considerations as they apply to the manufacture of the product will be taken up.

Bul. 245, 1915.

The building may be constructed of wood, stone, various bricks or concrete. The kind of material will depend on the relative cost of materials in the local market and on the amount of money available for building.

285. Heating plant.—Many of the older factories have no heating plants and some are so poorly constructed that they cannot be warmed. Means of heating should be provided, either by steam or a stove. The loss due to freezing is an item which is entirely avoided in factories properly heated.

286. Curing-rooms.—The size of the curing-rooms will depend on the amount of cheese to be handled and its location on the variety of cheese to be manufactured. In every case, some provision should be made to control humidity and temperature. If the room becomes hot and dry, evaporation from the cheese will be much more rapid. In a hot curing-room, undesirable types of ferments are more likely to develop and to injure the quality of the cheese.

287. Light.—The importance of light should be emphasized. It acts as a stimulant to keep things clean. It also makes the factory more cheerful. There should be numerous windows to give plenty of light. A skylight may often serve both as a source of light and ventilation.

288. Ventilation.—Plenty of ventilation should be provided. This may be accomplished by means of the windows or skylight. However, it is a good precaution to have at least one ventilator to carry off the steam and control the circulation of air. All openings should be carefully screened to keep out flies.

289. Boiler-room.—The boiler-room should be easily accessible from the manufacturing rooms. A gauge located in the latter should tell the steam pressure. Windows or doors should be so located that the flues of the boiler can be cleaned. The coal supply should be handy. Great care should be exercised to keep the boiler-room clean for otherwise the dirt will be tracked all over the factory.

290. Whey tanks should be kept clean. Daily washing is absolutely necessary to prevent offensive odors. Pasteurization of whey has been found requisite to prevent the spread of disease if raw milk is used.[131] This is required by law in some states. It is sometimes accomplished by heat with steam coils; in other cases by running live steam directly into the whey. Whey tanks may be made of wood or steel. The acid of the whey seems to eat and decompose concrete.

291. Store-room.—There should be a separate room or a place in the attic where the supplies can be kept. This saves much waste and keeps the factory cleaner and more tidy.

292. The floors.—The floor is the most important part of the building. It should be of non-absorbent material, which can be easily cleaned, and it should not leak. Concrete makes the best floor of any material used at present. It should slope very gently to the drain. The corners between the floor and side walls should be rounding to make cleaning easy. The drain should be provided with bell traps to prevent the entrance of sewer gas into the factory. If the traps and floor about them are

---

[131] Dotterer, W. D., and R. S. Breed, Why and how pasteurize dairy by-products, N. Y. (Geneva) Exp. Sta. Bul. 412, 1915.

slightly depressed, it will help to make the floor drain more quickly. A catch-basin should be provided just outside the factory for all solid material which might clog the sewer pipe. This should be cleaned three or four times a year.

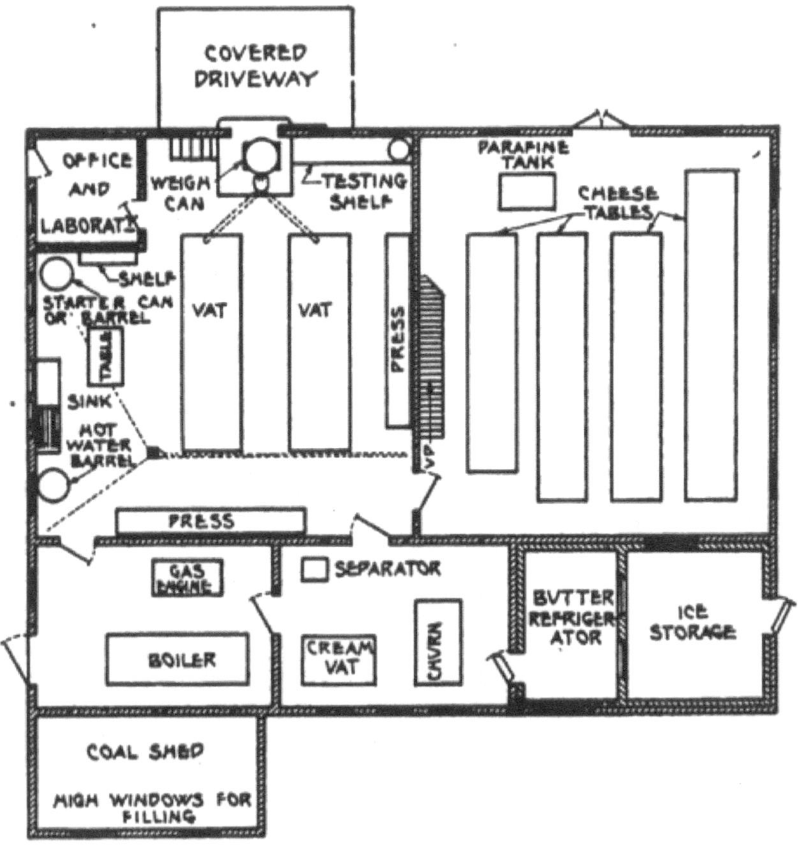

Fig. 60.—A well arranged Cheddar cheese factory, including the equipment for the manufacture of whey butter.

293. Arrangement of machinery and rooms.—The rooms and machinery should be arranged so that the work will follow the natural sequence of the process with as little inconvenience as possible. Some of the points to be observed in this connection are: vats should be near the weigh-can; boiler-room near the work room; cheese presses near the vats; cheese presses near the curing-rooms and the like.

Fig. 60 shows a well arranged Cheddar cheese factory. The necessary machinery and rooms for the manufacture of whey butter are included. In this plan, the attic contains the store-room and the whey tanks. The whey is forced from the vats into the tanks with a steam jet and then runs by gravity to the separator. Slides are provided in the walls of the ice storage to regulate the flow of air into the curing-room and butter refrigerator. In order to have a smaller boiler, a gasolene engine is used to run the separator, churn and curd-mill. The plan can be modified to use the upstairs for a curing-room so that the size of the factory may be reduced. The whey butter could be shifted to a small room where the curing-room now is and the boiler-room added as a "lean-to" at one side of the building. This would materially reduce the size of the main building.

Another plan (Fig. 61) shows the arrangement of a Cheddar cheese factory without the whey butter apparatus. The location of the drain between the vats might be criticized. In Fig. 62 is shown the arrangement of a combined butter and cheese factory. Fig. 63 shows the possible arrangement of a Limburger factory. The size of this factory could be reduced by having the salting tables closer together.

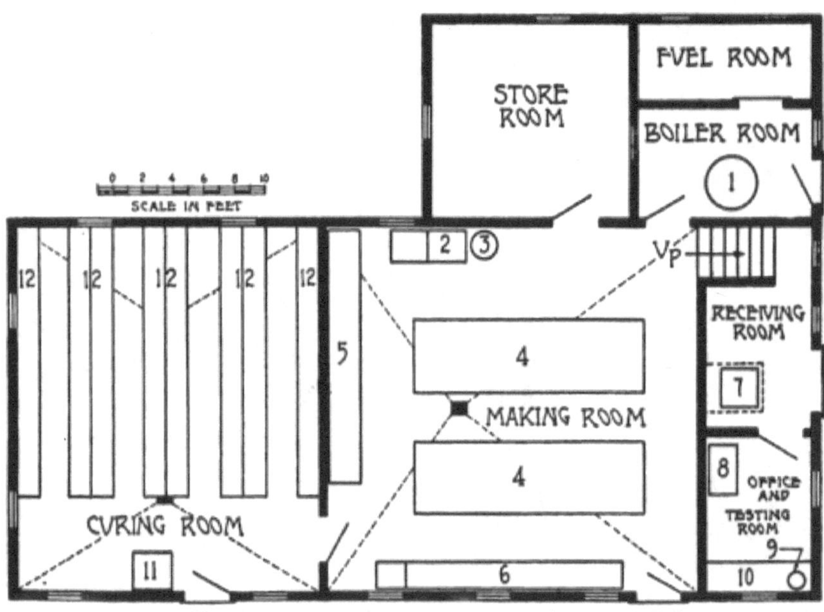

Fig. 61.—Plan of Cheddar cheese factory without whey butter equipment. 1, Boiler; 2, sink; 3, hot water barrel for scalding utensils; 4, cheese vats; 5, 6, cheese presses; 7, weigh-can; 8, desk; 9, Babcock tester; 10, shelf; 11, paraffine tank; 12, cheese shelves.

In a Cheddar cheese factory, the curing-room may be over the manufacturing room. This makes considerable work in carrying the cheese up and down. A small elevator may be used for this purpose. The same principle holds in cheese factories in which other varieties of cheese are made; the floors should be on one level so far as possible. There is danger of the overhead curing-room becoming too hot and causing the cheese to leak fat. Shelves or tables should be provided on which to put and keep the utensils. The utensils should never be placed on the floor.

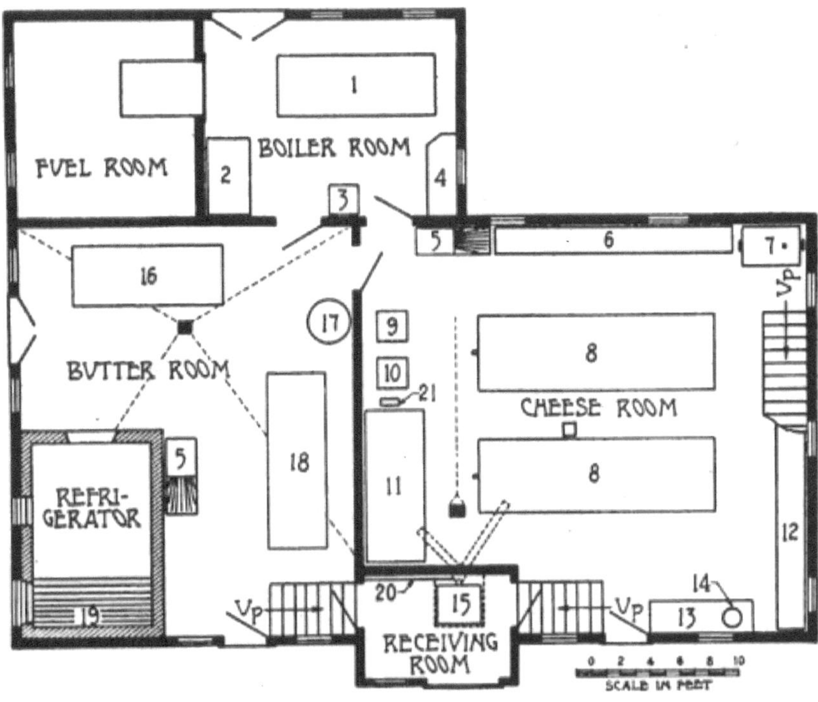

Fig. 62.—1, Boiler; 2, engine; 3, water pump; 4, work bench; 5, wash sink; 6, press; 7, elevator; 8, cheese vats; 9, separator; 10, milk heater; 11, milk receiving vat; 12, press; 13, shelf; 14, Babcock tester; 15, weigh-can; 16, churn; 17, starter; 18, cream ripener and pasteurizer; 19, refrigerator; 20, milk sheet and sample jar; 21, milk pump.

294. Arrangements for cleanliness.—A sink for washing the utensils should be provided and boiling water to scald them after washing. After being scalded, tin utensils dry quickly without rusting. The boiling water may be obtained by placing a steam pipe in a barrel of water and turning on the steam. The utensils can then be washed clean, dipped in this barrel of boiling water and put in their place. Too much emphasis cannot be laid on keeping the factory itself, the utensils and the surroundings clean. This will prevent the development of mold. Cases are known in which the cheese factory was allowed to become very dirty, so that a red mold developed. This eventually got into the cheese and caused red spots.[132] They are called rust spots. All doors and windows should be screened to keep out flies.

---

[132] Harding, H. A., and G. A. Smith, Control of rust spots in cheese, N. Y. (Geneva) Exp. Sta. Bul. 225, 1902.

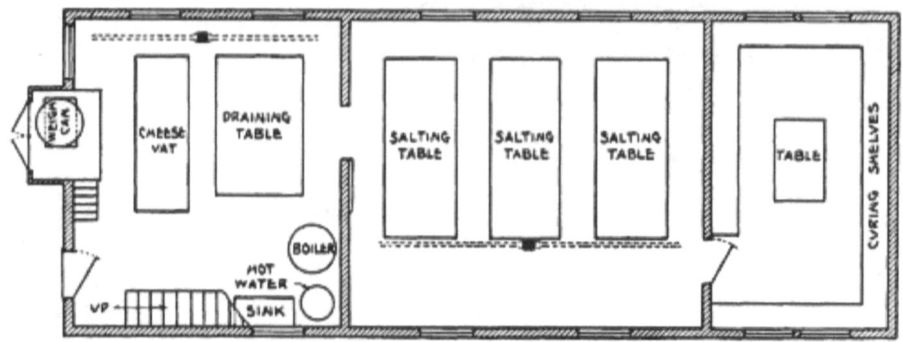

Fig. 63.—A Limburger cheese factory.

295. Equipment and supplies list.—The following utensils will be needed in a Cheddar cheese factory to handle 10,000 pounds of milk daily: 1 5-H. P. boiler; 1 60-gallon weigh-can; 1 conductor head and trough; 1 platform scale; 1 Babcock tester, glassware and sample bottles; 2 700-gallon cheese vats; 2 gang cheese presses; 1 curd-mill; 2 curd-knives; 30 cheese hoops; 1 whey strainer; 1 curd scoop; 1 long-handled dipper; 1 strainer dipper; 1 siphon; 1 cheese knife; 1 glass graduate; 1 cheese-trier; 1 speed knife; 1 paraffine tank; 1 Marschall rennet test; 1 lactometer; 1 milk can hoist; 1 acid test; 1 sink; 1 40-quart milk can; 3 pails; 3 shot-gun cans for starter; 3 thermometers; brushes and brooms; 1 Wisconsin curd test or fruit jars for same; 1 set counter scales; 2 curd rakes.

If whey butter is made, the equipment should include: Tanks to hold the whey; separator; cream ripening vat; churn; butter-worker; butter refrigerator; large boiler and steam engine or gasolene engine.

The following supplies will be needed for the making of the cheese: Bandages; boxes; scale boards; starched circles; rennet extract or pepsin; cheese color; press cloths; paraffine; formaldehyde; alkali; indicator; sulfuric acid.

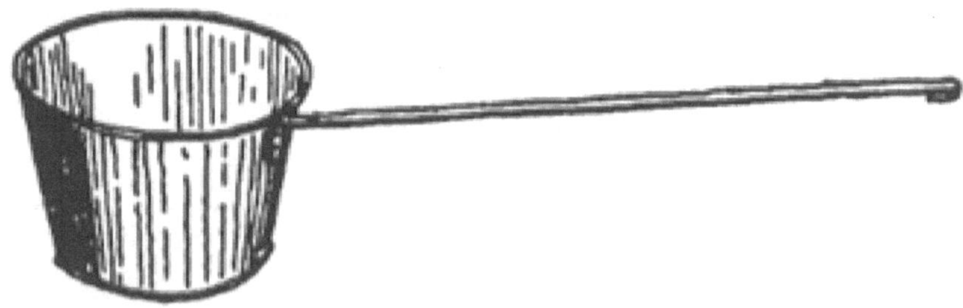

Fig. 64.—A sanitary dipper with a solid handle.

When choosing the utensils, the ease of cleaning and sanitary construction should not be overlooked. One of the most unsanitary utensils in a factory is a dipper with a hollow handle. Fig 64 shows a dipper with a solid handle which any tinsmith can make. The seams of all utensils should be flushed full of solder, to make cleaning easy. When ready to clean or wash any utensils which have come in contact with milk or its products, the steps are as follows: rinse in cold water, wash in warm water in which some washing-soda has been dissolved, rinse clean, scald in boiling water. Never use a cloth to wash utensils; a brush is more sanitary.

296. Factory organization.—There are two general classes of organizations[133] to operate cheese factories, one the proprietary and the other the coöperative. Unless the kind of organization is what the dairy-men desire, dissatisfaction is sure to result.

(1) *Proprietary organization.*—Under this form of organization, one person owns and operates the factory. The dairy-men are paid a stated price for milk, or the milk is made into cheese for a stated price a pound. The proprietor receives all profits and assumes all losses.

So far as the dairy-man is concerned, the stock company is a proprietary organization. The gains and losses are shared by each member according to the amount of money invested.

(2) *Coöperative organization.*—In a true coöperative cheese factory each patron is an owner, as the name indicates. The object of this organization is to reduce the cost of manufacture rather than pay large dividends, so that the dairy-man with a large herd and small capital invested in the factory obtains more returns than the one who owns considerable capital and has a small herd. Many cheese factories are coöperative in name only and proprietary in operation. The state of Wisconsin has a law which tends to stop this defect and defines what organizations may use the term or name, coöperative.

The constitution of a coöperative organization should state: 1, Name; 2, object; 3, officers and duties of officers; 4, manager or other person to run business; 5, capital stock; 6, meetings; 7, voting power; 8, amendments.

Some of the most important statements which should appear in the constitution are mentioned in the following sentences. A statement should show what persons are eligible to membership in the organization. It is a careless plan simply to say that the duties of the officers are those usually defined in such an organization. This may lead to confusion and neglect, or both. Direct statements should be made explaining the exact duties of each officer. The limits of the authority of the manager or person who runs the business should be explicitly stated. The manager then knows just what his duties are and what matters or parts of the business must be considered by other officers or committees. The amount of capital stock and the number and value of each share should be exactly stated. The constitution should state when and where the regular meetings must be held and by whom and when special meetings may be called. This gives every member ample notice

[133] Elliott, W. J., Creameries and cheese factories, Mont. Exp. Sta. Bul. 53, 1904.

Farrington, E. H., and E. H. Benkendorf, Origination and construction of cheese factories and creameries, Wis. Exp. Sta. Bul. 244, 1915.

of the regular meetings. Some method or means should be provided to notify each member of the special meetings.

The voting power should be definitely stated, whether it is limited to shares of capital stock or by members or by number of cows owned by each member. It is necessary to indicate just how amendments to the constitution may be made. Each member should know before the final vote just what changes are being proposed. Types of constitutions may be found in the following references:

ELLIOTT, W. J., Creameries and cheese factories; organization, building and equipment, Mont. Exp. Sta. Bul. 53, 1904.

FARRINGTON, E. H., and G. H. BENKENDORF, Organization and construction of creameries and cheese factories, Wis. Exp. Sta. Bul. 244, 1915.

VAN SLYKE, L. L., and C. A. PUBLOW, The science and practice of cheese making, pages 447-453, 1909.

Iowa Exp. Sta. Bul. 139, 1913. Creamery organization and construction.

CHAPTER XVIII
HISTORY AND DEVELOPMENT OF THE CHEESE INDUSTRY IN AMERICA

The factory system; Introduction of factory system in Canada; Introduction of cheddaring; Introduction of Swiss and Limburger; Number and distribution of cheese factories; Total production of cheese in the United States; Rank of the leading cheese-producing states; Exportation and importation of cheese by the United States; Average yearly price of cheese; Canadian cheese statistics; Introduction of cheese-making into new regions.

Just when the first cheese was made is not known. By the time the first immigrants came to America, cheese-making was rather generally known in Europe, so that the early settlers brought with them and practiced established methods. The countries of Europe developed different kinds of cheese and have since become noted for such particular varieties, for example: France, Camembert and Roquefort; Switzerland, Swiss cheese; England, Stilton and Cheddar; Germany, Limburger; Holland, Edam and Gouda; Italy, Parmesan and its allies, also Gorgonzola cheese. The manufacture of these various cheeses has been attempted in this country. Because of the difference in climatic conditions and in some cases the use of milk of sheep or goats, it was and still is difficult to manufacture some of the European cheeses in America. Since the climatic conditions of this country and certain parts of England are somewhat similar, the manufacture of the cheeses of England predominated, and there was also more information on their manufacture. These are probably the reasons why the United States and Canada have become famous for Cheddar cheese.

The first cheeses of the Cheddar group were made on the farms. The work was usually performed by women, and the process was very simple. The methods were crude, and the cheeses were made in a more or less haphazard way. The milk of the evening was placed in a cheese tub in the dairy room and cooled to a temperature that would prevent souring. In most cases the cream that had raised to the surface of the night's milk was removed in the morning. This was considered an act of economy, for it was thought that in the process of manufacture it would all pass off in the whey and be lost. The morning's milk was then mixed with that of the evening and warmed to the setting temperature by placing a portion in a tin pail and suspending it in a kettle of hot water. When hot, it was emptied into the tub of cold milk. By transferring back and forth, the setting temperature was finally reached. Few of these settlers owned thermometers. Consequently, cheese-makers were obliged to depend on the sense of feeling to determine temperature.

One of the serious difficulties of the early manufacture was the production of rennet of a uniform strength. After the addition of the rennet and as soon as the coagulated milk became firm enough, it was broken into as small pieces as could be conveniently made, a wooden knife being used for the purpose. After standing ten minutes it was stirred by hand, breaking the pieces finer, and the temperature was gradually brought to 98° F., aiming as near blood heat as could be judged by the sense of feeling. It was kept at this temperature until the moisture was out of the curd and it would squeak between the teeth. The whey was drawn off and the curd stirred until dry, salted and put to press. All the curd of one day was made into a cheese. This resulted in small uneven-sized cheese. Since such cheeses were made from the milk of single dairies with all the surroundings clean, the flavor was usually good but the texture was open and soft. The method of caring for the cheese and marketing was entirely different from that practiced at the present time. All the cheeses made during the entire season were held until fall and marketed at one time. They were packed in casks four to six in a package, one on top of the other. The earliest date when single boxed cheeses were on the market was 1841.

Between 1820 and 1840, a small export trade in cheese was started. As this demand for cheese increased, particularly in England, it became necessary to change the methods employed in manufacture. The farm dairy cheese was rather an open-textured sweet curd product. If not, it was due more to accident than to any intention of the cheese-maker to improve the quality. One of the early complaints from England was that the cheeses were too small and uneven in size. The practice of making on the farm continued until about 1851, when the factory system was started, although home manufactures continued after that time. Following are the reasons for the change from the farm to factory system: (1) England demanded larger cheese; (2) the farm product was not uniform; (3) the quality of the farm cheese did not suit the English trade; (4) factories saved much labor on the farms; and (5) could secure higher prices.

297. The factory system.—Where and by whom the first Cheddar cheese factory in America was started is not definitely known. Jesse Williams of Oneida County, New York, is supposed by many to have been the first to build and operate under the factory system, in 1851. Cheese factories were opened in Ohio and Wisconsin about 1860. In the period 1860 to 1870, a large number of cheese factories were built in the various states, especially New York, Ohio and Wisconsin.

298. Introduction of factory system in Canada.—In 1863, Harvey Farrington of Herkimer, New York, was so impressed with the opportunity of developing the cheese factory system in Canada that he sold out his business in New York and established the first Canadian cheese factory in the town of Norwich, Ontario. It was accepted at once by Canadian farmers, and factory cheese-making increased rapidly. In 1866, a small quantity of cheese was exported and from that time the export trade of Canada has been large and growing. Ontario and Quebec are now the leading provinces in the production of cheese.

299. Introduction of cheddaring.—The factories at first used the same process as the farms, namely the stirred-curd process. In 1867, Robert McAdam introduced the English Cheddar system in a factory near Herkimer, New York. This is the Cheddar system as known to-day. It produces the closer bodied cheese demanded by the export trade. This introduction made Herkimer County famous for its cheese.

300. Introduction of Swiss and Limburger.—In 1870, factories for Limburger, Swiss and Brick cheese were started and have gradually increased. In New York such plants are located around Boonville in Oneida County, and Theresa, in Jefferson County. In Wisconsin, Swiss cheese-making was begun by a colony of Swiss who came to New Glarus, Green County. It is now made in Green, Lafayette, Iowa, Grant, Dane and Rock counties. Limburger and Brick are manufactured in Dodge, Fond du Lac, Winnebago, Marathon, La Crosse, Buffalo, Trempealeau, Clark, Washington, Dunn, Barron and Lincoln counties. In the southeastern part of Ohio Swiss cheese is produced. Ohio and Wisconsin have manufactured more of these cheeses, especially Swiss, than any other states. This is probably due to the fact that the conditions are more nearly like those of Switzerland.

When the cities in New York began to grow, an increased demand for market milk was felt. The result was that the dairy-men could not supply both the cities and the cheese factories with milk. A large part of the cheese was being exported and most of it had always been partly skimmed. The amount of skimming, therefore, was largely increased. Then other animal fats were substituted for the milk-fat. This product was known as "filled" cheese. The delay in controlling the practice of making skimmed-milk and filled cheese ruined the export trade. In Canada laws prohibited the making of filled cheese and as a consequence Canadian Cheddar cheese is still very popular in England. However, with the control of skimmed-milk cheese-making and the elimination of filled cheese, the volume continued to grow and to find outlet in local consumption. New York probably exported more cheese than any other state. Wisconsin shipped cheese into other regions, especially the southern states in which no cheeses were made. Some Wisconsin cheeses were shipped to the New York market from time to time, but in October, 1913, the first quotations[134] were made in New York City for Wisconsin products.

301. Number and distribution of cheese factories.—The following list and maps (Figs. 65, 66) compiled in 1914 by the United States Department of Agriculture Dairy Division, show the number of cheese factories in the different states and their location:

---

[134] From N. Y. price current.

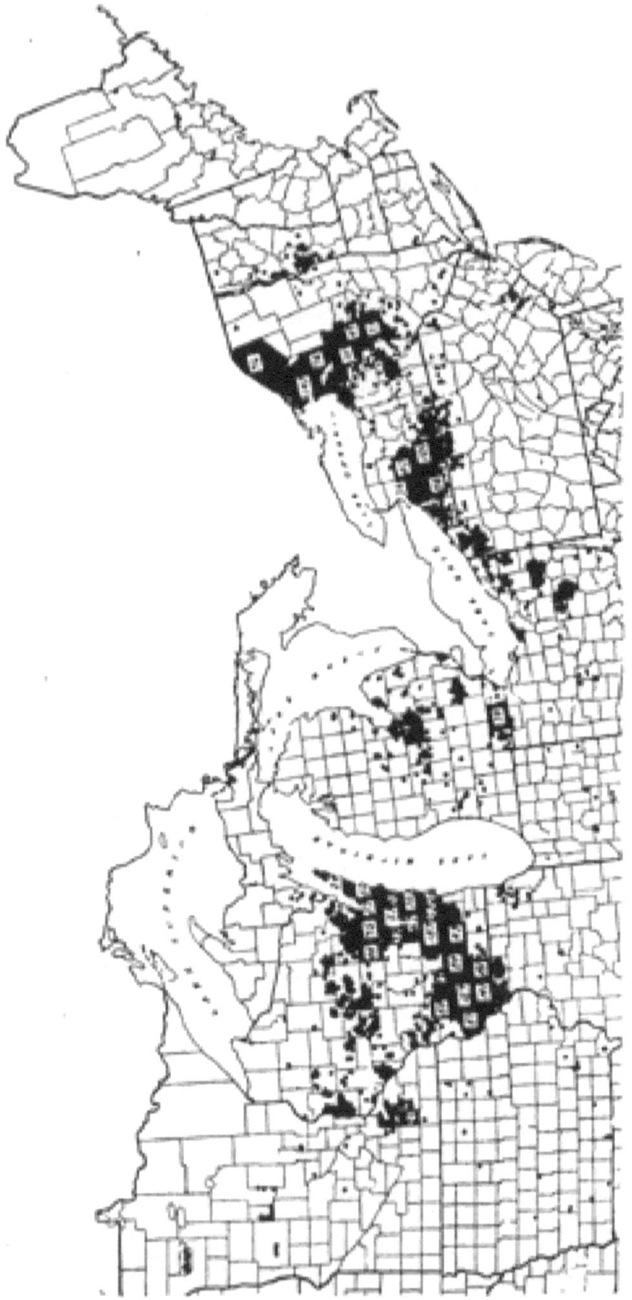

Fig. 65.—Map showing the distribution of cheese factories in the principal cheese-producing states.

Arizona	3	New Hampshire	2
California	93	New York	995
Colorado	8	North Dakota	3
Connecticut	2	Ohio	111
Delaware	1	Oklahoma	1
Illinois	50	Oregon	42
Indiana	13	Pennsylvania	106
Iowa	25	South Dakota	1
Kansas	1	Utah	8
Maine	5	Vermont	35
Michigan	196	Virginia	3
Minnesota	74	Washington	15
Missouri	4	West Virginia	1
Montana	1	Wisconsin	1720
Nebraska	1		— —
			3520

302. Total production of cheese in the United States.—The following figures (Table XX) compiled by the United States Census show the total production of cheese and the amount made on farms and in factories in the United States by ten-year periods:

TABLE XX

SHOWING THE TOTAL PRODUCTION OF CHEESE AND PART MADE ON FARMS AND IN FACTORIES IN THE UNITED STATES BY TEN-YEAR PERIODS

1849	Total	103,663,927 pounds
1859	Total	105,535,893 pounds
1869	Total	162,927,382 pounds
1879	Total	243,157,850 pounds
1889	On farms	18,726,818 pounds
	In factories	238,035,065 pounds
	Total	256,761,883 pounds
1899	On farm	16,372,330 pounds
	In factories	281,972,324 pounds
	Total	298,344,654 pounds
1909	On farms	9,405,864 pounds
	In factories	311,126,317 pounds
	Total	320,532,181 pounds

Fig. 66.—Showing the cheese factories in the Pacific coast states.

Comparing the figures of 1899 with those of 1909, it is seen that the total production of cheese in the United States increased 22,187,539 pounds, or an increase of 7.4 per cent in 1909 over 1899. During the same years the amount made on the farms decreased 6,966,454 pounds, or a decrease of 42.6 per cent, while the amount made in factories increased 29,153,933 pounds or 10.3 per cent.

303. Rank of the leading cheese-producing states.—The rank of the leading cheese states according to the number of factories in 1914 was: Wisconsin 1720, New York 995, Michigan 196, Ohio 111, Pennsylvania 106.

The table on the opposite page (Table XXI) shows the amount of cheese produced by the five states with the largest number of factories. This table indicates that New York led in the production of cheese until some time between 1899 and 1909. This is probably because, New York having so many cities, the demand for market milk is so large that it is sold as such instead of being manufactured into cheese. There is about the same number of milch cows in New York and Wisconsin. However, Wisconsin is credited with more cheese in 1909 than New York ever produced and this output probably will increase, as there are considerable areas of undeveloped agricultural land in Wisconsin. It is also interesting to note that Ohio is falling off in cheese production. This may be due to the increased demand for market milk. On the other hand, production has increased in Pennsylvania.

TABLE XXI

Showing the Amount of Cheese Made in five Leading States by Ten-year Periods

State	Year 1859	Year 1869	Year 1879	Year 1889	Year 1899	Year 1909	Year 1914
	Amount in pounds	Amount in pounds	Amount in pounds	Amount in pounds	Amount in pounds	Amount in pounds	Amount in pounds from factories only
Wisconsin	1,104,300	3,288,581	19,535,324	54,614,861	79,384,298	148,906,910	205,920,915
New York	48,548,289	100,776,012	129,163,714	124,086,524	130,010,584	105,584,947	97,614,024
Michigan	1,641,897	2,321,801	3,953,585	5,370,460	10,753,758	13,673,336	13,267,145
Ohio	21,618,893	24,153,876	32,531,683	22,254,054	19,363,528	12,473,834	8,717,996
Penn.	2,508,556	2,792,676	8,966,737	5,457,897	11,124,610	12,676,713	14,808,573

304. Exportation and importation of cheese by the United States.—The accompanying table shows the exports and imports of cheese from 1851 to 1916 and their values, in so far as the figures are available.

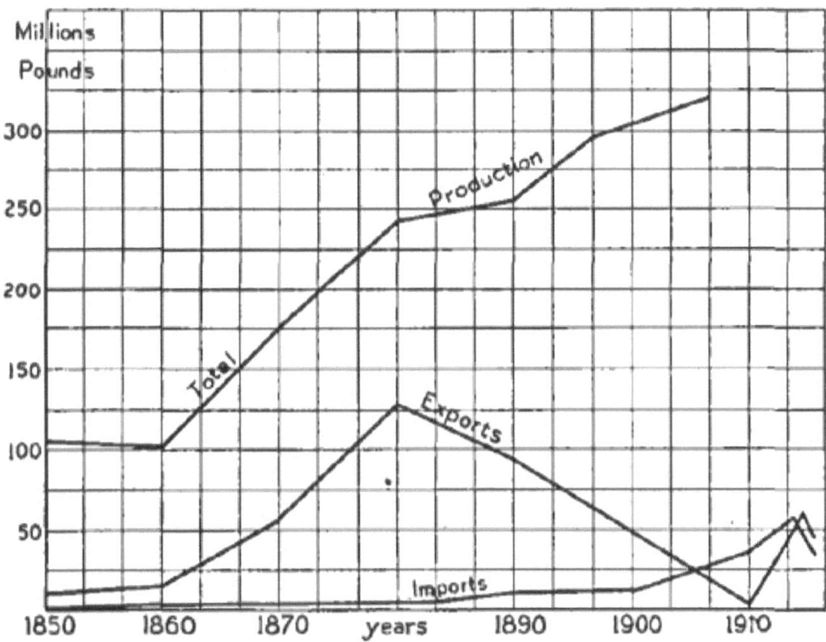

Fig. 67.—Showing relationship of total production, exports and imports of cheese.

One noteworthy item in Table XXII is that the exports have gradually decreased and imports increased. This is probably because immigrants have demanded the cheeses of their native country which were not made in America. The exports for the years 1915 and 1916 are interesting as they show the effect of the war on the cheese industry, the imports being gradually decreased and the exports greatly increased.

TABLE XXII

SHOWING THE IMPORTS AND EXPORTS OF CHEESE BY THE UNITED STATES FROM 1851-1916

YEAR	IMPORTS		EXPORTS	
	Amount in pounds	Value in dollars	Amount in pounds	Value in dollars
1851	603,398	——	10,361,189	——
1852	514,337	——	6,650,420	——
1853	874,949	——	3,763,932	——

1854	969,417	— —	7,003,974	— —
1855	1,526,942	— —	4,846,568	— —
1856	1,384,272	— —	8,737,029	— —
1857	1,400,252	— —	6,453,072	— —
1858	1,589,066	— —	8,098,527	— —
1859	1,409,420	— —	7,103,323	— —
1860	1,401,161	— —	15,515,799	— —
1861	1,090,835	— —	32,361,428	— —
1862	594,822	— —	34,052,678	— —
1863	545,966	— —	42,045,054	— —
1864	836,127	— —	47,751,329	— —
1865	985,362	— —	53,154,318	— —
1866	— —	— —	36,411,985	— —
1867	1,738,657	— —	52,352,127	— —
1868	2,997,994	— —	51,097,203	— —
1869	— —	— —	39,960,367	— —
1870	— —	— —	57,296,327	— —
1871	— —	— —	63,698,867	— —
1872	— —	— —	66,204,025	— —
1873	— —	— —	80,366,540	— —
1874	— —	— —	90,611,077	— —
1875	— —	— —	101,010,853	— —
1876	— —	— —	97,676,264	— —
1877	— —	— —	107,364,666	— —
1878	— —	— —	123,783,736	— —
1879	— —	— —	141,654,474	— —
1880	— —	— —	127,553,907	— —
1881	— —	— —	147,995,614	— —
1882	— —	— —	127,989,782	— —
1883	— —	— —	99,220,467	— —
1884	6,243,014	— —	112,869,575	— —
1885	6,247,560	— —	111,992,990	— —
1886	6,309,124	— —	91,877,235	— —
1887	6,592,192	— —	81,255,994	— —
1888	8,750,185	— —	88,008,458	— —
1889	8,207,026	— —	84,999,828	— —
1890	9,263,573	— —	95,376,053	— —
1891	8,863,640	— —	82,133,876	— —

1892	8,305,288	— —	82,100,221	— —
1893	10,195,924	— —	81,350,923	— —
1894	8,742,851	— —	73,852,134	— —
1895	10,276,293	— —	60,448,421	— —
1896	10,728,397	— —	36,777,291	— —
1897	12,319,122	— —	50,944,617	— —
1898	10,012,188	— —	53,167,280	— —
1900	13,455,990	— —	48,419,353	— —
1901	15,329,099	— —	39,813,517	— —
1902	17,067,714	$2,551,366	27,203,184	$2,745,597
1903	20,671,384	3,183,224	18,987,178	2,250,229
1904	22,707,103	3,284,811	23,335,172	2,452,239
1905	3,379,600	3,284,811	10,134,424	1,084,044
1906	27,286,866	4,303,830	16,562,451	1,940,620
1907	33,848,766	5,704,012	17,285,230	2,012,626
1908	5,586,706	5,704,012	8,439,031	1,092,053
1909	35,548,143	5,866,154	6,822,842	857,091
1910	40,817,524	7,053,570	2,846,709	441,017
1911	45,568,797	7,053,570	10,366,605	1,288,279
1912	46,542,007	8,807,249	6,337,559	898,035
1913	49,387,944	9,185,184	2,599,058	441,186
1914	63,784,313	11,010,693	2,427,577	414,124
1915	50,138,520	9,370,048	55,362,917	8,463,174
1916	30,087,999	7,058,420	44,394,301	7,430,089

The graph (Fig. 67) represents the total production and the exports and imports of cheese into the United States.

305. Average yearly price of cheese.—The following table shows the average yearly price of Cheddar cheese in the United States:

TABLE XXIII

SHOWING THE AVERAGE YEARLY PRICE OF CHEESE, 1892-1916

YEAR	CENTS
1892	9.4
1893	9.4
1894	9.7
1895	9.1
1896	8.4
1897	9.1

1898	8.6
1899	8.6
1900	10.2
1901	9.9
1902	11.9
1903	11.9
1904	10.5
1905	10.7
1906	11.7
1907	11.6
1908	12.9
1909	12.6
1910	15.5
1911	12.4
1912	14.2
1913	17.0
1914	17.1
1915	15.3
1916	16.7

The graph (Fig. 68) shows that the average yearly price has increased from 9.4 cents a pound to 16.7 cents.

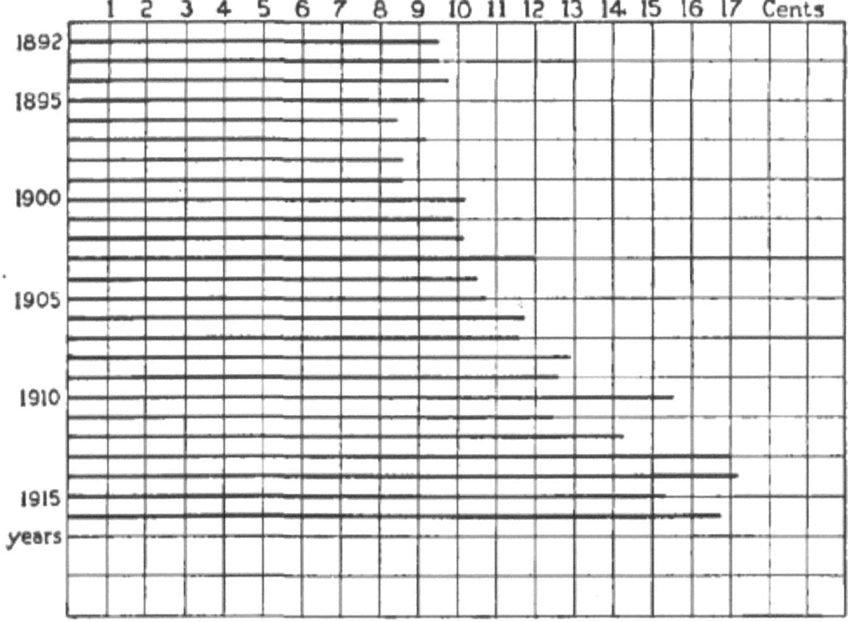

Fig. 68.—Average yearly price of cheese.

306. Canadian cheese statistics.—The following statistics show the development of the industry in Canada. The figures in Table XXIV show the number of cheese factories, the amount of milk received and the total production in Canada.

Table XXIV indicates that the number of cheese factories has decreased but that the production has increased. Because of the scarcity of figures, conclusions would not be accurate.

The figures in Table XXV of the exports and imports show that the exports gradually decreased and the imports increased. If the production has increased, as shown in Table XXIV, more cheese must be consumed by the Canadians. The effect of the war is probably seen in the year 1916, when the imports are decreased and the exports increased.

TABLE XXIV

SHOWING THE NUMBER OF CHEESE FACTORIES, AMOUNT OF MILK RECEIVED
AND THE FACTORY PRODUCTION OF CHEESE

YEAR	NUMBER OF CHEESE FACTORIES	POUNDS OF MILK DELIVERED	FACTORY PRODUCTION OF CHEESE
1900	— —	— —	220,833,269
1907	— —	— —	204,788,583
1910	2291	— —	199,904,205

1915	1871	1,501,946,221	183,887,837
1916	1813	1,503,997,215	192,968,597

TABLE XXV

SHOWING THE AMOUNT AND VALUE OF CANADIAN EXPORTS AND IMPORTS OF CHEESE				
YEAR	NUMBER OF CHEESE FACTORIES		POUNDS OF MILK DELIVERED	
	Amount in Pounds	Value in Dollars	Amount in Pounds	Value in Dollars
1880	40,368,000	$3,893,000		
1890	94,260,000	9,372,212		
1900	185,984,000	19,856,324		
1910	180,859,000	21,607,692	683,778	— —
1911	181,895,000	20,739,507	866,653	— —
1912	163,450,000	20,888,818	919,189	— —
1913	155,216,000	20,697,000	1,495,758	— —
1914	144,478,000	18,866,000	1,512,108	— —
1915	137,601,000	19,213,000	1,162,456	— —
1916	168,961,000	— —	971,821	— —

If the total population of the United States is figured at 100 million and the difference between the exports and imports found and added to the total production, it shows that the average person must consume about three and one-half pounds of cheese in a year.

In the past few years there has been considerable demand for more of the foreign cheeses, such as Camembert and Roquefort.

307. Introduction of cheese-making into new regions.—The manufacture of Cheddar cheese is being encouraged in new regions, in the Alleghany Mountains, in Virginia, West Virginia, North Carolina, Tennessee and in the western states. There has also sprung up a considerable demand for the lactic acid group of cheeses, especially Neufchâtel and Cottage, so that while the cheese industry may decline in certain sections, the total production will probably increase. In the proper locations or sections, the cheese industry has a very bright future. The development of the skimmed-milk cheeses will undoubtedly be given considerable attention in the next few years.

REFERENCES

N. Y. Dept. Agr. Bul. 54, The Dairy Industry in New York State.

N. Y. Produce Rev. and American Creamery.
    Vol. 34, No. 3, page 108.
    Vol. 37, No. 16, page 684.
    Vol. 37, No. 16, page 666.

Vol. 37, No. 9, page 411.
Vol. 33, No. 11, page 482.
Vol. 36, No. 23, page 1078.

Wis. Exp. Sta. Rept. 1897, pages 113-149.

U. S. Census.

U. S. Dept. Agr. Year Books.

Bureau of Foreign and Domestic Commerce.

Statistical abstract of the U. S.

Canadian Dept. Agr. 1915, Report of the dairy and cold storage commissioner.

Dominion of Canada, Census and Statistics office, Rept. 1915.

CHAPTER XIX

TESTING

The fat test; Sampling the milk; Adding the acid; Centrifuging; Reading the test; testing whey for fat; testing cheese for fat; Reading the test; The Hart casein test; Solids in the milk; the lactometer; Calculating the solids not fat in the milk; Testing cheese for moisture.

In connection with marketing, a certain amount of testing of the products should be practiced, to determine exactly the results and grades of products. This includes the testing of the whole milk, whey and cheese for fat, the milk for casein, and the cheese for moisture. In factories in which the milk is bought on the fat basis, it is necessary to test each patron's milk for fat. If there is a cheese-moisture law in the state, it is necessary to test for moisture. The whey should be tested to learn the loss of fat in the manufacturing process and to ascertain whether the losses have been reduced to the minimum.

308. The fat test.—The test commonly used to determine the fat in milk is known as the Babcock. The principle of this test is as follows: Fat exists in the form of very small globules. Because the fat globules are lighter than the other milk constituents, under the influence of the force of gravity most of them rise to the surface. There, mixed with the other milk substances, these globules form a layer of cream. Babcock found that by adding to the milk sulfuric acid of proper strength and temperature, the casein, the milk-sugar and the albumin are decomposed and the sticky quality of the milk is destroyed. The acid does not decompose the fat but leaves it free to come to the surface of the mixture. Under centrifugal force, this fat is quickly brought to the surface. By using a known quantity of milk and having a scale graduated in percentage of the amount of milk, the percentage of fat can be determined. Fig. 69 shows the necessary equipment.

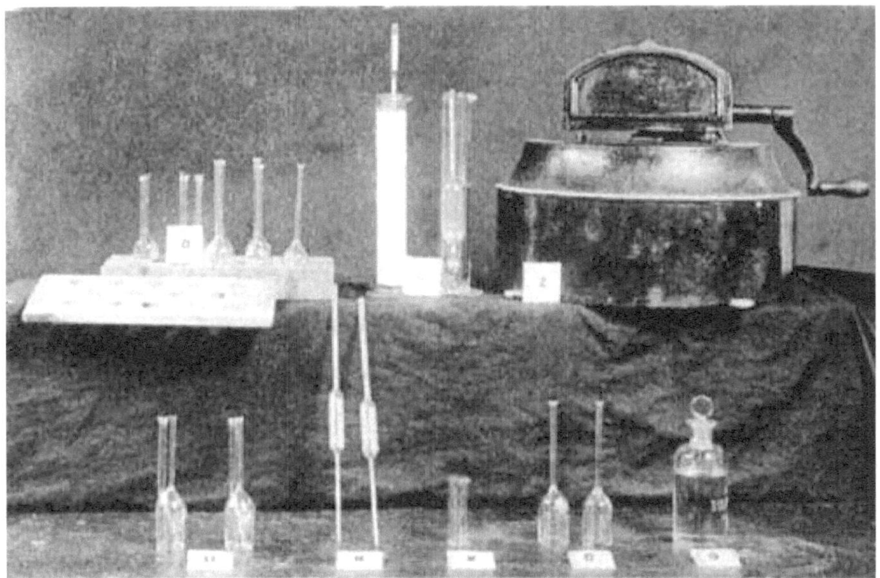

Fig. 69.—Apparatus necessary to test milk and whey for fat and total solids.

There are three kinds of bottles employed in making the test, one with a very large neck which is used when testing materials high in fat-content such as cream, butter and cheese. This is generally called a cream-test bottle. It is graduated from 0 to 50 per cent. When testing materials with a small amount of fat such as whey, skim-milk and buttermilk, a test bottle with two necks is used, one with a small bore for the fat and the other neck with a larger bore to add the milk, acid, water. It is graduated from 0 to 0.5 of 1 per cent. There is a third bottle between the other two to test whole milk. This is known as a whole-milk bottle. It is graduated from 0 to 8 per cent. All of the glassware should comply with the laws.

309. Sampling the milk.—One of the most important parts of testing is to obtain a fair sample of the milk. The milk to be tested may be in a vat or in a farmer's can or a composite sample jar. If the milk is bought on the fat basis, that of each patron is not tested daily, but a small quantity, about half an ounce, is taken each day and placed in a jar; this is known as a composite sample. It is the usual practice to number the patrons and have a sample bottle for each patron with his number on it. Some substance must be added to preserve the milk and to keep it from souring or coagulating. It is difficult to secure a fair sample of sour milk. A wide-mouthed jar is preferred for keeping milk samples. This must be kept closed to prevent evaporation. Each day when milk is added to the composite sample, the bottles should be shaken to prevent the cream drying. Composite samples are tested at least twice a month. The milk may be mixed to obtain a fair sample, by stirring in the vat or by pouring from one bottle to another. Vigorous shaking should be avoided as this is likely to cause churning. One should see that all the cream is removed from the sides of the sample bottle and that it is evenly distributed through the milk. The sample of milk is now measured out with the pipette. This is graduated to deliver 18 grams of milk, and holds 17.6 c.c. Hold the pipette between the thumb and second finger of the right hand with the tip below the surface of the milk, draw the milk by suction with the lips until it is filled well above the graduation. Quickly place the forefinger over the opening and at right angles to the pipette. By gently and carefully raising the forefinger, allow the milk to run down until the surface is exactly level with the graduation. To obtain an accurate reading, the pipette should be on a level with the eye. Then with the left hand, hold the milk test bottle in a slanting position and place the tip of the pipette into it about one-third of an inch and at a slight angle. Now let the milk slowly flow down the side of the neck of the bottle, making certain that none is blown out by the escaping air. When all has run out of the pipette, blow out the drop which remains in the tip. Then measure out another sample in the same way, as the test should be made in duplicate.

310. Adding the acid.—The sulfuric acid should have a specific gravity between 1.82 and 1.83. It should be kept in glass-stoppered bottles or carboys to prevent the absorption of moisture from the air, which will reduce its strength. Acid that is too strong might burn the fat. The acid is a strong poison and will burn if it comes in contact with the flesh or the clothing. In such case, it should be removed by washing with plenty of water. An alkaline substance such as ammonia or bicarbonate of soda should be applied to remove any acid not washed away.

The acid measure holds 17.5 c.c. and it should be filled to the graduation. Then this acid should be added to the test bottle. The bottle should be held at an angle and slowly rotated so that the acid will rinse down any milk remaining in the neck of the bottle. Immediately mix the acid and milk by whirling the body of the bottle in a circle five or six inches in diameter. The mixture should not be allowed to go into the neck of the bottle while mixing. Continue shaking for about a minute after all the curd has disappeared. One should avoid pointing the neck of the bottle toward any person in the mixing operation. The acid unites with all the milk substances except the fat and generates much heat.

311. Centrifuging.—There are two machines in common use for centrifuging, one that runs by mechanical power and the other smaller and runs by hand. If the machine and atmosphere are very cold, the apparatus can be warmed by placing hot water in it. This is not necessary in a steam machine. In a factory where there are a number of samples to test, a power machine is usually employed. In this machine there are pockets or cups in which to set the test bottles. The machine or disk must be balanced by placing bottles in opposite pockets. These pockets are hinged so that when standing still the bottle is in an upright position and when the centrifuge is running, it is in a horizontal position. The machine should then be covered and started running. It should be run at the speed indicated. After five minutes, stop the machine and fill the bottles with boiling water up to the neck. This can be done without taking the bottles out of the machine. A pipette or slender-spouted vessel may be used to add the water. Whirl the bottles two minutes, then add more boiling water to bring the fat column into the graduated part of the neck of the bottle. Then whirl one minute. The test should be read at once or the bottles kept at a temperature of 130° to 140° F. until ready to read.

312. Reading the test.—To read the test, subtract the reading at the bottom of the fat column from that at the highest point. The curved meniscus which always forms at the top of the fat column should be included in the reading. Duplicate samples should not vary more than O.2 of 1 per cent. Standard Babcock test bottles and pipettes should always be used. In some states the agricultural experiment stations examine all glassware and mark it to make certain that it conforms to the requirements of the state law. In New York, glassware found to be correct is branded "S. B.," which means State Brand. In some states a person must have a license to test milk or cream, when it is paid for on the fat test. Such a person must pass an examination to show that he understands the test before a license, will be granted. The license may be revoked if the work is not honestly performed.

313. Testing whey for fat.—Because of the small amount of fat in whey, it is difficult to obtain a representative sample. The best way, if the entire amount cannot be placed in a vat and stirred, is to catch a little of the whey at intervals as it is being drawn from the vat. The sample to be tested is measured with the pipette the same as the milk and placed in the skimmed-milk test bottle. The same acid is used to test whey as to test milk but because there are not so many solids to destroy, not so much is used. If as much acid is used with whey as with milk, it will burn the fat and so interfere with the reading of the test. Just enough acid is added to destroy the milk substances except the fat, or enough to turn the contents of the test bottle dark brown. This usually requires filling the acid measure one-quarter of an inch under the graduation. The remainder of the test is the same as for whole milk.

314. Testing cheese for fat.—The sample of cheese to test for fat is obtained by removing the sample with a cheese-trier. This sample is called a "plug." Different plugs from the same cheese will test various percentages of fat so that it is difficult to secure a representative sample. The usual practice is to take three plugs, one near the center, another near the outside and the third between the first two. The plugs should be put into glass-stoppered bottles to prevent the evaporation of moisture. These plugs are then chopped up very fine. It is of course impossible to measure the cheese as with milk and whey, but it is weighed (Fig. 70). If the cheese is soft it can be stirred with a spatula until well mixed. A soft cheese usually sticks to the neck of the test bottle. After being weighed, it can be dissolved in a little sodium hydroxide and poured into the bottle. Different amounts may be used, commonly 4½ or 6 grams, but 6 grams is to be preferred. This is placed in the Babcock cream bottle since there will usually be more fat than can be read in a milk bottle. After the material has been placed in the test bottle, about two-thirds of an acid-measure of warm water is added to assist in dissolving the cheese.

Fig. 70.—Apparatus necessary to test cheese for fat.

The acid is added the same as with the milk. If all the cheese particles are not destroyed, and therefore do not disappear, a little more acid will complete the solution. Centrifuging is performed as with the milk.

315. Reading the test.—In a cream-test bottle the neck is so much wider that there is a much larger meniscus. In order to obtain an accurate result, the meniscus should be removed. This is done by carefully adding a substance called glymol, which is a mineral oil colored red. Usually about one-quarter of an inch of glymol is added to the fat column. This should not mix with the fat. The bottles should be placed in a hot water bath 135° to 140° F. for four minutes before reading. The temperature at reading should be 135° to 140° F. The reading is then taken from the bottom of the fat column to the line between this and the glymol. The bottle is graduated for 18 grams of material, but as only a part of 18 grams of cheese was used for the test, the reading should be multiplied by the part of 18 grams used. For example, suppose 6 grams of cheese were used and the test read 12 per cent fat. Since 6 is one third of 18, the actual percentage of fat is 3 times 12, or 36 per cent.

316. The Hart[135] casein test was devised to determine the percentage of casein in milk. A special test bottle and centrifuge are necessary. The method of making the test is as follows: Place 2 c.c. of chloroform in the casein test tube, add 20 c.c. of a 0.25 of 1 per cent solution of acetic acid at a temperature of 65° to 75° F. This solution of acetic acid is made by diluting 10 c.c of glacial acetic acid with 100 c.c. of water, then dilute 25 c.c. of this solution to 1000 c.c. with water; 5 c.c.

____

[135] Hart, E. B., A simple test for casein in milk and its relation to the dairy industry, Wis. Exp. Sta. Bul. 156, pages 1-22, 1907.

of milk at a temperature of 65° to 75° F. is then run into the bottle. The bottle is then covered with the thumb and inverted and the mixture shaken vigorously for exactly twenty seconds. It is then centrifuged within twenty minutes at a speed of 2000 revolutions a minute. The bottle should stand ten minutes before reading the percentage of casein. There are other tests for casein but they are very complicated.

Fig. 71.—A Quevenne lactometer.

317. Solids in the milk.—Because not only the fat but all the solids are utilized in cheese-making, it is important to know the amount of the solids in the milk. This is ascertained by determining the specific gravity of the milk and knowing the fat-content; the solids not fat can then be calculated.

318. The lactometer. — The specific gravity of liquids is measured by an instrument called a hydrometer. Its use is based on the fact that when a solid body floats in a liquid, it displaces a volume of liquid equal in weight to its own. Hydrometers are in many cases so made that the specific gravity can be read at the point where the scale is even with the upper surface of the liquid. A hydrometer that is especially adapted to milk is called a lactometer. There are two lactometers in common use, the Quevenne and the Board of Health.

The Quevenne lactometer. — This is a long slender hollow piece of glass weighted at the bottom to make it float in the milk in an upright position (Fig. 71). The upper end is slender and contains the scale. This scale is graduated from 15 at the top to 40 at the bottom. Each reading on the scale corresponds to the point marked specific gravity on a hydrometer, except that the figures are not complete. For example, 15 on the Quevenne scale means a specific gravity of 1.015; a reading of 30 on the Quevenne scale means a specific gravity of 1.030, and so on. The Quevenne lactometer is graduated to give correct results at a temperature of 60° F. The milk should be at this temperature. If the temperature is below or above this, a correction must be made to the reading. The temperature should not be more than 10 degrees above or below 60° F. The correction for each degree in variation of temperature can be made by adding 0.1 or subtracting 0.1 from the lactometer reading, as the case may be. If the temperature is above 60° F., the correction is added to the lactometer and if it is below 60° F., the correction is subtracted from the lactometer reading. The reading should be taken when the lactometer is floating free in the milk. The scale is read exactly at the surface of the milk. The better lactometers have a thermometer with the scale just above or opposite the lactometer scale.

Fig. 72.—A Board of Health lactometer.

The Board of Health lactometer.—This is very similar to the Quevenne lactometer except that the scale is graduated from 0 to 120 (Fig. 72). The point on the scale of the lactometer that floats at the surface in water is represented by 0, and 100 represents the specific gravity of 1.029. On the Board of Health lactometer, the 100 degrees or divisions from 0 to 100 equal 29 divisions on the Quevenne. Therefore, one division on the Board of Health equals 0.29 of a division on the Quevenne. To convert Board of Health reading to Quevenne, multiply by 0.29 and to convert Quevenne to Board of Health, divide by 0.29. The correction for temperatures above or below 60° F. is made the same as with the Quevenne, except 0.3 is added or subtracted from the reading instead of 0.1 as with the Quevenne.

319. Calculating the solids not fat in the milk.—When the lactometer reading and fat-content of the milk are known, there are several formulas for calculating the solids not fat. In the following formulas, L equals Quevenne lactometer reading at 60° F., and F equals the percentage of fat in the milk:

$$\frac{L + 0.7\,F}{5} = S.N.F$$

$$\frac{L + F}{4} = S.N.F$$

$$\frac{L}{4} + 0.2\,F + 0.14 = S.N.F$$

320. Testing cheese for moisture.[136]—There are two methods of testing cheese for moisture. The following is a simple test devised by H. C. Troy:

The ordinary butter moisture test, in which a metal cup is heated over a flame, cannot be used for determining the percentage of water in cheese because the high temperature developed in operating that test drives from the cheese other substances with the water. Also, particles are lost by spattering when the cheese is heated with any degree of rapidity in the shallow butter-moisture cups. To overcome these difficulties, the new method here described has been developed for the purpose of determining the percentage of moisture in cheese. The apparatus consists of:

    1 double-walled copper drying cup
    1 centigrade thermometer registering to 200°
    1 alcohol lamp
    1 tripod
    1 special flask
    1 scales sensitive to 0.01 gram
    1 set of weights, 0.01 to 100 grams

The body of the copper drying cup may be made in two parts. One of the parts is a jacket that forms the outer wall of the apparatus. It has a flat bottom 4½ inches in diameter, and the perpendicular wall is 4½ inches in height. The inner part of the cup must have a flat bottom 2¾ inches in diameter and a side wall 3¾ inches high. A flange attached to the upper rim of the inner part extends out at right angles to the cup wall and forms a cover for the space between the walls when the two parts are put together. The flange is bent down around its outer edge to make it fit snugly over the upper rim of the outer jacket. It thus holds the inner cup securely in place, leaving a space about ¾ inch wide for oil between the walls and bottoms, and permits the apparatus to be taken apart readily. A circular opening

[136] Sammis, J. L., The moisture test in the cheese factory, Wis. Exp. Sta. Circ. 81, 1917.

Troy, H. C., A cheese moisture test, N. Y. (Cornell) Exp. Sta. Ext. Bul. 17, 1917.

about ½ inch in diameter is made through the flange to permit the insertion of a thermometer for taking the temperature of the oil or the melted fat which is used in the space between the walls. Lard or tallow serves best for use in this space; a readily inflammable oil should not be employed. The thermometer may be permanently held in place by passing it snugly through a hole bored in a cork, the cork being then fitted into the hole through the flange. A flat metal cover is placed on the cup when making a test. This cover has a hole through the center just large enough to permit the neck of the drying flask to extend up through it. The cover assists in keeping the body of the flask at a constant temperature by preventing the entrance of cold air currents. The thermometer should register changes in temperature between zero and 200° C. The alcohol lamp should yield a flame about ¼ inch in diameter and ¾ inch high. The tripod should be about 6 inches high and of proper diameter at the top to support the oil bath.

An ordinary flat-bottom glass Erlenmeyer flask, of such a diameter as to fit neatly into the oil-bath cup, may be used to hold the cheese during the drying operation; but a special glass flask serves better. It is made with a flat bottom 2½ inches in diameter, which will fit into the cup of the drying apparatus. The side walls of this flask should be perpendicular for about 1 inch, when they should begin to slope in toward the base of the neck, which should be located about 2 inches above the bottom. The neck of the flask should be 1 inch in diameter, with perpendicular walls, and its length should give the flask a total height of 4¾ inches. When the apparatus (Fig. 73) is put together for the first time, the melted fat or oil may be placed in the outer jacket and the inner cup may then be fitted into position, or the parts may be put together first and the oil then poured into the space between the cup walls through the opening where the thermometer is to be placed. The oil should fill the space to within an inch of the top. The cork through which the thermometer has been passed is then fitted into the opening. The thermometer bulb should be placed in the oil about half an inch above the bottom of the outer jacket. The apparatus is then placed on the tripod over the alcohol lamp. A flame ½ inch in diameter and ¾ inch high will give sufficient heat to hold the bath at the proper temperature. The temperature may be regulated by raising or lowering the lamp or by changing the size of the flame by adjusting the wick. Hundreds of tests may be run without taking the apparatus apart or changing the oil. The copper drying cup can be made by any tinsmith. The other parts may be ordered through any dairy or chemical supply company.

Fig. 73.—Apparatus necessary to test cheese for moisture.

In operating the test, the alcohol lamp is first lighted, so that the oil bath may be warming while the test sample is under preparation. A representative sample of the cheese, which may be taken with a cheese-trier and held in a glass-stoppered sample jar, is then cut into particles about the size of kernels of wheat without removing it from the jar. This may be accomplished with an ordinary table knife that has had the end squared and sharpened. The clean dry flask is then accurately balanced on the scales and a 5-gram weight is placed in the opposite scale pan. Particles of cheese from the prepared sample are put into the flask until the scales comes to an exact balance. Great care should be taken to avoid loss of moisture from the cheese in the preparation of the sample.

With the thermometer in the oil bath registering between 140° and 145° C. (or between 284° and 293° F.), the flask is placed in the cup of the oil bath and the flat disk-shaped cover is adjusted over the apparatus. The flask should remain in the bath for fifty minutes, the temperature being kept between 140° and 145° C. all the time. The flask is then removed, covered and allowed to cool to room temperature in a dry place. It is then weighed, and the quotient obtained by dividing the loss in weight by the original weight, multiplied by 100, gives the percentage of water in the cheese. The following shows the method of computation:

Problem: Five grams of cheese was heated until the water contained in it was evaporated. The remaining substance weighed 3.15 grams. What percentage of water did the cheese contain?

Answer: 5.00 - 3.15 = 1.85
           1.85 ÷ 5 = 0.37
           0.37 × 100 = 37 (percentage of water in cheese)

A butter-moisture scales with an extra 5-gram weight may be used for weighing out the 5 grams of cheese. If the scales indicates the amount of moisture in 10 grams of butter by percentage graduations on its beam or by percentage weights, then it will be necessary to multiply by 2 the percentage indicated by such scales or percentage weights when only 5 grams of cheese is used.

The moisture may be determined by weighing out a small sample of cheese and drying it in an oven and calling the loss moisture. Many such ovens have been devised.

New York and Wisconsin have laws limiting the amount of water which may be incorporated in Cheddar cheese. New York places the limit at 39 per cent and Wisconsin at 40 per cent. If the moisture-content is above this, the cheese must be branded adulterated.

CHAPTER XX

MARKETING

Buying milk; Cheese yield basis of buying milk; Fat basis for payment of milk; Weight basis or pooling method for payment of milk; Fat-plus-two method for payment of milk; Comparison of methods; Laws governing the production and sale of milk; Marketing of cheese; Mercantile exchanges; Marketing perishable varieties; Distribution of price; Standards; Laws relating to cheese marketing.

Marketing is related to cheese in two ways: First, the purchase of the raw material, the milk; and secondly the sale of the finished product, the cheese.

321. Buying milk.—The method of paying for the milk differs in the various cheese sections and factories. At some factories a stated price is paid for the milk or the fat. This is usually in terms of 100 pounds of milk or for each pound of fat. This is the practice with concerns possessing large capital. Other factories make the milk into cheese and after each sale, the expenses necessary for operating the factory are deducted and the remainder of the money divided among the patrons. This money is divided either on the basis of the number of pounds of milk or of fat delivered. The question arises as to which is the better method to buy milk for cheese-making, or the fairest way to divide the money received from a sale of cheese.

322. Cheese yield basis of buying milk.—Let us suppose that at a cheese factory there were five patrons: (A) delivered 100 pounds of milk testing 3 per cent fat; (B) 100 pounds of milk testing 3.5 per cent fat; (C) 100 pounds of milk testing 4.0 per cent fat; (D) 100 pounds of milk testing 4.5 per cent fat; and (E) 100 pounds of milk testing 5.0 per cent fat. Table XXVI shows the actual number of pounds of cheese containing 37 per cent moisture which 100 pounds of milk containing different percentages of fat will produce. The cheese sold net for 20 cents a pound.

TABLE XXVI

SHOWING PAYMENTS FOR MILK BASED ON THE ACTUAL YIELD OF CHEESE					
PATRON	POUNDS OF MILK DELIVERED	PER CENT OF FAT IN MILK	YIELD OF CHEESE CONTAINING 37% MOISTURE	PRICE A POUND	AMOUNT DUE EACH PATRON

A	100	3.0	8.30	$.20	$1.66
B	100	3.5	9.45	.20	1.89
C	100	4.0	10.60	.20	2.12
D	100	4.5	11.74	.20	2.34
E	100	5.0	12.90	.20	2.58
Total	20.0	5.0	52.99	.20	10.59

This table shows the amount of money each patron should receive if the money were divided on the basis of the actual yield of cheese.

323. Fat basis for payment of milk.—Let us suppose that the same five patrons delivered the same quantity of milk testing the same percentages of fat and that the cheese sold for the same price. A total of 20 pounds of fat was delivered and the cheese sold for $10.598; by dividing this amount by the pounds of fat delivered, the price or value of one pound of fat is found to be $.5299. Multiplying the pounds of fat each patron delivered by the price a pound would give the amount of money due each patron.

TABLE XXVII

SHOWING PAYMENTS FOR MILK BASED ON FAT-CONTENT OF MILK					
PATRON	POUNDS OF MILK DELIVERED	PER CENT OF FAT IN MILK	POUNDS OF MILK DELIVERED	VALUE OF POUND OF FAT	AMOUNT DUE EACH PATRON
A	100	3.0	3.0	$.5299	$1.58
B	100	3.5	3.5	$.5299	$1.85
C	100	4.0	4.0	$.5299	$2.12
D	100	4.5	4.5	$.5299	$2.38
E	100	5.0	5.0	$.5299	$2.65

324. Weight basis or pooling method for payment of milk.—By this system, each patron would receive an equal price for 100 pounds of milk. If the same supposition is taken as before, there would be 500 pounds of milk delivered and the cheese sold for $10.59; each 100 pounds of milk would be worth $2.12. As each patron delivered an equal weight of milk, each would receive an equal amount of money, or $2.12.

325. Fat-plus-two method for payment of milk.—Some workers have thought that by adding two to the fat test, the division of money would be more nearly the true cheese-producing value of the milk. The amount due each patron is figured as in the fat basis, except that two is added to the fat test and this is used as the basis of division. If the same suppositions were used as before, each patron would receive the amount shown in Table XXVIII.

326. Comparison of methods.—The best way to judge the different methods of paying for milk is to compare them with the true value based on the actual cheese yield as shown in Table XXIX.

TABLE XXVIII

	Showing Payments for Milk by Fat-Plus-Two Methods					
Patron	**Pounds of Milk Delivered**	**Per Cent of Fat in Milk**	**Fat Plus Two**	**Pounds of Fat Delivered**	**Value of Pound of Fat**	**Amount Due Each Patron**
A	100	3.0	5.0	5.0	$.353	$1.78
B	100	3.5	5.5	5.5	.353	1.94
C	100	4.0	6.0	6.0	.353	2.12
D	100	4.5	6.5	6.5	.353	2.29
E	100	5.0	7.0	7.0	.353	2.47

TABLE XXIX

	Showing the Comparison of the Different Methods of Paying for Milk at Cheese Factories			
	Percentage of Fat in Milk	**Initial**		
Patron		**Pooling System**	**Fat Basis**	**Fat-Plus-Two Method**
A	3.0	+ $0.46	- $0.08	+ $0.10
B	3.5	+ 0.23	- 0.04	+ 0.05
C	4.0	0.00	0.00	0.00
D	4.5	- 0.23	+ 0.04	- 0.05
E	5.0	- 0.46	+ 0.08	- 0.10

A careful study of the above table shows that the pooling system is in favor of the dairy-man with the poor milk, and that the fat basis favors the dairy-man with the rich milk. This is due, of course, to the fact that the casein does not increase in the milk quite in proportion to the fat. With the pooling system or fat basis of payment, no account is taken of the casein; but the fat-plus-two system is an attempt to recognize the casein, but considers the percentage of casein in all milk to be the same. This method is in favor of the dairy-man with milk low in fat, but not to the extent of the pooling system. The latter system considers the cheese-producing power of all milk to be the same. It favors the dairy-man with low-testing milk. The fat basis for payment recognizes only the fat and is an advantage to the dairy-man with the high-testing milk but not to the extent that the pooling system is in favor of the low-testing milk. The fat-plus-two method recognizes 2 per cent of casein in the milk. This favors the dairy-men with low-testing milk. Other methods[137] of paying for milk have been devised. Because the actual yield of cheese from the milk of different herds cannot be easily determined at the cheese factory, this method of payment cannot be employed. In localities in which all the dairy-men have the same breed of cattle and there is not a wide variation in the fat percentage, the fat basis is usually found to be the most satisfactory way to pay

[137] Sammis, J. L., Correct payment for cheese factory milk by the Babcock test, Wis. Exp. Sta. Bul. 276, 1917.

for the milk.

327. Laws governing the production and sale of milk.—Many states have laws regulating the sanitary conditions under which the milk may be produced. These laws relate principally to the condition of the stables, the health of the cow, the food given the cow, and the care of the milk. The following law[138] of Wisconsin is a good example:

"Adulterated milk, what constitutes. Section 4607a. In all prosecutions under the preceding section, or any other section of these statutes, or laws amendatory thereof or supplementary thereto, relating to the sale of adulterated milk or adulterated cream, the term adulterated milk shall mean: milk containing less than three per centum of milk fat, or milk containing less than eight and one-half per centum of milk solids not fat, or milk drawn from cows within eight days before or four days after parturition, or milk from which any part of the cream has been removed, or milk which has been diluted with water or any other fluid, or milk to which has been added or into which has been introduced any coloring matter or chemical or preservative or deleterious or filthy substance or any foreign substance whatsoever, or milk drawn from cows kept in a filthy or unhealthy condition, or milk drawn from any sick or diseased cow or cow having ulcers or other running sores, or milk drawn from cows fed unwholesome food, or milk in any stage of putrefaction, or milk contaminated by being kept in stables containing cattle or other animals. The term adulterated cream shall mean cream containing less than eighteen per centum of milk fat, or cream taken from milk drawn from cows within eight days before or four days after parturition, or cream from milk to which has been added or introduced any coloring matter or chemical or preservative or deleterious or filthy substance or any foreign substance whatsoever, or cream from milk drawn from cows kept in a filthy or unhealthy condition, or cream from milk drawn from any sick or diseased cow or cow having ulcers or other running sores, or cream from milk drawn from cows fed unwholesome food, or cream contaminated by being kept in stables containing cattle or other animals, or cream to which has been added or into which has been introduced any coloring matter or chemical or preservative or deleterious or filthy substance or any foreign substance whatsoever, or cream in any stage of putrefaction, provided, that nothing in this act shall be construed to prohibit the sale of pasteurized milk or cream to which viscogen or sucrate of lime has been added solely for the purpose of restoring the viscosity, if the same be distinctly labeled in such manner as to advise the purchaser of its true character; and providing that nothing in this act shall be construed as prohibiting the sale of milk commonly known as 'skimmed milk,' when the same is sold as and for 'skimmed milk.' Milk drawn from cows within eight days before or four days after parturition, or milk to which has been added or into which has been introduced any coloring matter or chemical or preservative or deleterious or filthy substance, or milk drawn from cows kept in a filthy or unclean condition, or milk drawn from any sick or diseased cow or cow having ulcers or other running sores, or milk drawn from cows fed unwholesome food, or milk contaminated by being kept in stables containing cattle or other animals and cream from any such

------

[138] Dairy Laws of Wisconsin, 1916, section 4607a.

milk, or cream in any stage of putrefaction are hereby declared to be unclean and unsanitary milk or unclean and unsanitary cream, as the case may be."

Most states have laws which determine the legal standard of milk. Any one selling milk which does not meet this standard is liable to be fined. The laws of most states prohibit the taking of anything from the milk or the adding of anything to it. This prohibits the skimming and watering. Skimmed-milk must be sold as such.

328. Marketing of cheese.—There are many different methods[139] of selling cheese. Each is adapted to certain conditions and each has its advantages and disadvantages. In cheese sections, the customary method of selling is on the board of trade, which is the meeting of the cheese-buyers and factory salesmen. They meet at a given place at a certain day and hour each week. Every board has its officers. There are different ways in which a board of trade may be operated. In some cases there is a large blackboard divided into columns. In the first column, the salesman writes the name of the factory and the number and kind of cheese offered for sale. At the top of the other columns are the names of the different cheese-buyers. The president usually opens the sale at a stated time and asks that all cheese be placed on the blackboard. When this is done he states that they are ready to receive bids on the cheese. The buyers then write the price a pound they wish to pay opposite each lot of cheese and in the column headed by their names. After all the bids have been received and placed on the board, the presiding officer states that a certain length of time, usually fifteen minutes, will be given the salesman to withdraw his cheese if he does not think a high enough price has been offered; this is indicated by the salesman stepping to the blackboard and erasing the factory name and number of boxes. At the close of the stated time, the presiding officer declares the cheese offered on the board sold to the highest bidder. The purchaser then gives the salesman directions for shipping.

Sometimes a board of trade has a committee of one member elected by the factory salesmen and one elected by the cheese-buyers. These two members elect a third and these three constitute the price committee. This committee meets each week and determines what the price shall be. This is known as the ruling. The factory salesmen and cheese-buyers then try to make private sales. By this method no one, except the persons concerned, knows exactly what price is paid for the cheese. Usually, a price above the ruling is paid.

At Quebec, Canada, there is a cheese-selling organization with government assistance. On paying a certain fee, any cheese factory may join. All the factories belonging to the organization ship their cheese to a central cold storage where the cheeses are examined and graded by a government inspector. A cheese from each vat is tried. These cheeses are separated into white and colored lots, then graded according to quality. When the total number of cheeses in each lot is known, the lots are sold at auction. The purchaser must accept the cheese as graded. The better

[139] Sammis, J. L., The improved system of selling cheese, Hoard's Dairyman 52 (1916), 15, pages 5, 11-12.

Hibbard, B. H., and A. Hobson, Markets and prices of Wisconsin cheese, Wis. Exp. Sta. Bul. 251, pages 1-56, 1915.

grades of cheese bring about the same price as on the market, but the advantage lies in the selling of the lower grades. Ordinarily, the purchaser takes advantage of the salesman when the cheeses are undergrade. The success of this plan depends on the accuracy of the person grading the cheese. This method seems to be growing in popularity, because the cheese-buyer can purchase large amounts of cheese at one time and be sure of the quality. A small fee, about one-twelfth of a cent a pound, is charged for handling the cheese. Similar organizations are in operation in Wisconsin. The boards of trade and selling organizations deal almost entirely in Cheddar cheese.

329. Mercantile exchanges.—In the larger cities are exchanges where cheese is bought and sold by jobbers. This cheese is mostly Cheddar. The prices paid these jobbers tend to fix the daily price of cheese. These prices are published daily, for example, in New York Price Current. Some factories ship their cheese directly to these jobbers. The following are the cheese rules of the New York Mercantile Exchange adopted May 4, 1915:

CHEESE RULES OF THE NEW YORK MERCANTILE EXCHANGE

Rule 1. At the first regular meeting of the Executive Committee in each year, the President shall appoint, subject to the approval of the Executive Committee, a Cheese Committee to consist of seven members of the Exchange, who are known as members of the cheese trade, to hold office until their successors are appointed. It shall be the duty of the Cheese Committee to formulate such rules and regulations as may be necessary for the government of transactions between members of the Exchange, and to revise the same as circumstances may require. Such rules and revisions shall be subject to the approval of the Executive Committee.

Rule 2. All transactions in cheese between members of the Exchange shall be governed by the following rules, but nothing therein shall be construed as interfering, in any way, with the rights of members to make such special contracts or conditions as they may desire.

Rule 3. If a sale is made from dock, or platform, or to arrive, the buyer shall assume the same relations toward the transportation line by which the cheese arrives, as the seller previously held as regards its removal from the place of delivery within the time granted by such lines for that purpose. Transactions between members of this Exchange shall be governed as follows: Any member negotiating for any lot of cheese belonging to another member, the price having been agreed upon, shall examine such lot of cheese within twenty-four (24) hours after such negotiation takes place. Failure to examine within said time releases the seller from any obligations to make delivery thereafter, if he so wishes.

Rule 4. In the absence of special agreement, all cheese purchased "in store" shall be understood as being ready and designed for immediate delivery, but the buyer shall have twenty-four hours in which to have the cheese inspected, and weight tested, and shall not be liable for the storage and insurance, if removed within two days.

Rule 5. When cheese are sold to arrive, or from depot or dock, the cheese must be accepted or rejected within six business hours after notice of actual arrival to buyer. Business hours shall be understood to be from 10 A.M. to 4 P.M. If buyer rejects the same, he shall state the reasons for rejection. Should the rejection be considered unfair, the seller shall at once notify the buyer that he declines to accept such rejection; and he may call for a Committee, which shall be composed of three members of the cheese trade; the seller choosing one, the buyer one, and the third selected from the cheese trade by these two, or, they failing to agree, the third shall be appointed by the Chairman of the Committee on Cheese. The Examining Committee shall at once inspect the lot of cheese in dispute, sampling not less than five (5) per cent of each mark or factory, and they shall immediately give their decision in writing to both parties. Either party failing to abide by the decision of the Committee may be summoned by the other party before the Complaint Committee under Section 24 of the By-laws. The fees for each examination shall be six ($6) dollars, to be paid by the party adjudged to be in fault.

Rule 6. The weight of all cheese shall be tested by a regularly appointed official weigher, and his certificates shall accompany the document conveying the title of the property. Said official weigher to be appointed by the Committee on Cheese, subject to the approval of the Executive Committee.

Rule 7. The weigher's fee shall be twenty-five (25) cents per factory except where the owner requires more than ten (10) boxes be tested in which case the fee shall be fifty (50) cents, which shall be paid by the seller.

Rule 8. Unless otherwise agreed upon in testing the weight of cheese, not less than five (5) boxes or more than ten (10) per cent of the whole lot shall be a test, and said test shall be considered good for three (3) business days, including day test is made.

Rule 9. In testing weights, all over and short weights shall be taken into the average on each particular factory. Single Daisies shall be tested on half pounds, Double Daisies and all other sizes on even pounds.

Rule 10. Where a lot of cheese is found to test irregular in weights, either the buyer or seller may require the entire lot to be reweighed. The charge for same shall be three (3) cents per box.

Rule 11. Boxes of cheese which may be found largely at variance from original weights shall not enter into the average, but their weight shall be separately ascertained and certified to by the weigher.

Rule 12. Where sales are made, and the buyer finds damaged or sour cheese in excess of fifteen (15) per cent it shall be optional with him to refuse or receive the remainder of the lot purchased. But, in the event of his accepting the remainder of the lot, the sour or damaged cheese shall revert to the seller.

Rule 13. The Committee on Cheese shall appoint subject to the approval of the Executive Committee, a Cheese Inspector and also a Deputy Inspector, whose duties shall be, when called upon by members of the Exchange, to inspect the quality and condition of such lots of cheese as may be required and to render a certificate of such inspection. Where the cheese in the lots are reasonably uniform in quality, the examination of 10 per cent of the lot shall be considered sufficient, but this shall not prevent the Inspector examining a larger percentage of the lot, when he deems it necessary. The fee for inspection shall be fifty (50) cents for lots consisting of fifty (50) boxes or less. Lots exceeding fifty (50) boxes shall be one cent per box, which shall be collected from the member ordering the inspection.

Rule 14. The Cheese Inspector's certificate shall be made to read as follows:

NEW YORK MERCANTILE EXCHANGE

Cheese Inspector's Certificate

Inspection No.............

This is to certify that I have this day inspected for M...........
the following cheese, now located at...........................
Factory and identification marks.......................
Quantity in lot..boxes
Quantity inspected...boxes
and find as follows:
Flavor..
Body and Texture..
Color...
Condition..
Boxes..
Grade..
Inspection charges.................................

....*Inspector*

The certificate to have a blank margin of three inches at the bottom, for the purpose of inserting specifications of Institutions, also for cheese sold under the Call, so that the Inspector may certify that cheese inspected fill the requirements as specified and the Inspector shall brand one impression on both boxes and cheese.

NEW YORK MERCANTILE EXCHANGE

OFFICIAL INSPECTION

Number...............   Date...............................
....*Inspector*

Rule 16. The Weigher's Certificate shall be made to read as follows:

This is to certify that the following is the actual test of ....
boxes, out of shipment of...........**boxes**
Factory Mark...
Marked Weights...
Actual Weights..
Loss...
Average loss...................**lbs. on**...**boxes**
New York...19......
....*Weigher*

and the Cheese Rules numbered 6 to 11 inclusive be printed on the back thereof.

Rule 17. Members offering cheese for sale under the Call shall describe each lot, as to number of boxes, color, texture (open or close made), body, flavor, size, and how boxed, section where made, whether whole milks or skims and the average weight of each lot. Cheese sold under the Call to be accepted, or rejected, as a good delivery, or otherwise, based on the description given at the sale.

Rule 18. When cheese are sold under the Call, unless otherwise stated, they shall be ready for immediate shipment.

Rule 19. All cheese offered under the Call, with Inspector's Certificate attached, shall be accompanied by such Certificate and be accepted by the buyer unconditionally, provided the cheese are branded according to Rule 13.

Rule 20. When cheese are offered under the Call, without Inspector's Certificate, should the buyer not consider the cheese a good delivery, according to description by seller, he may notify the seller, and if the seller is unwilling to make another delivery, the buyer may call upon the Inspector to decide whether or not the delivery shall stand. If the Inspector decides it is a good delivery, the buyer shall accept the cheese. If the Inspector decides it is not a good delivery, then the seller shall have twenty-four (24) hours in which to make a good delivery. But if the seller, after twenty-four (24) hours, fails to make a good delivery, then the buyer shall notify the Superintendent of the Exchange, who shall collect a penalty of three per cent of the amount of the transaction, the Exchange retaining twenty-five per cent of this sum, and seventy-five per cent shall be paid to the buyer.

Rule 21. Spot sales under the Call shall be for spot cash unless otherwise agreed.

Rule 22. All failures in meeting contracts shall be reported to the Superintendent of the Exchange, and announced at next regular session of the Exchange.

330. Marketing perishable varieties.—Soft cheeses, such as Cream, Neufchâtel, Cottage, are usually sold to jobbers or directly to retail stores. They have a very short commercial life, hence cannot be held long before delivery to the consumer. From the jobber, cheese usually goes to the wholesale grocer and then to the retail dealer and finally the consumer. Most jobbers have cold storages so that they can hold cheese without injury to quality. (See Fig. 74.) The kind of cheese marketed in any locality depends on the tastes of the residents. For example, the South usually desires a highly colored product, thinking this color indicates more fat; in the Cheddar group New England demands a soft pasty quick-curing cheese, thinking that softness is a sign of more fat and richness; England wants a rather dry, well-cured, highly flavored cheese. Canadian Cheddar cheese has been standardized as far as possible to appeal to the English market. A long ripening period keeps capital tied up through the further time required for delivery. This has led to the sale of much of the cheese almost or entirely unripe. So much of the product has reached the consumer without characteristic varietal flavor that large numbers have acquired the habit of purchasing and even preferring cheese only partly ripe.

Fig. 74.—A cheese cold storage room.

The time during which cheese should be held at the factory depends on the variety. Some are shipped as soon as made, including those cheeses with sour-milk flavor only. Others have to be cured in the factory from six to eight weeks. Cheeses in paper or tin-foil should be neatly wrapped and carefully put in the boxes. The box of cheese should be neat, clean and attractive. Cheeses not wrapped should have a firm rind to hold them in shape. The boxes should be clean and the weight of cheese neatly and plainly marked. In the case of Cheddar cheese, it may be paraffined at the factory, but if not, this is usually done at the cold storage of the jobber. The cheeses usually have some time to cure or ripen while being handled by the various dealers.

331. Distribution of price.—The final selling price of cheese is a composite of all the changes that have gone before; or conversely, the farmer, the maker, the carrier and the distributors (wholesale, jobbing and retail dealers) must all be paid from the final price of the product. A study of this problem in Wisconsin has been made by Hibbard, and Hobson.[140] The general facts as determined for Wisconsin

[140] Hibbard, B. H., and Asher Hobson, Markets and prices of Wisconsin cheese, Wis.

have fairly wide application to the manufacture and sale of cheese.

Economic success in handling cheese is dependent on proper provision for the sale of the product. Where the output is small, a personal market can be created and maintained. This eliminates all profits intervening between the maker and the retailer. If the business reaches a volume beyond the possibilities of direct sale to the retailer, some selling organization is necessary. Where the number of producers is great and the selling machinery is well organized, the cheese factory becomes a producer of a commodity which is turned over to existing selling agencies. This condition is well established for Cheddar, Swiss, Brick and Limburger cheese. The soft cheeses other than Limburger have thus far been handled principally by large companies, each of which has developed an expensive selling organization. A study of the map (Fig. 65) shows how the cheese industry is localized in particular sections of certain states. Individual factories have maintained themselves in widely separated places. This localization is due to the geographical conditions which make certain regions specially adapted to dairying, modified by the proximity to markets for milk as milk. There are many regions, however, well adapted to cheese production in which there is no development of the industry at present. New developments are now taking place in the mountain areas of the South, notably North Carolina and adjacent states, and in several centers of the western mountain states. Many other areas should develop the making of cheese in some form.

The actual costs of making and selling cheese were found by the Wisconsin investigators to vary approximately as follows: (1) cost of making, 1.2 to 1.75 cents; (2) storage, ⅛ cent a pound a month, or ⅜ to ½ cent for the season; (3) transportation to distant points, $.20 to $2.50 for 100 pounds according to distance; (4) the local dealer, about 1 cent a pound; (5) the wholesale dealer, 2 cents; (6) the jobber or broker who occasionally intervenes, about ⅛ to ¼ cent; and the retailer, 5.5 to 9 cents. The entire cost of selling at the time this investigation was made represented about one-half of the retail price of the cheese. The producer of milk received the other half of that price.

332. Standards.—Legal standards in the United States are thus far largely based on the specifications of American Cheddar. In so far as they are applied to other products, they operate merely to prevent or reduce the use of skimmed-milk. The analyses and limits proposed in the discussion of varieties or groups in this book represent the range of composition actually known to be associated with cheeses of typical quality. Efforts are now being made to establish definitions and standards of composition which will limit the use of cheese names to products conforming to the requirements for such varieties. Practically the only federal requirement thus far enforced in the United States is that 50 per cent of the water-free substance of the cheese must be milk-fat. Various states have local requirements but most of them include the federal rule as to fat. New York and Wisconsin now restrict the amount of water in Cheddar cheese to 40 per cent. Most states have laws regulating the manufacture and sale of skimmed-milk cheese.

333. Laws relating to cheese marketing.—A cheese of foreign origin if made

Exp. Sta. Bul. 251, 1915.

in this country must be branded to show that it is not imported. For example, Camembert made in America is labeled Domestic Camembert. Some manufacturers call it Camembert type of cheese. The same applies to other varieties of foreign cheese. If a variety is made under a trade-marked name, this prevents any other manufacturer from using that name. For example, a concern may make "Philadelphia" cream cheese; other concerns may make cream cheese, but they must call it by some other name.

The committee on definitions and standards for the Association of Official Agricultural Chemists has now undertaken to define the proper use of type names. This is intended to determine the proper limits of composition of cheeses in each variety and such essentials of physical identification as will insure the proper use of these names.

Certain states have laws which relate to the branding of the cheese to denote quality. If the cheese is made from whole milk, a brand may be applied to show this fact. This is usually called the state brand. If made from skimmed-milk, the cheese must be branded to show this. The following[141] illustrate the laws relating to the state brand and skimmed-milk cheese:

Sec. 48. Manufacturer's brand of cheese. "Every manufacturer of whole-milk cheese may put a brand or label upon such cheese indicating 'whole-milk cheese' and the date of the month and year when made; and no person shall use such a brand or label upon any cheese made from milk from which any of the cream has been taken. The Commissioner of Agriculture shall procure and issue to the cheese manufacturers of the state, on proper application therefor, and under such regulations as to the custody and use thereof as he may prescribe, a uniform stencil brand or labels bearing a suitable device or motto, and the words 'New York state whole-milk cheese.' Every such brand or label shall be used upon the outside of the cheese and shall bear a different number for each separate factory. The commissioner shall keep a book, in which shall be registered the name, location and number of each manufactory using the brands or labels, and the name or names of the persons at each manufactory authorized to use the same. No such brand or labels shall be used upon any other than whole-milk cheese or packages containing the same. (As amended by chapter 207 of the Laws of 1910.)

Sec. 49. Use of false brand prohibited; branding of skim-milk cheese regulated. No person shall offer, sell or expose for sale, in any package, butter or cheese which is falsely branded or labeled. No person shall sell, offer or expose for sale cheese commonly known as Cheddar cheese made from skimmed or partially skimmed milk unless the same is branded to show that it is skim-milk cheese. All such cheese so sold, offered or exposed for sale shall be branded with the words 'skim-milk cheese,' or if such cheese contains thirteen per centum of milk fat or over, it may be branded 'medium skim-milk cheese,' or if it contains eighteen per centum of milk fat or over, it may be branded 'special skim-milk cheese.' Such branding shall be upon the sides of both the cheese and the container. The branding herein provided shall be in block letters at least one-half an inch square. (As amended by chapter 456 of the Laws of 1913.)"

[141] N. Y. Agricultural Laws, Sect. 3, paragraphs 48 and 49.

Filled cheeses are those from which the milk-fat has been removed and other animal fats substituted. The laws of some states prohibit the manufacture of this product. The federal law relating to filled cheese permits its manufacture under license, taxes and government inspection.

The various states have laws regulating the length of time that the cheese may be held in cold storage.

Another important law in some states requires the cheese-maker to have a license. He must pass an examination to show that the principles and practices of cheese-making are understood.

CHAPTER XXI
CHEESE IN THE HOUSEHOLD

Food value of cheese; Digestibility of cheese; Cheese flavor; Relation to health; Cheese poisoning; Proper place in the diet; Care of cheese; Food value and price; Methods and recipes for using cheese.

Although cheese in some form is familiar to every household, it has been widely regarded in America as an accessory, almost a condimental substance rather than as a staple food worthy of comparison with meat or eggs. Statistics of the annual production, importation and exportation of cheese indicate that the total consumption in the United States is about 300,000,000 pounds—perhaps three pounds per capita. The household manufacture and consumption of cottage cheese would add a small amount to these figures.

Cheese is used as a staple source of food values among many peoples of Europe. Such use of cheese increases rather than decreases with the density of the population. France with a small fraction of the land area and one-half the population of the United States produces and consumes about the same amount of cheese. In America, cheese-making has been developed with the advance of settlement into unoccupied territories only to be dropped as increasing population produced greater demands for milk in other forms. If cheese had been accepted as a regular part of the food supply in such communities, some form of cheese-making would have survived the economic changes.

334. Food value of cheese.—A consideration of the nutritive components of cheese shows it to be a rich source of fat, protein or both, according to the variety under examination. It is low in carbohydrates, and aside from salt (sodium chloride) compares favorably with other substances in mineral constituents. The following discussion with an amplified table is taken from Langworthy and Hunt:[142]

"In order, however, that the question of the use of cheese in the diet may be adequately discussed, knowledge of its composition in comparison with other foods is desirable, and there is an abundance of data available on this subject, since the composition of cheese and other foods has often been investigated at the Department of Agriculture, in experiment station laboratories and in many other places where nutrition problems are studied. An extended summary of analyses of cheese of different sorts is included in an earlier publication of this department.[143]

[142] Langworthy, C. F., and C. L. Hunt, Cheese and its economical uses in the diet, U. S. Dept. Agr. Farmers' Bul. 487, 1912.

[143] See also, Reich, R., Cheese as a food and its judgment from standpoint of the food

"Data regarding the composition of cheese and a few other common foods are summarized in the following table.

"It will be seen from the table (Table XXX) that cheese has nearly twice as much protein, weight for weight, as beef of average composition as purchased and that its fuel value is more than twice as great. It contains over 25 per cent more protein than the same weight of porterhouse steak as purchased, and nearly twice as much fat.

chemist, Arch. f. Hyg. 80 (1913), no. 1/6, pages 169-195.

TABLE XXX

AVERAGE COMPOSITION OF CHEESE AND SOME OTHER COMMON FOODS AS PURCHASED, AND ALSO ON THE BASIS OF EDIBLE PORTION								
FOOD MATERIALS	REFUSE %	WATER %	PROTEIN %	FAT %	CARBO HY-DRATES %	ASH %	FUEL VALUE PER POUND CALORIES	FUEL VALUE COMPARED TO CHEESE[144]
Cheese, American Cheddar[145]	— —	34.2	25.2	33.7	2.4	3.8	1,950	1.00
Beef of average composition as purchased	18.6	50.5	15.2	15.5	— —	.7	935	0.48
Edible portion	— —	62.2	18.8	18.8	— —	.9	1,145	0.58
Porterhouse steak as purchased	12.7	52.4	19.1	17.9	— —	.8	1,110	0.57
Edible portion	— —	60.0	21.9	20.4	— —	1.0	1,270	0.65
Loin steak, broiled, edible portion	— —	54.8	23.5	20.4	— —	1.2	1,300	0.66
Dried beef	— —	53.7	26.4	6.9	— —	8.9	790	0.45
Eggs as purchased	11.2	65.5	13.1	9.3	— —	.9	635	0.32
Edible portion	— —	73.7	13.4	10.5	— —	1.0	720	0.37
Milk	— —	87.0	3.3	4.0	5.0	.7	310	0.16
Bread	— —	35.3	9.2	1.3	53.1	1.1	1,215	0.62
Potatoes as purchased	20.0	62.6	1.8	.1	14.7	.8	295	0.15
Edible portion	— —	78.3	2.2	.1	18.4	1.0	385	0.20
Apples as purchased	25.0	63.6	.3	.3	10.8	.3	190	0.10
Edible portion	— —	84.6	.4	.5	14.2	.3	290	0.15

[144] This calculation was added by the authors.
[145] Varietal name added by authors.

"As shown by the figures in the following table, cheese contains 3.8 per cent ash. Of this a considerable part may be salt added in cheese-making. Like the milk from which it is made, cheese ash is characterized chiefly by the presence of calcium (lime), magnesium, phosphorus and iron, the average values as given in earlier bulletins of the department[146] being 1.24 per cent calcium oxid, 0.049 per cent magnesium oxid, 1.49 per cent phosphorus pentoxid, and 0.0015 per cent iron."

It is clear from the calculations shown in the last column, that Cheddar cheese takes first rank among the foods compared as to fuel value. The estimate of food values in terms of calories may not completely express the value of that food to a particular individual. It is generally conceded that one great function of food is the production of energy and this function is probably more closely determined by the number of calories produced than in any other known way. Such calculation has become an essential factor in the preparation of dietaries. The calculation here given necessarily applies only to Cheddar cheese. By easy use of the last column, the caloric value of this cheese can be compared with that of any competing food and the relative economy determined, whatever the price asked. Another recent calculation with reference[147] to the same cheese follows:

"One pound of American Cheddar cheese contains as much protein as—

    1.57 pounds of sirloin steak.
    1.35 pounds of round steak.
    1.89 pounds of fowl.
    1.79 pounds of smoked ham.
    1.81 pounds of fresh ham.

"In order to judge the value of foods fairly not only the protein but the energy also must be compared. To supply energy cheese is one of the best of food products. On the basis of energy supplied, 1 pound of cheese equals—

    1.98 pounds of sirloin steak.
    2.61 pounds of round steak.
    2.52 pounds of fowl.
    1.17 pounds of smoked ham.
    1.29 pounds of fresh ham."

All these discussions have applied to whole-milk Cheddar cheese. With minor reductions, much the same figures will hold for Swiss, Limburger, Brick, Munster, Edam.

On the other hand, very little has been published until recently on the skimmed-milk cheeses. The food value lost in skimmed-milk has at times been enormous. Many households purchase milk by the bottle, use the top-milk as cream and lose a part of the remainder. Similarly creameries have wasted tons of skimmed-milk. The recovery of the protein of this milk for human food is both good economy and an important addition to the dietary. The United States Department of Agriculture has recently published the following: "Cottage cheese is richer in protein

[146] Doane, C. F., and H. W. Lawson, Varieties of cheese, U. S. Dept. Agr. Bur. An. Ind. Bul. 146.

[147] U. S. Dept. Agr. Bur. An. Ind., Dairy Div. A. I. 21, 1917.

than most meats and is very much cheaper. Every pound contains more than three ounces of protein, the source of nitrogen for body building. It is a valuable source of energy also, though not so high as foods with more fat. It follows that its value in this respect can be greatly increased by serving it with cream, as is so commonly done."

It is an open question whether the decline of cheese-making in America is not due to our failure to develop the use of skim and part-skim cheeses. The whole-milk cheeses are very rich in fat. Use of such cheese in quantity in connection with ordinary foods quickly leads to the ingestion of too much fat. The skimmed-milk cheeses are primarily protein food and as such substitutes for lean meat.

"The following table shows that cottage cheese is much cheaper than most meats in furnishing protein for the diet.

"For supplying protein, one pound of cottage cheese equals:

    1.27 pounds sirloin steak.
    1.09 pounds round steak.
    1.37 pounds chuck rib beef.
    1.52 pounds fowl.
    1.46 pounds fresh ham.
    1.44 pounds smoked ham.
    1.58 pounds loin pork chop.
    1.31 pounds hind leg of lamb.
    1.37 pounds breast of veal.

"In addition to protein, energy for performing body work must be furnished by food. As a source of energy also, cottage cheese is cheaper than most meats at present prices. The following table shows the comparison when energy is considered.

"On the basis of energy supplied, one pound of cottage cheese equals:

    8⅓ ounces sirloin steak.
    11¼ ounces round steak.
    11¼ ounces chuck rib beef.
    10¾ ounces fowl.
    5½ ounces fresh ham.
    5 ounces smoked ham.
    6 ounces loin pork chop.
    7⅓ ounces hind leg of lamb.
    12¾ ounces breast of veal."

335. Digestibility of cheese.—Although it has been a staple food with many races for uncounted years, there is a widespread belief that cheese is suitable for use chiefly in small quantities as an accessory to the diet, and that in large quantities it is likely to produce physiological disturbances. The question of digestibility was made the subject of a special investigation by the United States Department of

Agriculture.[148] Calorimeter experiments[149] were made to test the digestibility of several varieties of cheese and some of these varieties at various stages of ripening. All forms of cheese were found to be digested as completely as most of the usual forms of food. Approximately 90 per cent of the nitrogenous portion (casein) was retained in the body. Unripe cheese in these experiments was apparently digested as completely as the ripened forms. These experiments make clear the possibility of making cheese a more prominent article in the regular dietary than is usual in America. They especially point to the desirability of the use of the skim and partially skim cheeses, which as cheap sources of protein when properly combined with other foods, may be made to replace meats as a less costly source of proteins. Cheese is then to be classed with meat and eggs, not with condiments. An ounce of Cheddar[150] cheese roughly is equivalent to one egg, to a glass of milk, or to two ounces of meat. It is properly to be combined with bread, potatoes and other starchy foods, lacking in the fat in which the cheese is rich. These experiments included Roquefort, fresh-made and ripe Cheddar, Swiss, Camembert and Cottage cheese.

336. Cheese flavor.—"Cheese owes its flavor to the fatty acids and their compounds which it contains and to ammonia-like bodies formed during ripening from the cleavage of the casein, to salt added to the curd, and in some varieties, like Roquefort, to bodies elaborated by molds which develop in the cheese. In the highly flavored sorts some of the fatty acids of a very marked odor are present in abundance, as are also the ammonia-like bodies. Indeed, in eating such cheese as Camembert a trace of ammonia flavor may often be plainly detected.

"The cleavage of the nitrogenous material of the cheese and other changes are brought about chiefly by the action of enzymes originally present in cheese or by micro-organisms and are to be regarded as fermentative and not as putrefactive changes.

"The liking for highly flavored cheeses of strong odor is a matter of individual preference, but from the chemist's standpoint there is no reason for the statement often made that such cheeses have undergone putrefactive decomposition."

337. Relation to health.—In connection with the use of cheese as a food, its relation to the health of the consumer must be considered. The presence of the bacillus of tuberculosis in milk has led to careful study of its possible presence in cheese. When American Cheddar cheese was specially inoculated for this purpose, the living organism was recovered from it after about five months by Schroeder of the United States Department of Agriculture. This danger is much greater from cheeses, such as Cream and Neufchâtel, which are eaten when comparatively freshly made. The disease has been produced in guinea pigs from such cheese often enough to emphasize the desirability of developing methods of making every variety possible from thoroughly pasteurized milk. This would remove the danger of tuberculosis and with it eliminate the possibility of transmitting other diseases.

[148] Doane, C. F., et al., The digestibility of cheese, U. S. Dept. Agr. Bur. An. Ind. Circ. 166, pages 1-21, 1911.

[149] Langworthy and Hunt, loc. cit.

[150] U. S. Dept. Agr. Farmers' Bul. 487, page 38.

338. Cheese poisoning[151] cases occasionally occur. These take two main forms: (1) an enteritis (caused by *Bacillus enteritidis*) or some other member of that series which while painful and accompanied by purging is rarely fatal; (2) acute toxæmias which, although rare, usually result in death. From the latter type a variety of *Bacillus botulinus*, an organism usually associated with meat poisoning, was isolated by the New York State Department of Health. The occurrence of such cases is frequent enough to emphasize the desirability of using every precaution to reduce the number of bacteria that are allowed to enter milk when drawn and to prevent the development of those which actually gain access to it. When possible, pasteurization should be introduced.

339. Proper place in the diet.—It has already been noted that cheese is used "in general in two ways—in small quantities chiefly for its flavor and in large quantities for its nutritive value as well as for its flavor. Some varieties of cheese are used chiefly for the first purpose, others chiefly for the second. Those which are used chiefly for their flavor, many of which are high priced, contribute little to the food value of the diet, because of the small quantity used at a time. They have an important part to play, however, in making the diet attractive and palatable. The intelligent housekeeper thinks of them not as necessities, but as lying within what has been called 'the region of choice.' Having first satisfied herself that her family is receiving sufficient nourishment, she then, according to her means and ideas of an attractive diet, chooses among these foods and others which are to be considered luxuries.

"Those cheeses, on the other hand, which are suitable to be eaten in large quantities and which are comparatively low priced are important not only from the point of view of flavor, but also from the point of view of their nutritive value." Among such cheeses are American Cheddar, Swiss, Brick, Limburger and the lower priced forms of Neufchâtel.

It is clear that in buying cheese, the housekeeper should know definitely the dietary purpose of the purchase, and then choose the variety of cheese best suited. To a very large degree the personal tastes of the family determine the kinds of cheese which will be tolerated when served uncooked. In some families, the strong flavors of Roquefort or Limburger are not acceptable. However, there is a range of choice in which much judgment can be used. Cheese to be served with mild-flavored foods should as a rule be also mild-flavored. For most sandwiches, for example, Cheddar or Swiss is usually very acceptable; Brick or partly ripe Limburger still hard enough to slice cuts into thin rectangular slices and is very attractive to many consumers because it has somewhat more flavor without being too strong. With proper handling it is good policy to buy the cheapest of these forms for this purpose. The selection of dessert cheeses offers the widest range. If served with mild-flavored crackers, very many persons prefer Cream, Neufchâtel or mild Cheddar; a little stronger taste calls for club cheese, or Camembert. If tobacco smoke is present, Roquefort, Gorgonzola, Limburger and related types will satisfy many consumers better than mild cheeses. The intensity of flavor to be

[151] Levin, W., Cheese poisoning—a toxicogenic bacillus isolated from cheese, Jour. Lab. Clin. Med. 2 (1917), page 761.

sought in the cheese should thus be adjusted to the food served with it. A person with an aversion to strong-smelling or strong-tasting cheese has been frequently known to approve over-ripe Camembert, or Limburger when served without label but spread upon a ginger cracker.

For cooking purposes, some recipes prescribe cheese of special quality. In large markets, old Cheddar ripened carefully for two or three years is commonly purchasable for Welsh rabbit. (Ask for "rabbit" cheese.) An expert housekeeper familiar also with cheese ripening has demonstrated that almost any cheese, whether ripened to its best, part ripe or over-ripe, can be used in many cooking formulas without injuring the acceptability of the product to most consumers. In canning Camembert, it has been shown[152] that over-ripe cheese so strong as to be objectionable, when sterilized loses the objectionable flavor of the raw product. No cheese should be wasted; any not used when served the first time should be served at a closely following meal or used in cooking. No matter what the variety, it will add to the food value and palatability of some one of the common dishes served within forty-eight hours.

340. Care of cheese.[153]—"One of the best ways of keeping cheese which has been cut is to wrap it in a slightly damp cloth and then in paper, and to keep it in a cool place. To dampen the cloth, sprinkle it and then wring it. It should seem hardly damp to the touch. Paraffin paper may be used in place of the cloth. When cheese is put in a covered dish, the air should never be wholly excluded, for if this is done, it molds more readily.

"In some markets it is possible to buy small whole cheeses. These may be satisfactorily kept by cutting a slice from the top, to serve as a cover, and removing the cheese as needed with a knife, a strong spoon, or a cheese scoop. It is possible to buy at the hardware stores knobs which inserted in the layer cut from the top make it easy to handle. The cheese with the cover on should be kept wrapped in a cloth."

341. Food value and price.—There is little relation between the price and food value of standard varieties of cheese. The higher-priced varieties claim and hold their place because they possess particular flavors. These may or may not accompany high comparative food values. Even among low-priced varieties discrimination into grades is largely based on flavor. Of the low-priced cheeses, those made from skimmed-milk commonly command the lowest prices. As noted above, a choice may be based either on purpose or on price. If the purpose is fixed, the price should not change the selection. If, however, a particular quality of cheese is purchasable at a low price, some satisfactory form of utilizing it is clearly available to the housekeeper. Some standard recipes are given in the following paragraphs.

342. Methods and recipes for using cheese.—(1) As a meat substitute. Meat is wholesome and relished by most persons, yet it is not essential to a well-balanced meal and there are many housekeepers who for one reason or another are interest-

---

[152] Thom, C., Camembert cheese problems in the United States, U. S. Dept. Agr. Bur. An. Ind. Bul. 115.

[153] Langworthy and Hunt, loc. cit.

ed in lessening the amount of meat or to substitute other foods. The problem with the average family is undoubtedly more often the occasional substitution of other palatable dishes for the sake of variety, for reasons of economy, or for some other reason than the general replacement of meat dishes by other things.

Foods which are to be served in place of meat should be rich in protein and fat and should also be savory. Cheese naturally suggests itself as a substitute for meat, since it is rich in the same kinds of nutrients that meat supplies, is a staple food with which every one is familiar and is one which can be used in a great variety of ways. In substituting cheese for meat, especial pains should be taken to serve dishes which are relished by the members of the family. A number of recipes[154] for dishes which contain cheese are given below. They are preceded by several recipes for cheese sauces which, as will appear, are called for in the preparation of some of the more substantial dishes. In the first list of recipes, cheese means Cheddar.

Cheese Sauce No. 1

1 cupful of milk. 1 ounce of cheese (¼ cupful of grated cheese).
2 tablespoonfuls of flour. Salt and pepper.

Thicken the milk with the flour and just before serving add the cheese, stirring until it is melted.

This sauce is suitable to use in preparing creamed eggs, or to pour over toast, making a dish corresponding to ordinary milk toast, except for the presence of cheese. It may be seasoned with a little curry powder and poured over hard-boiled eggs.

Cheese Sauce No. 2

Same as cheese sauce No. 1, except that the cheese is increased from 1 to 2 ounces.

This sauce is suitable for using with macaroni or rice, or for baking with crackers soaked in milk.

Cheese Sauce No. 3

Same as cheese sauce No. 1, except that two cupfuls of grated cheese or 8 ounces are used. This may be used upon toast as a substitute for Welsh rabbit.

Cheese Sauce No. 4

Same as cheese sauce No. 2, save that 2 tablespoonfuls of melted butter are mixed with the flour before the latter is put into the milk. This sauce is therefore very rich in fat and has only a mild flavor of cheese.

Among the recipes for dishes which may be used like meat, the following give products which, eaten in usual quantities, will provide much the same kind and amount of nutritive material as the ordinary servings of meat dishes used at dinner. In several cases there is a resemblance in appearance and flavor to common

[154] Langworthy and Hunt, loc. cit.

meat dishes, which would doubtless be a point in their favor with many families.

(2) For general cooking purposes:

Cheese Fondue No. 1

1⅓ cupfuls of soft, stale bread crumbs.	4 eggs.
6 ounces of cheese (1½ cupfuls of grated cheese or 1⅓ cupfuls of cheese grated fine or cut into small pieces).	1 cupful of hot water. ½ teaspoonful of salt.

Mix the water, bread crumbs, salt and cheese; add the yolks thoroughly beaten; into this mixture cut and fold the whites of eggs beaten until stiff. Pour into a buttered baking dish and cook 30 minutes in a moderate oven. Serve at once.

The food value of this dish, made with the above quantities, is almost exactly the same as that of a pound of beef of average composition and a pound of potatoes combined. It contains about 80 grams of proteids and has a fuel value of about 1300 calories.

Cheese Fondue No. 2

1⅓ cupfuls of hot milk.	⅓ of a pound of cheese (1⅓ cupfuls of grated cheese or 1 cupful of cheese cut into small pieces).
1⅓ cupfuls of soft, stale bread crumbs.	
1 tablespoonful of butter.	
4 eggs.	½ teaspoonful of salt.

Prepare as in previous recipe.

The protein value of this dish is equal to that of 1⅓ pounds of potato and beef, the fuel value, however, being much in excess of these.

In making either of these fondues, rice or other cereals may be substituted for bread crumbs. One-fourth cupful of rice measured before cooking, or one cupful of cooked rice or other cereals, should be used.

Corn and Cheese Soufflé

1 tablespoonful of butter.	1 cupful of chopped corn.
1 tablespoonful of chopped green pepper.	1 cupful of grated cheese,
¼ cupful of flour.	½ teaspoonful of salt.
2 cupfuls of milk.	

Melt the butter and cook the pepper thoroughly in it. Make a sauce out of the flour, milk and cheese; add the corn, cheese, yolks and seasoning; cut and fold in the whites beaten stiffly; turn into a buttered baking dish and bake in a moderate oven 30 minutes.

Made with skimmed-milk and without butter, this dish has a food value slightly in excess of a pound of beef and a pound of potatoes.

Cheese Soufflé

2 tablespoonfuls of butter.	A speck of cayenne.
3 tablespoonfuls of flour.	¼ cupful of grated cheese.
½ cupful of milk (scalded).	3 eggs.
½ teaspoonful of salt.	

Melt the butter; add the flour and, when well mixed, add gradually the scalded milk. Then add salt, cayenne and cheese. Remove from the fire and add the yolks of the eggs, beaten until lemon colored. Cool the mixture and fold into it the whites of the eggs, beaten until stiff. Pour into a buttered baking dish and cook 20 minutes in a slow oven. Serve at once.

The proteid of this recipe is equal to that of half a pound of beef; the fuel value is equal to that of three-fourths of a pound.

Welsh Rabbit

1 tablespoonful of butter.	½ pound of cheese, cut into small pieces.
1 teaspoonful of corn-starch.	¼ teaspoonful each of salt and mustard.
½ cupful of milk.	A speck of cayenne pepper.

Cook the corn-starch in the butter; then add the milk gradually and cook two minutes; add the cheese and stir until it is melted. Season and serve on crackers or bread toasted on one side, the rabbit being poured over the untoasted side. Food value is that of about three-fourths of a pound of beef.

Macaroni and Cheese No. 1

Macaroni and Cheese No. 1

1 cupful of macaroni, broken into small pieces.	2 tablespoonfuls of flour.
2 quarts of boiling salted water.	¼ to ½ pound of cheese.
1 cupful of milk.	½ teaspoonful of salt.
	Speck of cayenne pepper.

Cook the macaroni in the boiling salted water, drain in a strainer, and pour cold water over it to prevent the pieces from adhering to each other. Make a sauce out of the flour, milk, and cheese. Put the sauce and macaroni in alternate layers in a buttered baking dish, cover with buttered crumbs, and heat in oven until crumbs are brown.

Macaroni and Cheese No. 2

A good way to prepare macaroni and cheese is to make a rich cheese sauce and heat the macaroni in it. The mixture is usually covered with buttered crumbs and browned in the oven. The advantage of this way of preparing the dish, however, is that it is unnecessary to have a hot oven, as the sauce and macaroni may be reheated on the top of the stove.

Baked Rice and Cheese No. 1

1 cupful of uncooked rice and	2 tablespoonfuls of flour.
4 cupfuls of milk;	½ pound of cheese.
or,	½ teaspoonful of salt.
3 cupfuls of cooked rice and	
1 cupfuls of milk	

If uncooked rice is used, it should be cooked in 3 cupfuls of milk. Make a sauce with one cupful of milk, add the flour, cheese and salt. Into a buttered baking dish put alternate layers of the cooked rice and the sauce. Cover with buttered crumbs and bake until the crumbs are brown. The proteids in this dish, made with rice cooked in milk, are equal to those of nearly 1¾ pounds of average beef. If skimmed-milk is used, the fuel value is equal to nearly 3½ pounds of beef. Whole milk raises the fuel value still higher.

Fried Bread with Cheese No. 1

6 slices of bread.	½ teaspoonful of salt.
1 cupful of milk.	½ teaspoonful of potassium bicarbonate.
2 ounces of cheese,	Butter or other fat for frying.
or ½ cupful of grated cheese.	

Scald the milk with the potassium bicarbonate; add the grated cheese, and stir until it dissolves. Dip the bread in this mixture and fry it in the butter. The potassium bicarbonate helps to keep the cheese in solution. It is desirable, however, to keep the milk hot while the bread is being dipped.

Plain Cheese Salad

Cut Edam or ordinary American cheese into thin pieces, scatter them over lettuce leaves and serve with French dressing.

Olive and Pimiento Sandwich or Salad Cheese

Mash any of the soft cream cheeses and add chopped olives and pimientos in equal parts. This mixture requires much salt to make it palatable to most palates, the amount depending chiefly on the quantity of pimiento used. The mixture may be spread between thin slices of bread or it may be made into a roll or molded, cut into slices and served on lettuce leaves with French dressing.

Cheese and Tomato Salad

Stuff cold tomatoes with cream cheese and serve on lettuce leaves with French dressing.

Cheese and Pimiento Salad

Stuff canned pimientos with cream cheese, cut into slices and serve one or two slices to each person on lettuce leaves with French dressing.

(3) Ways to use cottage cheese. Cottage cheese alone is an appetizing and nutritious dish. It may also be served with sweet or sour cream, and some persons add a little sugar, or chives, chopped onion or caraway seed.

The following recipes[155] illustrate a number of ways in which cottage cheese may be served:

Cottage Cheese with Preserves and Jellies

Pour over cottage cheese any fruit preserves, such as strawberries, figs or cherries. Serve with bread or crackers. If preferred, cottage cheese balls may be served separately and eaten with the preserves. A very attractive dish may be made by dropping a bit of jelly into a nest of the cottage cheese.

Cottage Cheese Salad

Mix thoroughly one pound of cheese, one and one-half tablespoonfuls of cream, one tablespoonful of chopped parsley and salt to taste. First, fill a rectangular tin mold with cold water to chill and wet the surface; line the bottom with waxed paper, then pack in three layers of the cheese, putting two or three parallel strips of pimiento, fresh or canned, between the layers. Cover with waxed paper and set in a cool place until ready to serve; then run a knife around the sides and invert the mold. Cut in slices and serve on lettuce leaves with French dressing and wafers or thin bread-and-butter sandwiches. Minced olives may be used instead of the parsley, and chopped nuts also may be added.

Cottage Cheese Rolls

(To be used like meat rolls.)

A large variety of rolls, suitable for serving as the main dish at dinner, may be made by combining legumes (beans of various kinds, cowpeas, lentils or peas) with cottage cheese, and adding bread crumbs to make the mixture thick enough to form into a roll. Beans are usually mashed, but peas or small Lima beans may be combined whole with bread crumbs and cottage cheese, and enough of the liquor in which the vegetables have been cooked should be added to get the right consistency; or, instead of beans or peas, chopped spinach, beet tops or head lettuce may be added.

Boston Roast

1 pound can of kidney beans, or equivalent quantity of cooked beans.
½ pound of cottage cheese.
Bread crumbs.
Salt.

Mash the beans or put them through a meat grinder. Add the cheese and bread crumbs enough to make the mixture sufficiently stiff to be formed into a roll. Bake in a moderate oven, basting occasionally with butter or other fat, and water. Serve with tomato sauce. This dish may be flavored with chopped onions cooked until

[155] U.S. Dept. of Agr. Bur. An. Ind. A. I. 18.

tender in butter or other fat and a very little water.

Pimiento and Cottage Cheese Roast

2 cupfuls of cooked Lima beans.   3 canned pimientos chopped.

¼ pound of cottage cheese.   Bread crumbs.

Salt.

Put the first three ingredients through a meat chopper. Mix thoroughly and add bread crumbs until it is stiff enough to form into a roll. Brown in the oven, basting occasionally with butter or other fat, and water.

Cottage Cheese and Nut Roast

1 cupful of cottage cheese.   2 tablespoonfuls of chopped onion.

1 cupful of chopped English walnuts.   1 tablespoonful of butter..

1 cupful of bread crumbs   Juice of half a lemon.

Salt and pepper.

Cook the onion in the butter or other fat and a little water until tender. Mix the other ingredients and moisten with the water in which the onion has been cooked. Pour into a shallow baking dish and brown in the oven.

Cheese Sauce

(For use with eggs, milk toast or other dishes.)

One cupful of milk, 1 tablespoonful of cottage cheese, 2 tablespoonfuls of flour, salt and pepper to taste.

Thicken the milk with the flour and just before serving add the cheese, stirring until it is melted.

This sauce may be used in preparing creamed eggs or for ordinary milk toast. The quantity of cheese in the recipe may be increased, making a sauce suitable for using with macaroni or rice.

INDEX

W. L. Carlyle *8*
W. R. Wright *28*
W. W. Fisk *29*
W. White *28*

Y

Yeasts *4, 9, 13, 34, 55, 87, 98*
Young America *147*

Z

Zumkehr *89*

Lector House believes that a society develops through a two-fold approach of continuous learning and adaptation, which is derived from the study of classic literary works spread across the historic timeline of literature records. Therefore, we aim at reviving, repairing and redeveloping all those inaccessible or damaged but historically as well as culturally important literature across subjects so that the future generations may have an opportunity to study and learn from past works to embark upon a journey of creating a better future.

This book is a result of an effort made by Lector House towards making a contribution to the preservation and repair of original ancient works which might hold historical significance to the approach of continuous learning across subjects.

HAPPY READING & LEARNING!

LECTOR HOUSE LLP
E-MAIL: lectorpublishing@gmail.com